Operatic Afterlives

Operatic Afterlives

Michal Grover-Friedlander

ZONE BOOKS · NEW YORK

2011

ZONE BOOKS
1226 Prospect Avenue
Brooklyn, NY 11218

Printed in the United States of America.

Distributed by The MIT Press,
Cambridge, Massachusetts, and London, England

Library of Congress Cataloging-in-Publication Data

Grover-Friedlander, Michal.
    Operatic afterlives / Michal Grover-Friedlander.
        p. cm.
    Includes bibliographical references and index.
    ISBN 978-1-935408-06-2
        1. Opera. 2. Voice in opera. I. Title.

    ML1700.G84 2011
    782.1–dc22

                                    2010029420

To Norman, Rita, and Roni Grover,
with love

Contents

Acknowledgments

This book has taken many years to write. Part of the book was completed in 2004–2005 during my membership year at the School of Historical studies at the Institute for Advanced Study in Princeton. My stay at the Institute was made possible by the generous support provided by the E. T. Cone Fellowship for musicologists. It was an outstanding environment in which to write. Each of the chapters has drawn on vastly different sources and fields of knowledge. I would like to thank the following scholars for their indispensable advice and valuable assistance: Oded Assaf, Michael Ching, Boaz Huss, Ronit Meroz, Gerda Panofsky, Freddie Rokem, Ronit Seter, Peter Schäfer, and Stefanie Tcharos. My research assistances, Ofer Gazit and Yaniv Baruh, provided essential help with bibliography, typography, and the preparation of the musical examples. I would also like to thank Ramona Naddaff for her support and encouragement as well as for her insightful comments on different versions of the manuscript. The style editor, Jim Gibbons has, as always, done a wonderful job of editing the manuscript. Meighan Gale at Zone Books made the process of transforming my manuscript into a book both meaningful and pleasurable. Finally, I would like to express my admiration, deep appreciation and affection to those scholars who inspired me and whose influence on my writing is lasting: Carolyn Abbate, Caroline Bynum, Stanley Cavell, Eli Friedlander, and Michela Garda. Without them, this book and many thoughts and ideas surrounding it would not have materialized. I dedicate this book with love to Rita, Norman, and Roni Grover.

Introduction

Am I hearing voices within the voice? But isn't it the truth of the voice to be hallucinated? Isn't the entire space of the voice an infinite one?

—Roland Barthes, "The Grain of the Voice"

Surely the operatic voice is the grandest realization of having a signature, the world, as Emerson puts it, wearing our color—as the sign of abandonment to your words, hence of your mortal immortality.

—Stanley Cavell, "Opera and the Lease of Voice"

Singing

This book follows the most extreme implications of what opera entails, founded as it is on the myth of Orpheus: an attempt to revive the dead with the power granted to singing. The course of the history of opera is determined according to stylistic manifestations of the power of singing in lyricism, virtuosity, dramatic force, synchronization with text, etc. Opera's Orphic legacy is located in almost all aspects of singing, starting from the very fact that singing is its characters' mode of utterance. If characters are the source and origin of their utterances, if song stems from them (which is how we conceive of the dramatic personae's thinking and conversing), then they all speak and think in songs. Their utterances, that is, their music, must be perceived—and this is E. T. Cone's famous proposition—as their own compositions. In other words, operatic characters are all descendents of Orpheus; all are granted the gift of inspiration.

What exactly this intuition entails has generated the most fascinating questions and insights about opera. What would it mean to say that music originates in operatic characters? If this is the case, how do we account for moments specifically marked as song in operas (serenades, ballades, and so on, performed by the characters)? Do they differ from their surroundings as, in theater, speaking does from singing? Do characters compose the music *and* the text? And are they also the originators of the orchestral accompaniment to their singing? But then do we want to say that they hear the accompaniment? And do they do so as if they were hearing their own thoughts? Do they hear the accompaniment of other characters, or only their own? And what happens in duets, terzets, quartets? Whose music is it—who composes it? Do characters hear what they are doing as singing—that is, do they know they are singing? Are their utterances and those of others perceived as song, as music, or do they live in a cinemalike world in which, for most of the time and for most of the characters, there is no soundtrack?

These concerns and the ways they are dealt with lie at the bottom of our perception and conception of the medium. Melody, theme, and tonality determine character; musical transformations deepen, alter, or reveal that characterization. Music articulates the drama, as Joseph Kerman has long argued. Opera's texts throughout its history have been problematized because music adheres to rules of composition that differ from those of poetry and prose. But even though clashes of simultaneous signifying systems, linguistic and musical, determine opera, what accounts, in the deepest sense, for the specificity of opera is singing that is unlike any other. Not only is operatic singing excessive, stylized, artificial, extravagant, exaggerated, absurd, irrational, grotesque, and situated at the limits of human capacities; not only does it call for special production techniques and aspire to projection powers that can overcome a huge orchestra and fill the vastest auditorium (priding itself in doing so without technological amplification); not solely does it exercise concentrated intensity while impressing on us an ease of execution. Above all, such singing is what it is because it bears in unique ways on our conception of *who* is doing the singing.

Here is the core of my intervention, which I will develop throughout the arguments of this book: in opera, singing as such is not a straightforward expression of an already established character, but has the most indirect and circumvented ways of forming an identity. Such complications occur when singing grows independent of character and its utterance, when, in effect, it becomes more determining of the drama, more powerful than any delivered utterance. Specifically, it is when singing emanates from one no longer living that we need to reconceive who or what is singing.

Isn't a character in opera determined by singing—if one sings, one cannot be dead, and if one is dead one cannot sing? What would it mean for singing to be severed from character? And if this possibility is granted, further questions immediately arise: Can this seeming exception reveal something essential about opera, can it exemplify, after all, what we have all along expected of opera, namely its power to overturn mortality? Can singing's independence from character in the singing of opera's dead—unusual as it is—represent a revival of operatic singing as such? Has singing, as the medium has constructed it, enabled this unattainable exception? Is revitalization of the dead part and parcel of the power granted to singing, exhibiting singing as a presence beyond death? Put differently: are we, after all, in a realm not only of the Orphic power of artistic invention but also its forces of renewal, revival, resurrection? Isn't the passage between the world of the living and the dead always what opera has wished for?

Death Song

I adopt a view of the operatic as a phenomenon in which meaning is engendered in singing; and, through singing, the nature and significance of that very capacity is revealed. I join Abbate, Cavell, Starobinski, Poizat, and others in positioning the singing voice above all other constituents as what is essential to opera. Accordingly, the goal in and of opera is to emphasize singing above everything else. Notions such as the total work of art, multimedia work, and synesthesia—though central to certain styles and composers—are secondary to my inquiry.

The centrality of singing explains opera's attraction to liminal dramatic conditions, as these serve the expression of extreme singing. The quest for such singing brings about the excess of deaths in opera. Opera replays, ever again, the scene of death, releasing its central characters, one after the other, to that inner compulsion. The omnipresence of death is not just a matter of opera's plots. In opera, more than anything, an intimate association is established between singing and death. The climax of singing is the most extreme form of being-toward-death. The relation of opera to death is found most importantly in the placement of the apotheosis of singing, and thus of what we have termed operatic, precisely in its dependent relation to death: opera fashions what I have elsewhere called a death song. Whereas death is the end of opera, the mode in which that end is manifested is the death song. Whatever happens after the death of the protagonist—the one carrying such ultimate operatic singing—is, in more than one sense, totally insignificant.

The death song is the height of singing expressed in the face of death. It is the solitary singing that signifies the achievement of self-knowledge and closure. This is an expression in song of the awareness of approaching death. The knowledge of death, prophesied from the opera's outset, is what brings about the ultimate display of singing for the protagonist who is about to die. In such a scene the relation of music and meaning is reconfigured. It is the place where music overtakes narrative, the place where the plot lets go of its narrative logic in favor of singing. This is the operatic moment which the listeners have been waiting for: singing carries the burden of the work to the utmost. Such imminent death serves in canonical works as the occasion for what is most operatic in all operatic singing.

And yet there is also a sense of immortality that is consistent with the obsessive presence of death. The repetition of song in the face of death from one opera to the next can be seen as a manifestation of the fantasy that song's power can revive the world, even if momentarily. The origin of this duality in the medium can indeed be traced to what we opened with: the founding myth of Orpheus and Eurydice. It is as though the operatic voice wills precisely what is beyond human capacities—the reversal of death—but it does so indirectly, subversively. The myth's thematization of the failure to reverse death—Eurydice's revival, won by singing—is canceled out in a glance, thus revealing most acutely the predicament of song: its reviving powers cannot be sustained, and a dimension of immortality can be awakened only in and through the repetition of death. In my book *Vocal Apparitions*, I observed:

> The promise to bring back what is dead is supplemented by a more profound, less ecstatic acknowledgement that what is ephemeral and passing is also what can return. The gesture of endless dying signifies the failure of death to hold sway. The repetition of song questions the finality of death, introducing a dimension of immortality.

Endless dying is what opens to the dimension of immortality. It forms a kinship among works that subverts the recurring absoluteness of their individual deaths. Each opera kills anew, thereby exposing the failure of death to master song.

In *Vocal Apparitions*, I further suggested that the medium of film takes it upon itself to reenact and redeem the fate of opera. I traced the thematics of singing and death through films that reflect on opera and death in opera. The internality of death to the operatic is both retained and transformed when opera is translated into film. Films attracted to opera inherit and transform opera's attempt to achieve fulfillment in the face of death. This is true even when a film strives to rectify the ending and overtake it comically, as in the Marx Brothers' *A Night at the Opera*.

Afterlife: A New Configuration of Singing

What I turn to in the present book are peculiar cases of singing being granted power in the face of death, cases which I identify as exemplifying an afterlife of singing. These cases reformulate what operatic singing involves: death, the limit zone, is revisited or renegotiated and a new extremity, a beyond of death, emerges around which singing is reconfigured.

In my emphasis on operatic afterlives, I do not mean to point to the life a work takes in performance, criticism, staging, or translation; nor to the immortalization of ancestors within the work; nor am I drawing an analogy with attempts to arrest life and preserve it, as hoped for with the emergence of technologies such as photography or the gramophone; nor am I preoccupied with otherworldly communications through an interlocutor or medium, as in spirit photography; nor with transmissions between the worlds of the living and the dead. Operatic afterlives are, moreover, to be distinguished from religious genres of voicing the otherworldly, the dead, or the absent, as in glossolalia and shamanistic performance.

The notion of afterlife serves here to characterize a condition internal to singing. That is, it points to those cases in which a breach occurs and we find dissociation between the character's life trajectory and his or her singing. These are mostly cases in which singing itself takes on an afterlife in the face of the death of its carrier. Such misalignment between singing and meaning opens up a new array of possibilities.

In most works in the standard repertory, the entire opera prepares for and leads to the time of singing-toward-death in which nothing exists but singing. This is the highest expression of the operatic. Sometimes, to be sure, even in the more traditional scheme of things, the protagonist's singing can sound in the music heard after his or her death, as though singing may echo for a short, posthumous time (a striking example is found in Verdi's *Otello*, when Desdemona's death song is picked up by the orchestra). But, in the cases I turn to in this book, death is no longer the limit; it occurs within the space of the plot, but it does not mark a climactic moment nor a termination of singing. Rather, singing itself lingers.

Afterlives are exceptional cases of the space of opera being invaded by singing after death. These cases must be distinguished from famous operatic returns, such as ghosts that sing. For not all operatic ghosts exhibit the thematics of the afterlife outlined in what follows. In Britten's *The Turn of the Screw*, for instance, the ghosts of Quint and Miss Jessel indeed sing. But the effect, rather than problematizing the relation of song and death, in fact clarifies the ambiguity carefully preserved in the original story by Henry James about whether they exist or are figments of the imagination. The Commendatore in *Don Giovanni* returns from the grave singing from a surrogate body of stone. And at the end of Verdi's *Don Carlo*, a voice emanates from the grave. But both perform a narrative trick, a deus ex machina. They are voices that return to us from the beyond to intervene in the character's fate. However instrumental they may be for the unfolding of events, and however ominous or redemptive their message, they serve a narrative function, and their voices as such do not attain special status. What I have in mind, in contrast, are cases in which the entire space of the opera is affected by the presence of singing after death. Redrawing the boundaries of mortality through the notion of the afterlife of singing makes manifest a sphere of singing with its own qualities and conjoined meanings. When singing is driven by the protagonist's death but is not itself brought to an end by that death, we find ourselves in an alternate operatic world.

Embodiment

SINGING ITS OWN BEING   In the alternate space of opera I am
painting here, singing takes precedence over character; it overtakes character. If, in most cases, singing is taken to express
the innermost essence, the soul or interiority of the character,
here it takes on a life of its own. Singing, as it were, has its own
being, and is not the emanation of the character's subjectivity.
Such independence from character may manifest itself in various
forms. It can result in the multiplication of singing voices inhabiting the same body, or in disembodied singing (as when the character splits into multiple voices), or the merging of singing voices.
Singing can be a locus of unity of more than one voice, or it can
manifest itself through the (failure of the) attempt to put together
voice and person after their intimate unity has been severed.

Opera's expansion of the space of death, so that singing takes
place beyond the boundaries of life, is then at the same time a reart-
iculation, even a transgression of the boundaries of singing itself.
Singing as such becomes more present, becomes a being with its
own identity and soul. Singing is transformed when it is set free. It
sings from an absent body or emanates from a surrogate one. But
it does not become simply disembodied, as though a floating voice
retained its identity even when separated from a body. Singing
takes over and becomes what the body once was—it gets, as it were,
its own body. It may, to mention one of the more striking examples
I will consider, also take on the plasticity, the freedom from fate
that characterizes cartoon figures. Singing animates itself, breath-
ing life into itself to suspend its end, unfolding a realm between
life and death where death and non-death are undifferentiated. It is
remade into that which remains after one's death and which under
special circumstances may be retrieved and salvaged, as though a
voice from the past can sound from a present body. Singing not
only plays out the fantasy of reviving the dead, as in the myth of
Orpheus, but is itself what has been revived after death.

When singing is independent of the narrative trajectory leading to death, a peculiar sense of its indestructibility emerges.

One can hardly call this the immortality of the soul. For such immortality involves the retention of a stable identity after death. Here, it is as if singing, after paying dues to operatic death, takes on new signification as a result of the breach with character. Not immortality, then, but a temporary metamorphosis into something that is neither dead nor quite alive.

PLURAL VOCALITY Each of the examples dealt with in this book is a unique working-out of the possibilities opened up by the notion of afterlife. The diverse examples share several common themes, yet each takes a different feature to the extreme.

One of the common themes is plurality. Traditional operatic structure demanded a unique high point of singing: the death song, in which reconciliation and closure are achieved in the face of death. In the works I consider, singing lingers on, death no longer functions as a limit, climax, and end point. There is, then, no longer a unique climactic utterance with a perfect match to character. This moment is replaced by multiple occurrences in which singing is dispersed, split, multiplied, and endlessly echoed. Hearing, similarly, must be keyed to recurrent brief moments rather than absorbed in a single, self-enclosed scene. Singing simulates refrains, bare songs, or recurrent themes. The power of singing is in its resounding. Singing has become plurality. The most extreme example of this multiplicity I found in the singing of a host of angels. Theirs is a mode of unceasing singing, of endless echoes. I found other examples in cases when three singing voices are produced by a single body or a single voice dwells in more than one body and cannot be pinpointed in time, or when a pair of singers each simulates an authentic master voice. Or, finally, when a body part rather than a unified presence is emphasized as the origin of voice.

VOICE, SINGING, SONG It is surprising that voice, singing, and song can each become independent of the others. Obviously, this is quite paradoxical: What could possibly distinguish one's

voice as one sings and one's singing? There are operatic configurations that erect precisely such distinctions. Consider, for
example, impersonation. In Puccini's *Gianni Schicchi* (1918), the
main character impersonates another's voice. But for those who
stand to gain from this hoax and are threatened by its revelation,
something more lies in the impersonation. Gianni uses his usual
voice and a musical theme introduced earlier in the opera in the
midst of the impersonation. These serve as haunting reminders
of falsehood and thus become the voice of Gianni himself making his presence known. The foreign voice remains constantly
present even within the impersonated voice. Where, then, is a
character to be located? In a voice, in a song, in the imitation of
the dead? Or, take another example of dubbing: a film actress,
Fanny Ardent, attempts to impersonate a dead singer, Maria Callas. Dubbing here serves to "revive" a singer by matching a body
to a voice from another time. The voice placed in a foreign body,
however, is estranged, and the singing, though dubbed, does not
sound like that of the singer's.

Temporality
Afterlives of singing have their own expanse of possibilities,
intimate and at odds with traditional operatic temporality. Traditional operatic plots are often simple linear progressions of
events, but linear forward progression is not what most often
governs operatic time. Operatic time, in fact, works against linear sequence. Even in rare cases when everything is not already
familiar from repeated hearings, stock plots, conventions, and so
on, it is not the narrative but singing that dominates the experience of the passage of time. Traditional operatic singing creates
self-enclosed moments that stop time. The progression extends
from one distilled vocal moment to another. This explains the
ease by which opera is fragmented: an aria may be pulled out of
its dramatic surroundings and heard independently, as if it were
truly coherent unto itself on its own terms—not because, as many
would have it, the plot does not matter but because singing allows

for it. A single distilled scene can stand for the whole opera or for operatic singing as such. Operatic time manifests itself in such moments of stillness, moments when time is suspended. Everything is incorporated into the time of singing. Moreover, the centrality of the death scene to canonical tragic opera dictates that the end be foreshadowed at the outset. Let's return to Verdi's *Otello* once more. The timeframe of Shakespeare's play is not altered for the opera (everything occurs within twenty-four hours). But the opera is governed by another timeframe: the time span within which the opera unfolds begins with the premonition of doom in Desdemona's entrance aria and ends with her death song. The time of the opera involves the realization of what was presented in the entrance aria; the sense of time is the fulfillment of a preordained fate, fully uncovered in the death song. In other words, time does not flow forward in any customary sense; the unfolding narrative does not dominate the experience of time's progression.

With operatic afterlives there is a rethinking of this temporal template. The temporality of the afterlife does not develop from a structure of prophetic foretelling, nor does it depend on a climactic build-up. In this book's examples, the end is not foreshadowed but has *already occurred* at the outset: the character does not sing in conscious awareness of death from the first moment he sets foot onstage, but his singing already emanates from his dead self. An end is not a realization of an opera's beginning but is in fact its past; the future is embodied in the present. Thus opera's strange sense of progression, and the further distortion of its temporal idiosyncrasy—as when an opera's epilogue and prologue are nearly identical, each involving singing souls whose story is told in the course of the opera.

The notion of afterlife allows us to treat death as nonfinal, as something regarding which there is still a say. Instead of a fulfilled fatal prophecy, opera contains endings in which death is tricked, exposing a grotesque undertone. There occurs a loosening of the knot between singing, character, and event; different temporalities emerge. Singing is itself not necessarily modified, morphed, or new—it is often familiar, a resonance of something heard before. But then a fundamental aspect of its behavior has doubtless been transformed.

The examples presented here unsettle characters by problematizing the work's temporal boundaries, that is, by playing with beginnings and endings, with the edges of the work. For instance, in one work the central characters are introduced in the prologue by way of another's narration. Their voices are heard as a quote in that narration. The effect is to have the characters' voices present before they appear. They are present too soon, as sheer voices, before they play any role in the opera. Such a prologue thus functions to dissociate voice and character, or to present characters as spirits, and to form an intimate alliance with afterlife expressions. On the whole, beginnings and endings, often taking the form of prologue and epilogue, throw singing off course by replacing it with other forms of utterances, such as speaking or murmuring. They allow bits of reality, like biographical information or a voiceover, to enter the work, confronting the character with a double in the world outside the work or with her image as presented by an omniscient narrator. Such devices throw into question what it is for a work to begin and how it can reach an end. The work is burdened with an inheritance. Take another example: every biopic assumes the prior existence of its subject, yet in Zeffirelli's film *Callas Forever* (2002), the inheritance of the dead diva's voice becomes itself a problem internal to the film's plot: How can a past voice be synchronized with present existence?

Every opera also inherits its libretto's source-text and thus must internalize and control that inheritance. Puccini, for instance, in *Gianni Schicchi* builds on a few lines from Dante's *Inferno* and constructs an epilogue to subvert the great poet's severe verdict on *Gianni*. We are lured by the character constructed by the opera, even if Dante has put him in one of the lowest circles of hell. When another composer comes along to write a sequel to Puccini's opera, a further link in the chain of inheritances, appropriations, and epilogues is formed. One work serves as the other's epilogue or prologue, and voices of the dead are able to migrate between the two operas. Characters and their singing spill beyond the borders of the works.

Several works interpreted here rethink epilogues and prologues. The latter are used to question openings and closures and to doubt whether time has even passed at all, whether anything has in fact happened. These edges serve as pasts figuring the present, inventions of new pasts, and singing salvaged from the past of the singer.

Aesthetic Orbit

In many of the major contemporary reconfigurations of the aesthetics of opera, I find ideas that echo the notion of the afterlife of singing I develop here. Most prominently is the insight that opera's power derives from its hovering between worlds, one of which is either yearned for (Cavell), not directly present to us (Abbate), inaccessible (Tomlinson), or present at all costs (Žižek). In all these accounts, singing figures in some form as the passage, the in-between, the gate to something beyond itself.

What I offer as configurations of singing afterlives cannot simply be mapped onto an existing formulation of the aesthetics of the medium. I do not think of this book as a typical exemplification of an aesthetics of opera insofar as it is so bound up with the specific examples it explicates. The critical issues raised determining what the world of opera is about—the disembodiment of opera's voices, the power of voice to revive and to unveil as well as its frailty, the doubling of the world—are raised differently for every example. Each draws us into yet another alignment of voices and fugitive, impossible moments.

Three main premises from Stanley Cavell's ontology of opera are pertinent for thinking through the possibilities that operatic afterlives hold for opera: the peculiar relationship of voice and body, singing's power to revive the world, and singing as opening up to further meaning. Cavell's insight into opera's peculiar affinity between its voices and bodies facilitates our understanding of a voice achieving independence from character as experienced in relation to afterlives. Cavell develops his discussion of what is unique to opera against the background of his investigation of the relation of actor to character in media such as theater and film:

> On film the actor is the subject of the camera, emphasizing that this actor could (have) become other characters (that is, emphasizing the potentiality in human existence, the self's journeying), as opposed to theater's emphasizing that this character could (will) accept other actors (that is, emphasizing the fatedness in human existence, the self's finality or typicality at each step of the journey). In opera the relative emphasis of singer and role seems undecidable in these terms, indeed unimportant beside the fact of the new conception it introduces of the relation between voice and body, a relation in which not this character and this actor are embodied in each other but in which this voice is located in—one might say disembodied within—this figure, this double, this person, this persona, this singer, whose voice is essentially unaffected by the role.[1]

In Cavell's account, an operatic voice as such is disembodied within the body carrying it. For sure, the body determines voice in technical terms, what it can and cannot produce. But *character* in opera is not an outcome of the body and the voice of the singer. A loose link connects the two. The voice neither determines the character, nor the character determines the voice. A *singer* for Cavell has a unique body that cannot be detached from her very voice, but that voice is experienced as disembodied. This link is unreproducible because of "the utter contingency [of the diva's body] together with the ineluctable necessity in its being just this body that projects just that voice as beside itself, by itself—to imagine giving either of them up."[2]

A second aspect of Cavell's account of the medium's foundation is located in singing's power to cross over to the other world in an attempt to bring back the dead. Its origin should be sought, as mentioned, in the Orpheus myth. The power of singing to cross between worlds is also understood as the power to revive *this* world, to show it as transfigured, as though this world figured as the other. Reviving the world is coupled with an opposite notion of the world as lost and deadened. This is the realm of haunting, of enduring an existence in neither world, in limbo, neither dead nor alive.

A third aspect Cavell puts forth, and which I find pertinent to the configuration of operatic afterlives, is his account of singing as a figure for abandonment. Singing is not an expression of the inner life of the character. Instead, it is a figure for the exposure of what lies beyond the confines of the work: singing as opening up unbound reverberations of meaning. These tensions regarding the relation of voice to body might leave room to position operatic afterlives as expressive cases of what is nevertheless essential to opera's embodiment—rare, strange, yet compatible with the aesthetics of opera.

For Carolyn Abbate, too, disembodiment is fundamental to opera. But it is something opera defends itself against. It is not an essential condition of opera's voices as such, but a trick that may increase or diminish the power of the voice. The origin of opera in the myth of Orpheus's singing excludes a crucial moment, namely Orpheus's posthumous disembodiment. Orpheus is decapitated, yet his singing resonates after death. This very aspect of the originating myth of opera has repeatedly been left out of its history. Not wishing to acknowledge song's independence from the body or life of the singer, opera absents the singing head. But disembodiment finds its way back into opera in other forms. It serves, writes Abbate, as instances of impossible singing, "of a song that can never exist, sung by a creature no one can identify or see with human eyes."[3] In Abbate's implied (rather than present) moments of music, there is a glimpse of another world.

Doubleness of worlds is another feature shared in these views of opera. Two worlds is the critical determinant of opera for Gary Tomlinson as well: "Opera, through its history, has been a chief staging ground...for a belief in the existence of two worlds, one accessible to the senses, the other not. Operatic singing has supplied...a potent experience of a metaphysics as well as of a physics, of an immaterial as well as of a material world."[4] The two worlds acquire different manifestations throughout history in accordance with changing models of subjectivity. Tomlinson traces analogies among the approach of opera's voices to the limits of the phenomenal, their power to envoice the imperceptible, and the construction of the subject they embody. Doubleness of worlds has different manifestations for Abbate: "Opera will always give rise to two terms—whether 'speech versus music' or 'operatic music versus phenomenal performance.'"[5] Cavell's doubling of the world is reflected in a related figure for Abbate: that of the world above and the world below, what she also calls the flight and the fall, or the transcendental and the material. In writing on opera, according to Abbate, materiality and embodiment are dismissed in favor of an overemphasis on its transcendental, metaphysical nature. As a result, no true account has been given of opera's existence (and that of music as a whole) in and as live performance. But opera is a paradoxical amalgam of the two worlds. Abbate locates within the works themselves, in their different modes of singing, the very distinction between the material and the transcendental. Stage songs, for example, are special instances in opera in which a character really sings, something Abbate terms *phenomenal music* (as opposed to all other singing and music in opera, which she terms *noumenal*). In phenomenal music we get hints of the split between realms, between what characters inhabiting an opera are customarily conceived as hearing, what they are conceived as hearing when they sing a song, and how we, the audience, conceive of what we hear (the audience and the operatic character might not be hearing the same sounds). Another such example is the numinous intruder: a mysterious character, Faust for example, who breaches the opera and brings within its orbit the realm of the beyond. Opera stages more radical cases when it further imprints its performed nature within the works themselves: "Rather than accepting musical performances as ephemeral reflections of musical works," Abbate writes, "I toyed with a different idea. Perhaps it is the works that are the aftershocks, lingering shapes that give voice to an uncanny phenomenon. Acoustic images of performance press into musical works themselves; more specifically, opera takes into account the very means by which operatic works turn into sung reality."[6]

In the fictional space of an opera, death—that which would end a character's life and imply the end of singing—is overshadowed by the concern with the fading away of the work itself. Abbate reconceives the place of life and death in relation to the work to reveal the work's livelihood: "In opera, certain arias can convey a sense not that they are being sung, but they instead are reaching out to give life to a moribund body, making it sing. One could go further still: perhaps it is the musical works that are alive, and we who are dead."[7] Making an analogous insight to Cavell's third point about the ontology of opera, Abbate reveals a form of revival in the medium. The fading of every performance simultaneously carries its further resonances.

Slavoj Žižek's conception of opera, founded almost exclusively on his analysis of Wagner, relies heavily on Lacan's notion of the two deaths. The two deaths—"the biologically necessary demise and the so-called second death, the fact that the subject died in peace, with his accounts settled and with no symbolic debt haunting his or her memory"—form an economy that is different from what I think of as modes of afterlife.[8] We are in a zone where a hero is unable to die unhaunted. The Wagnerian hero is deprived of death, condemned to eternal suffering, yearning to die.

It is in this zone between the two deaths that Žižek locates the Wagnerian song. This in-betweenness is again a form of doubleness of the world that brings about the occasion for singing. It encompasses a sense of endlessness (for the Wagnerian hero, this undead existence, in which a second death is prevented, is an eternity of suffering). In Žižek's matrix, the Wagnerian exemplary song emerges from this condition of existing as an undead monster. Thus, it is an opening up, not of the conditions of an afterlife of singing but of the horror of immortality, an interminable existence of singing.

Inside the Book

This book comprises four main chapters interwoven with four shorter ones. Each chapter is self-sufficient and offers close scrutiny of a situation of singing; each addresses underlying questions about the possibility of afterlife singing. As the book progresses, the examples become gradually more radical. The book begins with a short prologue, outlining the chimeric example of Puccini's first opera, *Le villi* (1884), in which traits of singing-toward-death in the death song are found alongside, and only partially replaced by, traits of the afterlife of singing. In the prologue, an opera about singing after death is shown to still depend on and be bound to the death song. The book ends with an epilogue about a cartoon which transforms operatic death into endless multiplications of singing after death, reflecting the cartoon condition of undying. The epilogue and the prologue show cases in which two signification systems determine the work's thematics of afterlife: in the prologue, thematics of the death song clash with thematics of afterlife; in the epilogue, the systems of opera and the cartoon reinforce one another. In both cases, there are two aesthetics of death in question. Thus, the structure of the book, with its prologue and epilogue, echoes the importance of those sections for the thematics of afterlife in the works discussed in the book. Two interludes in the book function similarly: they are epilogues to the chapters that precede them.

The first chapter, "The Afterlife of Maria Callas's Voice," explores an afterlife that cinema has provided for a dead diva's voice. Franco Zeffirelli's film *Callas Forever* (2002) fictionalizes the last four months of Callas's life, a time when the opera star no longer possessed a singing voice. It tells of an attempt to recreate Callas's presence by pairing her wondrous bygone singing to her present self in a cinematic production. *Callas Forever* offers the diva two options for such a revival: she can make a comeback in a film in which she is dubbed by her own past recordings, or she can relearn an operatic role and find a novel interpretation for a character in hope of revitalizing her nearly nonexistent present voice. Each option of reanimating the body with the lost voice imagines a form of afterlife for that voice. I claim, however, that the plot, in effect, stages the failure of both these alternatives to recreate in cinema the presence and power of Maria Callas. It makes manifest that film itself, and Zeffirelli's film in particular, fails to preserve the presence of the operatic voice once it is removed from its body. The translation of the unity of the diva's embodied voice into a dubbed image powerfully attests to that impossibility. In the end, the film's desperate attempt to revive the voice has the opposite effect, and even the recordings Callas left behind seem to fade out. I argue, then, that in *Callas Forever*, profound loss is the price of a fantasy to arrest and hold onto the voice of the dead. The transposition of medium causes the voice to disintegrate and die out. The voice, we might say, has its own afterlife and cannot be forced to remain present by other means.

Letting go of the voice is what is offered in another film that gives the voice of Maria Callas a peculiar afterlife. Federico Fellini's *E la nave va* (*And the Ship Sails On*, 1983), a film I discuss at length elsewhere, offers a spectacle of the afterlife of Callas's voice by beginning rather than ending with the death of the singer.[9] The film stages an eccentric funeral rite in which her admirers gather aboard a ship to scatter her ashes at sea. She is a presence in the film only after her life has ended: the sound of her voice emanates only from a gramophone. And her singing is heard just once in the film, for the spreading of her ashes. Revitalizing the voice is unlike *Callas Forever*'s re-embodiment; in *E la nave va*, remains of a body and voice figure in the cult the singer leaves behind.

My second chapter, "Sung by Death," considers Puccini's 1918 opera *Gianni Schicchi* (the opera used in one of the scenes of *Callas Forever* to attempt the pairing of past voice to present self). *Gianni Schicchi*'s plot has the title character impersonate the voice of the

dead Buoso Donati in order to change Donati's will. It constitutes, on an obvious level, the revival of the voice of the dead. But
what is more interesting and important is that the final moments
of the opera are an apologia recited by Schicchi, supposedly many
years after the events depicted, from hell. I argue that the voice
given at the end to the dead in fact permeates the opera as a
whole. *Gianni Schicchi* undermines the presupposition that hell is
kept separate from the world of the living and is confined to the
opera's epilogue. Gianni Schicchi's afterlife in hell reflects back
from the epilogue to the whole opera and refashions the character's operatic self as one that is simultaneously living and dead. If
Gianni Schicchi is explicitly about a dead man being overtaken by
a voice of the living man who dubs him — about how the dead are
threatened by the living — then its implicit argument reveals the
world of the living as itself permeated by death.

In an interlude following chapter 2, I discuss an opera that
directly addresses *Gianni Schicchi*'s epilogue. Michael Ching's
Buoso's Ghost: Comic Sequel in One Act After Puccini's Gianni Schicchi (1996) offers itself, in fact, as *Gianni Schicchi*'s continuation,
indeed as an epilogue. Dominating the narrative and set of Puccini's opera is the dead corpse of Buoso that Gianni dubs. In the
sequel, *Buoso's Ghost*, both the dead and, temporarily, the living
feature as apparitions. The opera grants Gianni vocal abilities
above and beyond those granted him in Puccini's opera: he impersonates ghosts and conjures apparitions. *Buoso's Ghost* renegotiates
boundaries even beyond the already complex relation between
the realms in *Gianni Schicchi*.

The third chapter, "*Dybbuk*: Between Voice and Song," presents an even more extreme case. The chapter examines Lodovico
Rocca's opera *Il dibuk* (1934), in which a *dybbuk*, a wandering soul
of the dead, cleaves to and comes to inhabit his lover's body. The
spirit of the dead is not manifested in an imitation or dubbing
of the voice by the living, as in the examples of *Gianni Schicchi*
and *Callas Forever*. Rather, a distinction between voice and song
is drawn in which song comes to reflect a primordial core that

is aspired to but remains absent in the voice. The operatic *dybbuk* carves out an implication for singing that is distinct from voice—as if, indeed, that were possible, as if singing were dependent on neither a voice nor a voice's outcome. What makes the dead present to us takes the form of song; the operatic *dybbuk* is an invention of song within the medium of song.

In a brief interlude, functioning as an epilogue to chapters two and three, I show commonalities regarding the afterlife of singing in the examples of *Gianni Schicchi* and *Il dibuk*.

The fourth chapter, "Singing and Disappearing Angels," portrays a limit case in which distinctions no longer hold separating singing, dying, and the hereafter. In this example, we shift back and forth between human and angelic realms, as each echoes the other. The chapter originates in Walter Benjamin's evocation of a Jewish tradition according to which a host of angels is created daily in order to sing God's praises, only to then be destroyed. The angels die, but their singing remains incessant. Mordecai Seter's oratorio *Tikkun Ḥatsot* (*Midnight Vigil*, 1961), analyzed in this chapter, is shown to be a composition about music's ability to convey a passing away of song and the simultaneity of singing and dying; it considers the paradoxical idea of a perpetually evanescent song. In such a song, the fleeting dying out of song can be expressed in an unceasing flow. Through my discussion of *Tikkun Ḥatsot*, I investigate the simultaneity of death and life in a realm in which their opposition is annulled.

The book ends in an epilogue, "Cartoon-Animated Opera," presenting probably the most radical case of an afterlife of voice by means of the analogy of the cartoon body with the operatic voice. I argue that here is born a new life-form, a hybrid opera-cartoon creature that multiplies exponentially features of both opera and cartoon worlds. The cartoon figure, standing for opera, bypasses the death reserved for it from the world of opera. In the afterlife, its singing improves, multiplies, and is beautified. Death is central to the operatic aesthetic, but here it displays cartoon-like behavior: it does not bring singing to an end but perpetuates it. Opera takes it upon itself to become a cartoon so that its deaths will not overshadow the never-ending singing. The new creature dwelling in cartoon and opera worlds simultaneously dies (unlike a cartoon figure) and sings while dead (unlike an opera character). The construction unites operatic death and the undying cartoon character; operatic dying is made to mimic the undying condition of cartoon existence. The vehicle of this conflation is song. In other words, operatic death does not bring singing to an end. The perpetuity of the cartoon world gives body to an unending singing after death.

The notion of afterlife opens up hidden possibilities in the space of opera. It allows us to make intelligible a register of the voice that we intuitively sense to be essential to it. The extreme instances of the phenomenon interpreted in this book reflect back on the meanings of the operatic voice as such, and the sense of its resonating, unending, haunting presence.

Traces

Giacomo Puccini, *Le villi* (1884)

Death, Afterdeath

Hin und Zurück (*There and Back*, 1927), Paul Hindemith's twelve-minute opera, proceeds to a midpoint where a woman is killed and her murderer commits suicide. At this caesura, the scene darkens and a bearded sage rises through a trapdoor and sings about the intervention of a higher power:

> Looking down from above, no great difference exists
> if a man begins his life in the cradle,
> then proceeds 'til he meets death,
> or if he dies first, and follows from death to birth.
> Let us reverse this fate and make things turn back,
> then I will show you, the logic changes not a jot,
> and all will be well as it was before.

Then, in the opera's second half, the events are all undone. This trick is achieved by the opera going backwards both textually and musically, retracing its steps and ending exactly where it began. It is a metaphysical fantasy or, if you like, a cinematic trick: opera rewind. Beginning at birth and ending in death becomes interchangeable with dying first, then following from death to birth. In *Hin und Zurück*'s comic world, death has no bearing on singing: it leaves no residue, no trace. What happens up to the point of death is fashioned identically to what happens beyond that point.

But in Puccini's *Le villi* (1884), another opera with its death in the middle, the midpoint serves to gather characteristic traits of singing-toward-death, the death song, and what I call the afterlife of singing. Everything leads us to expect a death song, but it never materializes. Because death is placed in the middle, the death song is eschewed and loses its function as an end and apotheosis of singing. It is as though *Le villi* were a chimeric case: death unsung is transformed into a song after death. At the same time, traces of the expected yet undelivered death song are found in the delivery of singing in the afterlife. I will linger briefly on this mixed example as a prelude to the more detailed cases in this book.

Puccini's first opera, *Le villi* does not figure among the standard repertory, though one finds in it important precedents of Puccini's later style. In fact, scholars find the opera quite problematic.[1] There are, for instance, flaws in the construction of the libretto: the drama is not fully exploited, characters are underdeveloped, the main characters do not have solos, and there is no death scene; there are long orchestral *intermezzi* without singing (thus emphasizing a symphonic Germanic tendency, straying from Italian opera's view of song as supreme); important action is neither enacted in singing nor advanced by the main characters, but is instead recited by a narrator, and so on. Writing about the influence of German romanticism, with its supernatural themes, and French opera, with its abundance of dance, scholars refer to this opera as an example of Puccini's *Sturm und Drang* style[2] or simply as a "bizarrerie."[3] The opera, however, is also taken to be innovative. Julian Budden, for instance, writes that its novelty lies in a "conscious attempt to break down the barriers between the various artistic media."[4] This aim is exhibited in its very genre: it is a fusion between opera and ballet, where dance does not remain incidental, as in traditional Grand Opera, but is central to the drama itself. It is also innovative in its addition of declamation to narrate major happenings in the plot, replacing presentation in song. I do not wish to take sides in the debates about the merit of the work, nor claim that it is immature or underdeveloped, on the way to something else. But I do wish to argue that part of the praise (and criticism) given to the work can be traced to the conglomeration of death and after-death themes.

Le villi is about the lovers Anna and Roberto, who are about to marry; they sing of their love, though Anna has bad forebodings. Roberto must unexpectedly depart and, though he professes eternal love to Anna, he fails to return. The abandoned Anna dies. Up to this point, the storyline might have encompassed an entire typical operatic plot that leads inevitably to a death foreshadowed from the outset. If this were the entire opera, the supreme singing would have been reserved for Anna's death song.

Although we await this thematic cluster, it does not occur. We are in the middle, not the end of Le villi when Anna dies, and no death song takes place. Instead, her death is related by a narrator, and her funeral procession, accompanied by an unseen chorus, is viewed from behind a scrim. Anna dies "in" the orchestral *intermezzo*, and her very death is veiled. It happens in an in-between zone and is a death she does not sing; it is neither a high point nor a goal, and the coffin, rather than the voice, is objectified. In this deferral of the space of singing, there is already a hint of another kind of singing.

Substitute

Initially, Le villi was composed as a one-act opera for a competition in 1883. The competition aimed at changing the contemporary operatic scene by introducing shorter operas with fast action and direct expression.[5] Puccini did not win the competition but, following several alterations, the opera was performed and met with great success.[6] It was then expanded into a two-act opera.[7]

The extension of the opera entailed adding a solo scene for each of the lovers. (Originally, the main roles were conceived as duets. The absence of solos, central pieces expected in opera, is itself novel and weakens the death-song trajectory always projected onto the solo entrance aria.) In the expanded opera, Puccini and his librettist Ferdinando Fontana reintroduce an entrance aria for the heroine, indeed they overdo it: Anna's entrance aria does not merely foreshadow but resembles a death song: "Last night I dreamed I was dying," she sings. Another telling expansion is the addition of orchestral interludes to be played with the curtain raised. These orchestral passages are central to the drama rather than a distraction from behind-the-scenes stage business. Verses were also added to tell of Anna's death. These verses were not set to music, though they appear in the score and the libretto (recordings of the opera customarily provide a narrator to declaim them, as though the unsung portion were being staged). A women's chorus was added for the funeral prayer that accompanied Anna's body being borne across the stage in a funeral cortège behind the scrim. It seems that all additions and enlargements of the two-act version attest to the effort exercised to keep the death scene at bay and replace it with sounds other than Anna's.

Dance Detour

There is controversy whether Puccini's opera, with its libretto by Ferdinando Fontana, is based on Théophile Gautier's scenario for Adolphe Adam's famous ballet *Giselle*, or whether it shares with it a foundation in folk legend. Julian Budden argues that Puccini's libretto is based on Alphonse Karr's story "Les Wilis" (1852).[8] Michael Elphinstone, however, sees Karr's tale to be closely based on Heine (the ballet was inspired by Victor Hugo's poem "Fantômes"[9] and Heinrich Heine's *De l'Allemagne*).[10] Here as well I will not enter into the debate, but simply mention a point of comparison. There are differences between the ballet and the opera, most notably their opposite endings. In the ballet, the heroine's love remains after death and protects her lover from the *wilis*, while in the opera she, together with the other *wilis*, dances him to death. But though they have opposite outcomes, the works share a central feature regarding the heroine's death: they both strikingly underplay it. In the ballet, Giselle's death is so brief it is uncertain what has caused it. In "What Killed Giselle?," Marian Smith tries to decipher this mystery and asks whether she commits suicide with a sword or dies of a broken heart.[11]

This ambiguity makes space for another possible cause of death, originating in fact in both Hugo's "Fantômes" and Heine's *De l'Allemagne*, the sources for the opera and the ballet. This cause of death is most intriguing: it depends not on anything in the narrative but on the medium of enactment. In Hugo's "Fantômes," we encounter the following lines:

> Dancing causes her death: with eager, boundless love,
> Balls—dazzling balls—filled her with ecstasies;
> And now her ashes thrill and gently move.[12]

The love of dancing leads to her death; for the love of dance, the heroine turns into a *wili* and dances postmortem. In Heine's *De l'Allemagne* as well, an unfulfilled wish for dancing, not revenge, propels the narrative:

> In parts of Austria there exists a tradition...of Slavic origin: the tradition of the night-dancer, who is known, in Slavic countries, under the name Wili. Wilis are young brides-to-be who die before their wedding day. The poor young creatures cannot rest peacefully in their graves. In their stilled hearts and lifeless feet, there remains a love for dancing which they were unable to satisfy during their lifetimes. At midnight, they rise out of their graves, gather together in troupes on the roadside and woe be unto the young man who comes across them! He is forced to dance with them; they unleash their wild passion, and he dances with them until he falls dead. Dressed in their wedding gowns, with wreaths of flowers on their heads and glittering rings on their fingers, the Wilis dance in the moonlight.... Their faces, though white as snow, have the beauty of youth. They laugh with joy so hideous, they call you so seductively, they have an air of such sweet promise, that these dead bacchantes are irresistible.[13]

The dancing spirits of the dead lure the hero, who appears by chance while the *wilis* are dancing their fatal dance. Dancing kills; the dead return, dancing, to take others back with them. Indeed, in Karr's "Les Wilis," taken to be the direct source for the opera, emphasis is placed not only on dance but on music and the voice's sirenlike, destructive power—opera's mode of enactment.[14] When Heinrich (the name of Robert in Karr's story) unintentionally returns to the place where Anna lived, he hears a sound he recognizes as the music he once played (in Karr's tale he plays the horn) and danced to with Anna. In Karr's tale, when Heinrich returns, he is lured by the sound of music sung, to his amazement, to words of *his*. The music that draws him through its familiarity uncannily turns out to be that of the *wilis*. In the opera, though in a different way, his words and music are also returned to him voiced by Anna. In the opera, music and dance bring about death. And the opera ends fatally in a blasphemous hosanna sung by the *wilis*—a grotesque reference to Roberto's vow before departing that Anna may doubt God but not him.

Voice Recognition

The second half of the opera figures Anna's return. Dead, she has become a *wili*, and is joined by the others to take vengeance on Roberto, who has strayed into the vicinity of her house. Roberto feels that "weird voices pursue me"; he knows these voices to be those of the *wilis*. It is, in effect, Anna who has become a chorus of voices, made up of the spirits of abandoned maidens. All the *wilis* are in effect Anna, in plural; Anna multiplied and multivocal—a common feature encountered in postmortem singing.

What first marks her as specter is the voice. She is initially heard only offstage, her hiddenness reminiscent of her veiled death procession and the invisible voices accompanying it. Roberto recognizes her voice, but in fact the music she sings is in the *wilis'* musical style, not hers. Anna and the *wilis* now sound identical. Roberto recognizes her even though such singing has not previously been associated with her. How then does he recognize her? Is recognition a manifestation of her sirenlike seductive power? Or perhaps the differences between singing in life and singing after death are not detected by the opera's characters—only by us? The opera preserves a double stance: Anna's singing, once she is a *wili*, is conceived by Roberto as unchanged from that of the living Anna, but we hear that she has acquired the spirits' style and abandoned her own, that her singing is unrecognizable. Anna confirms *our* estranged hearing, not Roberto's, when she declares her transformation from the personification of love to the spirit of revenge: "I am no longer Love. I am Revenge!"

Character is abstracted into affect. Indeed how fixed or free the expression of singing becomes, how singing after death internalizes the effects of the opera it takes part in, is tied to questions of subjectivity. It depends on the meaning laid forth by each opera about what lies between living and dead selves. In each example of the afterlife of singing portrayed in this book, subjectivity is somehow eschewed, as though singing were capable of a degree of independence from its originating opera.

Returned Singing

Anna's voice is indirect in another way. In her entrance aria in act 1, not only does she dream of death, but she also sings of her wish that flowers be substituted for her voice; she wishes that they would deliver her words and thoughts to Roberto. Her estranged voicing and explicit dream, thus, like the entrance aria itself, already point to the thematics of afterlife.

When Anna returns in act 2, she does so accompanied initially by the *wilis*' music, then in her duet with Roberto she sings *his* words and *his* music. Anna has incorporated his expressions, which she quotes back to him. In fact, while she was alive, in act 1, she did the exact same thing in their first duet. Already then, she had committed to memory his vow of eternal love by reiterating and quoting it (this renders even the straightforward phrase "I love you" ambiguous: it can be a statement from either of the lovers, either hers or his as quoted by her).[15] Though typical of Puccini's early duets, here the near-interchangeability of the two parts of the duet play into the exhibition of indistinguishable

41

vocalities. The presence of multiple voices, another common feature encountered in expressions of the afterlife of singing, is hidden in Puccini's uses of convention and his operatic style, as well as in the specific narrative.

When Anna returns in the second act, she reminds him of their past by replaying her part of the duet, which was itself already a dubbing of him. She is being so very literal: to remind him of the past she sings what they sang, or what his singing sounds like as voiced by her. Voicing him, she tries to bring him back to that point, erasing any difference between her singing now and how it was while she was alive. But this attempt at reproducing what came before is not an enlivening of that past but a sign of death. This time, the duet's prophesizing text is directed at him, calling for Roberto's death. Both are now singing about their deaths: Anna accuses Roberto of responsibility for her death and calls for his, so that in his death he will again be hers.

In *Le villi*'s chimeric manifestations of the thematics of the afterlife of singing, death does not figure at the end. Death provides incentive and meaning; it propels the narrative and puts the entire space of the opera under its spell; and it renders singing ambiguous (are Anna and Anna-as-*wili* identical? Is Anna's singing itself multiplied in the *wilis*? Is the body-voice schism accentuated by Anna, *a dancing voice*? Is Anna, while singing, quoting Roberto or quoting herself quoting?).

To the charge of abandonment, Anna adds an accusation about the silence it has brought upon her:

I loved you: you betrayed me
I waited: you never came
But what a frightful sorrow
It is to suffer in silence!
With all hope gone from my heart
You made me die!

It is *silence* that was coerced. In his absence, indeed in his place, she memorizes his words and his music. But the words and

42

music that she now returns to him are in no way identical with what they were at their origin. Introjecting his singing does not allow it to be brought back as the singing it was. It only marks its loss and irretrievability as final. In *Le villi* — and we will encounter a related gesture of irretrievability in the next chapter, which deals with Maria Callas and her voice — singing, as such, is precisely that which cannot be called back or recalled.

CHAPTER ONE

The Afterlife of Maria Callas's Voice

Franco Zeffirelli, *Callas Forever* (2002)

Bygone Voices

> It is indeed impossible to imagine our own death; and whenever we
> attempt to do so we can perceive that we are in fact still present as
> spectators.... At bottom no one believes in his own death, or, to put
> the same thing in another way,...in the unconscious every one of
> us is convinced of his own immortality.
> —Sigmund Freud, "Thoughts for the Times on War and Death"

> [Maria Callas's] record company has succeeded in making people
> think she is still alive.... It's a little bit like conversations with the
> other world.
> —Manuela Hoelterhoff, *Cinderella & Company*

Franco Zeffirelli's film *Callas Forever* (2002) abounds with references to comebacks, second chances, the reclaiming of one's life,
the mourning for one's lost voice, and questions of immortality.[1]
It is a surprising film. Rather than reconstructing, twenty-five
years after her death, the diva's life, it depicts what could have
happened in her last few months. The fictionalized account is not
intended to correct Maria Callas's biography in any simple sense:
in fact, it tells of failures. To *Callas Forever*'s invented plot—about
a Callas comeback on film—Callas herself ultimately objects.
Here we have a case in which reality, our knowledge of Callas's
life, carries meaning for the work. The work as such, not a specific attribute, is an expression of the afterlife.

Callas Forever is not set during the diva's prime, but in 1977, when she no longer possessed a singing voice.[2] Pier Paolo Pasolini had cast Callas in *Medea* (1970), the diva's only (real) appearance in a film, but Callas famously did not sing in it.[3] Catherine Clément argues that Pasolini captures something essential to opera and to Callas precisely by not staging her singing.[4] This approach, Clément claims, is an attempt to separate Callas from her voice, as though extracting something from her that would not be overshadowed or violated by her song. Interestingly, Zeffirelli, in the narration for *The Callas Documentary*, authoritatively informs us that Pasolini's casting of Callas was unsuccessful. Pasolini, he says, misused the singer. By recreating Callas after her death, Zeffirelli, of course, also separates the singer from her voice, but, in contrast to Pasolini, he uses *only* Callas's voice. Zeffirelli, in creating an afterlife for Maria Callas, thus raises the question whether any representation of Callas—as herself, not in a role—is possible apart from her singing.

But can the human voice exist independently of the singing body? Sound recordings, at times, contain voices surviving the body that once produced them; invisible and devoid of body, the singer is somehow "there" in the presence of voice. Documentaries capture a sense of presence different from that preserved in sound recordings. Fragments of biographical information and interviews construct a different Callas from that heard in a role, a Lady Macbeth for instance. But now that Callas is dead, how can Zeffirelli recreate a sense of her presence? Can Callas be conjured, summoned, called back? And if so, what form of afterlife would that be? What is forever lost, and what is always preserved of the operatic voice after the singer's death? Can a different body seemingly "produce" the bygone voice, in an attempt thereby to recreate Callas, reanimate her, or would the new body refashion the voice itself? Or yet again, more uncannily, would the voice affect the image sounding it? Zeffirelli's film addresses these complex questions and oscillates between acknowledging the threat of the singing voice and abandoning itself to the ontology of cinema.

The use *Callas Forever* makes of Callas's voice emanating from recordings is not an obvious choice in films representing great dead opera singers. In *The Great Caruso* (1951), directed by Richard Thorpe, for example, the "remains" of Caruso's voice are not used. What replaces the sound of his voice is the *act* of singing; that is, Caruso is portrayed "in" the voice of Mario Lanza, another very famous singer: one singer is thus portrayed through the singing of another. Caruso's presence is invoked not through the sound of his own voice but through the performance of operatic singing as such, as though presence were recreated by an acoustic memory of the past. *The Great Caruso* and *Callas Forever* offer very different conceptions of the relationship between the voice and body of a dead singer.

There are a number of other films that, like *The Great Caruso* and *Callas Forever*, deal with the gap between the life of the voice and that of the singer's body, with operatic voices outliving the body that had once produced them or with bodies longing for the bygone voices they had once produced. These films interpret the notion of life sustained "in" or preserved "through" the voice. Daniel Schmid's *Tosca's Kiss* (1985) is one such example. The film follows elderly musicians in Milan's Casa Verdi, an old people's home for musicians established in 1902 in accordance with Verdi's Will. The musicians, mostly singers, have largely been forgotten; they no longer perform and have long since lost their singing voices. They are shown listening to their own voices emanating from old recordings, a striking testimony of the inevitable severance of the singing voice from the singer's body. *Tosca's Kiss* is a documentary about singers outliving their voices.

Another example, Fellini's *E la nave va* (*And the Ship Sails On*, 1983), is even more extreme in thinking through the conjunction of the singer's operatic voice and the cinematic body, in that Fellini dispenses with the singer's body altogether.[5] The film depicts a sea voyage to disperse the diva's ashes. We hear her voice only once, emanating from a gramophone as her ashes are blown away in the wind: her voice is "attached" to her disappearing body.

Thorpe, Schmid, Fellini, and Zeffirelli offer different solutions in their attempts to represent the disembodied operatic voice: Thorpe substitutes one singer for another; Schmid separates singers from their singing; Fellini demolishes the singer's body; and Zeffirelli, as we will see, has an actress mime the dead singer's song. These cinematic attempts, each in its own way, make manifest a fundamental problem with the embodiment of the operatic voice: it is as if the mismatch between voice and body brings out a haunting quality of that voice.

Paradoxically, it might be that another medium, such as cinema, attempts to inherit the operatic realm, but here is where the uncanniness of the operatic voice becomes most manifest. The relation between the two media must be elaborated bearing in mind a fundamental attraction of cinema to opera, as to a past beyond it, to which it yet returns and which it cannot quite incorporate. For sure, the transformation of opera into cinema occurs at times in cinema's self-effacement, in its merely reproducing operatic productions. But it is at its most ambitious when it is precisely aware of the tension between the two media and allows those tensions to be revealed and to work in favor of the self-understanding of both cinema and opera. Opera is linked to deep intimations of ephemerality, of the constant threat that singing will be terminated; film, on the other hand, is linked to remains, to intimations of immortality and the promise of continuity and inheritance. Which is to say that cinematic attempts to come to terms with the operatic voice often eventuate in the failure of the cinematic transposition and, in the most interesting cases, such as Zefirelli's *Callas Forever*, lead to cinema's own staging of its failure to return the operatic voice from the dead.[6]

In *Callas Forever*, Zeffirelli fictionalizes Callas's last few months—when she no longer possessed a singing voice—and invents her cine-operatic comeback. The making of the film and its plot mirror each other: recordings of the (real) dead diva emanate from the mouth of an actress resembling Callas (Fanny Ardant) and, at the same time, Callas as a fictional character relearns the gestures and motions that produced her former singing voice. *Callas Forever* employs two highly charged operas in the diva's career to mark her singing: *Carmen*, the opera she famously never performed on stage, and *Tosca*, the opera that is at once one of her most admired recorded works, a rare audio-visual documentation of her stage performance, the opera once intended for a film's soundtrack, and the opera that was to be Callas's last appearance on stage. But *Carmen* and *Tosca* are not simply the operas we hear in *Callas Forever*: they are the operas chosen to effect a revival of the dead diva's lost voice. *Carmen* plays out the first attempt to revive her voice; *Tosca*, the second. The two attempts to resurrect the diva's voice form the thrust of the film. In fact, most of the film concerns the production of the film *Carmen*, with less time devoted to the master class surrounding *Tosca*. There are a few side narratives. For instance, in a storyline parallel to the attempts made to persuade Callas to perform again, Larry (Jeremy Irons) is shown as an (aging) agent of a rock band (never seen in the film). He has an affair with a deaf painter, Michael, a fan of Callas who translates the vibrations he can feel from her singing into painted images. In another subplot, Maria tries unsuccessfully to seduce the singer performing Don José alongside her in the film of *Carmen*. Callas's seclusion and self-imposed isolation is portrayed through her relationship with Larry, an old reporter friend, her maid, and so on. But these narratives are all subordinate to the film's main theme, the re-creation of Callas's lost voice.

Carmen and *Tosca* are the operas chosen to effect a revival of the dead diva's lost voice. The film dramatizes two such attempts at revival. In the first attempt, Larry, her former agent, persuades Callas to act in a filmed opera, but since she no longer possesses a singing voice, she is to mime recordings of her voice at its prime. Callas chooses *Carmen*, an opera she had never performed on stage and, thus, as she explains to Larry, "I never completed her."

Larry is convinced of the successful marriage of the bygone voice to her present body, but to her it appears deceptive.

Turning Larry's initial idea on its head, Callas comes up with an alternative way to regain her lost voice. Callas wishes to really sing again, rather than mime her former singing. She wishes to once again explore the character of Tosca, a role she feels she had left incomplete. A novel interpretation, a fresh and renewed characterization, Callas advocates, will revive her voice. Larry's project is based on the technological capability to transport the voice from the past in a time machine, landing it in the body of Callas some two decades after it originally sounded; Callas's alternative is to travel backwards, and to expect the present voice to revive its past greatness. The first option offers to cover up the present, nonexistent voice; the second, to breathe new life into it.

Originally, the singer Teresa Stratas was asked to play the role of Callas but, at her own request, she was replaced by an actress. The part, as Stratas understood it, required not a singer but an actress: someone who would make believe she is singing rather than someone really singing. Stratas had "impersonated" Callas in the past, in the film of Verdi's *La Traviata* (1982) in which Zeffirelli cast her as a "Callas clone" in the role of Violetta, the consumptive courtesan. He had expected her to recreate the Violetta that Callas had once embodied, and indeed, Callas is present as a ghost singer in the film. As Wayne Koestenbaum has commented, the film is "an elegy, an homage to Callas, a memorial to her vanished voice."[7] Zeffirelli did not hide his intention of conjuring a Callas from Stratas: "Almost everyone on the film had at one time or another worked with Callas. To us she was Violetta and in making the film we were somehow giving ourselves a second chance to make the film with Maria. I was as much to blame as anyone: every gesture I had asked of Teresa and every detail of interpretation, no matter how I tried to disguise it, had been inspired by the work I had done with Callas so many years before. Now along came Piero [the film's costume designer] trying to resurrect, through her, the many memories and emotions Maria had given us." In response, according to Zeffirelli, Stratas cried out: "I'm not a ghost." And continued: "Just because I'm Greek and can sing, I'm not a ghost." And: "I'm not Callas, could never hope to be."[8]

Zeffirelli had planned to make a film of *La Traviata* with Callas, but the project was never realized.[9] Then, in 1982, Zeffirelli heard and saw Callas in the voice and image of Stratas enacting one of Callas's roles. In 2002, however, twenty-five years after Callas's death, it became far too oppressive for Stratas to impersonate for *Callas Forever* not only one of the diva's roles, but the dead diva herself—with the voice of the dead "sounding" from her throat.

Regaining the Lost Voice: First Attempt

Callas is deeply troubled by Larry's suggestion for regaining the lost voice (using an old recording to support her present acting in a film of *Carmen*): the body is hers, as is the voice, but can the technological outcome of matching a past voice and a present body reproduce "Callas"? After completing the film of *Carmen*—while agreeing that the outcome is magnificent—she requests that it be destroyed. *Carmen*'s problem, in the diva's eyes, is not due to any technical shortcoming, such as an unconvincing match between that voice and this body. On the contrary, the problem lies in the very success of the dubbing apparatus.

Callas formulates the problem in terms of legacy and inheritance: the film falsifies what it means to have a voice such as she once had. The voice, she implies, should remain "whole," "in its time." The dilemma is further complicated when we realize that the scenes of *Carmen* are the only scenes in *Callas Forever* that are colorful, grandiose, and "operatic" in style. These scenes recall Francesco Rosi's film (1984) of Carmen and Zeffirelli's own style in his film operas. In creating a Callas troubled by this *Carmen*, Zeffirelli casts suspicion on the very technique on which his film operas are based. In renouncing the filmic project of *Carmen*, Callas, as a character in *Callas Forever*, renounces what it had taken to create her in the first place.

Why invent a Callas that rejects what is common practice in filmed operas and a norm in Italian cinema? (Dubbing singers with their own prerecorded voices, and dubbing actors with singers' voices, are common practices in film operas and are repeatedly employed by Zeffirelli.) Why make her see the basic cinematic techniques of playback, dubbing, and post-synchronization as extraordinary yet unacceptable illusions? Why invent a filmic plot that depends on Callas's recordings, then stage the failure of their transformation into film? The answer is not to be sought solely in biography nor in a forthright rejection of the cinematic tricks of the trade. The (real) Callas, after all, had consented to make a film in which she would sing and record *Tosca*, a recording intended to become the soundtrack to a film by Zeffirelli himself.[10] Questioning the integrity of cinematic techniques by subverting a "cinematic Callas," as it were, is related, I suggest, to the status of Maria Callas's voice and the way it bears on the body — or any body.

Re-voicing

Before attempting to explicate the status of Callas's voice, let us remind ourselves of some of the re-voicing techniques central to *Callas Forever*.[11] Post-synchronization, dubbing, and playback usually belong to the final stage of making a film and are aimed at concealing themselves in the final product, which presents a coherent human subject on screen.[12] These procedures are considered to work best when they do not draw attention to themselves but effect a perfect match of the actors' facial gestures with the voice, even at the price of loss of meaning (when, for example, translation is involved).[13]

Re-voicing techniques reattach voices and bodies on screen, and though there are significant differences between these methods, they all, as Michel Chion says, evoke suspicion in cinema.[14] They reveal the unity of body and voice to be a "trick" that can be tampered with, that can only be yearned for, even if this yearning, as Chion intimates, is one of the things "cinema is best at telling us about."[15]

The illusory sense of unity in the foundation of cinema engenders two contrary film traditions: the American, in which revoicing is used sparingly, mostly for singing scenes; and the Italian, in which dubbing and post-synchronization are the norm.[16] Considered by many as the inventors of dubbing, the Italians are known as the world's "best dubbers."[17] In Italy, foreign films are always dubbed, suggesting that the familiarity of the Italian audience with Humphrey Bogart or Marlene Dietrich, for example, is not based on these actors' most prominent attribute. Because the general practice is to record the films' soundtracks separately (because only rarely is the sound recorded on the set satisfactory), the Italian way attests to the radical alienation of voices and bodies.[18] Only at the final stage, in the dubbing studio, is the entire film rerecorded and matched with the images. Different actors are sometimes taken for the "vocal parts," and for others, one dubber re-voices the parts of several actors.[19] The widespread practice of post-synchronization also results from Italian films often employing an international cast of actors whose parts will all be dubbed before the film's release (the most famous case being Fellini's *La Dolce Vita*, with actors speaking four different languages that were dubbed into Italian after the film was completed).[20] As Chion notes, Italian cinema is not concerned with perfecting the match of voice and body in order to create the illusion of wholeness; it is, he says, "far removed from any obsessive fixation with the matching of voices to mouths [as is the case in French and American film traditions]. The freedom allotted in Italy for the synching of voices is . . . enormous."[21] Both cinematic traditions—the American futile striving to simulate the human subject as a coherent whole with its investment in perfect synch, and the Italian ease of fragmenting it—are responses to the same phenomenon: the disclosure of the represented human subject as a visual-acoustic trick.

In *Callas Forever*, Zeffirelli makes conscious use of both the Italian and American re-voicing traditions. The film oscillates between concealing and exhibiting its own re-voicing procedures:

they are thematized within the plot and, at the same time, go into the making of the film. To begin with, the entire cast of *Carmen* sings to a playback, the actors' own singing voices remaining unheard. This becomes apparent when Marco, the singer in the role of Don José, asks Callas whether his voice will ever be good enough to be heard. In *Carmen* he is expected *to perform* the act of singing, giving it an aura of authenticity in the very act of re-voicing (an allusion to Zeffirelli's earlier aesthetic inclination to mute Stratas in order to emit the voice of Callas). But there is nonetheless an uncanny dependence on Marco's unheard voice: it should, we are told, be "beautiful" and "interesting." His unheard voice determines the success of the foreign voice, as if the very qualities of the former are important and must "fit" the latter, someone else's heard voice. Perhaps even more than the host body, the host voice must appear to "match" the guest voice.

But Callas is exhilarated that singing to a playback requires real singing, even if her singing is ultimately to be erased. Because flawless synchronization is almost impossible, close-ups are usually avoided in scenes of re-voicing. But Zeffirelli proceeds to do exactly that: there is a close-up on the mouth, a zoom-in on the impossible fit in a dubbing session. In *Callas Forever*, a mirror is positioned very close to Callas's mouth, and a technician supervises the fit between the movements and shapes her mouth makes and the singing it must appear to produce. Sometimes the fit is successful, but at other times it is less so, as when we see Callas relearning at what point in a given phrase she must pause for a breath. Thus the dubbing session takes us "behind the scenes" to witness the process of transforming Ardant into Callas, or, put differently, to see what it takes for Ardant to become Callas for 108 minutes. We become acutely aware that Ardant does not sing a single note of what we are hearing. But the scene also has the opposite effect: the attempt to simulate a perfect match, emphasized by the close-up on Ardant's mouth-with-the-Callas-voice, is so unsettling that we can "forget" that it is not Callas and *allow* Ardant to become Callas.

Paradoxically, Zeffirelli pays homage to both the American and the Italian re-voicing traditions: the dubbing session exhibits perfect and imperfect synch. We are shown the mismatch between the voice and the body through the attempt at their perfect match. Teaching Callas the perfect "American" way of re-voicing is achieved by making her act out the fact that the voice is not "hers" and, therefore, it does not perfectly fit: that is, it shows the "Italian" way of re-voicing.

In this scene there are constantly several levels to consider: there is Ardant trying to match her lip movements to Callas's voice, and there is Callas trying to match her movements to her former voice. Neither case fits the straightforward definition of re-voicing. Within the plot, Callas mimes her own earlier playback but, since the voice comes from so far back, it is a foreign voice, and thus her efforts approximate the conditions of dubbing. On the other hand, Callas's voice is there prior to the body of the actress, and it is the actress who must learn to accommodate the voice, unlike in traditional dubbing. In other words, we have an inverted dubbing situation which functions as playback in the plot. In *Callas Forever*, it seems, the plot not only mirrors but masks the cinematic techniques of its own making.

We assume that a voice searches for the right body to be anchored in, that it would remain incomplete if detached from a body, or were off-screen or disembodied. But as Christian Metz suggests and Rick Altman provocatively asserts, we should in fact be speaking of "aural objects" and the primacy of sound over image.[22] *Callas Forever*, I would argue, raises the theoretical question of the priority of sound or image in the cinematic matrix and affirms the primacy of sound over image. The film suggests that it is the *image* that struggles to satisfy the demands of the voice and that its epistemological power is diminished if not annulled by the voice. *Callas Forever* unleashes a "Voice-Callas" that overpowers its vessel and resists any anchoring in a body. This "Voice-Callas" disables Ardant-as-Callas to signify Callas. It reveals an impossibility inherent in the voice itself.

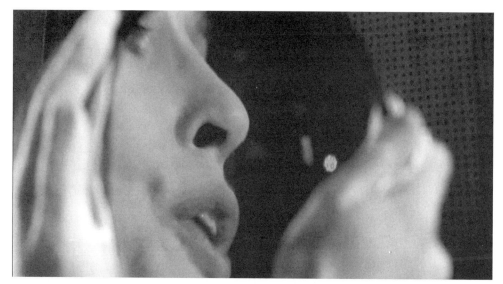

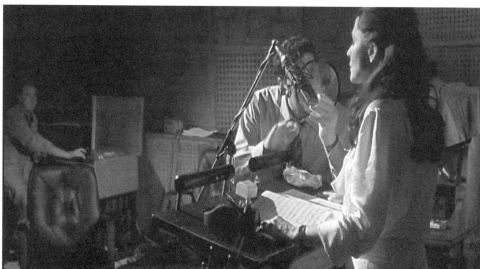

Still 1. The dubbing session: trying to synchronize Callas's past voice with Callas's (Fanny Ardant's) facial physiognomy, Zeffirelli, *Callas Forever.*

There are scholars who argue that re-voicing tricks give rise to the creation of inhuman combinations and impossible chimeras.[23] In the words of Jorge Luis Borges: "Hollywood has just enriched this frivolous, tautological museum [of chimeras]: by means of a perverse artifice they call dubbing, they offer monsters that combine the well-known features of Greta Garbo with the voice of Aldonza Lorenzo. How can we fail to proclaim our admiration for this distressing prodigy, for these ingenious audio-visual anomalies?"[24] Re-voicing techniques do indeed erect new combinations of imagined voices and fantastical bodies, creating monsters—or what we may call "vocal chimeras." In the words of Mikhail Yampolski: "Dubbing only leads the alienation of the voice from the body [present in cinema on the whole] to extremely paradoxical and therefore more tangible forms." Yampolski draws a radical conclusion from his analysis: "The body is absorbed by voice and becomes voice.... The voice is transformed into an all-absorbing monster.... The body, devouring voice, is in the end absorbed by it."[25]

Since, however, Callas's is no ordinary voice, these theories remain attractive but insufficient.[26] Elaborate as they are, re-voicing techniques and the theories explicating them fail to account for the uniqueness of the "Voice-Callas." There have been countless accounts of Maria Callas, a phenomenon unmatched in the world of opera. Zeffirelli's *Callas Forever* is a cinematic example, one in a long line of aural, textual, audio, and visual testimonies to the afterlife of the Callas phenomenon. What surfaces again and again in these accounts is a sense of bewilderment, a marveling at the Callas phenomenon and its inexplicability. Hers is still the supreme reigning voice, above and beyond any other voice of the twentieth century. This goes far beyond any explanation or description of her historical role in reviving opera, her unbeautified yet expressive timbre, her sense of theater, her opera-like biography that includes scandals and glamorous love affairs. It seems that what ultimately comes close to approaching the elusiveness of the icon are accounts such as Wayne Koestenbaum's, with its total absorption or abandonment in the Callas cult. His excess in writing provides a response in kind to Callas's mystery: there has been only one Voice and that is Callas's. Although taking a very different tone than Koestenbaum, Zeffirelli, in his film about Callas, cannot totally mask a similar predisposition to hear her as "the one and only one."

Vocal Pairs: An Overwhelmed Body

Dubbing, playback, and post-synchronization have little to do with voice-body accommodation, when it comes to Callas's voice, because reattaching a body to the voice of Callas does not put that voice to rest. Hers is a voice absolutely and unconditionally marked, a voice already uncomfortably hosted in its originating body (as the weight loss and the Hepburn fixation make manifest). *Callas Forever* tells the more haunting tale: pairs of *voices* ominously searching for, reliving, recalling, and remapping themselves one onto another.

The relation between a salient pair of voices orients the film's unfolding: the (real) Callas's two voices, the shot voice from the present and the wondrous voice from the past. The film accentuates the distinction between them by staging two attempts to retrieve the diva's lost voice: the first attempt utilizes her voice from the past; the second, her present voice. From the outset, these two voices are juxtaposed so as to persuade Callas to "regain" her singing voice by appearing with her past voice. Later, however, Callas opts for her lost present voice.

We first hear the shot voice when Callas is seen playing a video clip of what she calls her Japan tour, explaining to Larry that she repeatedly listens to it to "remind her never to sing on stage again."[27] The clip alludes to (the real) Callas's last world tour in 1974 that ended in Japan, where for the very last time she sang in public. The tour symbolizes the loss of her voice, but it also shows how the public's adoration exceeds the quality of her singing.

Zeffirelli recreates a clip of Callas's Japan concert and attaches to the image two soundtracks of "O mio babbino caro" from Puccini's *Gianni Schicchi*. In one of the soundtracks, Ardant mimes Callas's nearly nonexistent voice while, in the other, she mimes Callas's magnificent voice from the past. Zeffirelli thus attaches two voices that belong to the real Callas to one and the same image. Zeffirelli's Callas's bewildered reaction to the vocal "improvement" of the Japan concert turns into approval. She puts on her glasses to *see* better: what she hears should not yield an identical body image. At this early stage, the chimeric visual-acoustic outcome—one body sounding two voices—is both alarming and seductive. It is alarming because the "wrong" voice fits so well: Callas's voice fits Ardant's body, and Callas's past voice fits her present body, as though the aural image bypasses the visual image. The voice does not belong to the body and yet it is perfectly matched to what we see on screen. One could think of it as one voice being given up so that its past can be called back, summoned, and that which enables to bring this voice back is none other than the voice it replaces. *Gianni Schicchi*, the opera chosen to carry the burden of mismatched voices, is a perfect match for *Callas Forever*, as it is an opera about reassigning a voice to the dead and about dubbing that redirects inheritance. (*Gianni Schicchi* will be taken up in great detail in the following chapter.)

The second pair of Callas voices in the film consists of *Ardant* singing in her own voice as if it were Callas's present, ruined voice—above Callas's real voice from a past recording. Zeffirelli's scenes *superimpose* the two voices, parading the gap between them, with Ardant's voice illustrating the difference between Callas's two voices (or the metanarrative difference between actress and singer). The voices do not overlap, for we constantly hear two distinct timbres, Ardant's and Callas's. This pair is evident in a scene that, we are told, is reenacted over and over, in which Callas, troubled by insomnia, sings to her old recordings. We see the scene through the eyes of Larry and Bruna, agent and maid, as they eavesdrop on a Lady Macbeth–like sleepwalking scene, as though Callas were gesturing at a futile attempt to undo what has been done.[28] When the actress tries to sing like the singer, when the latter represents one voice trying to repeat or "return" as the other, to "be" it once again, we realize that the relationship of the first vocal pair, that of the real Callas's two voices, has metamorphosed. In other words, Callas's "bad" voice can be replaced by her "good" voice (through dubbing in the studio), but it cannot *become* the "good" voice. This difference may be the result of (the real) Callas's two voices being figured as a double soundtrack for one screened image or as two voices emanating from a single source. In the "Lady Macbeth" scene, however, the two voices emanate from two different sources. One is Ardant (singing Callas's present voice), and the other is the record player (from which Callas's past voice emanates). Clearly, the scene does not establish a "voice-body" affinity between Ardant's voice and the record player as "body," but rather presents the failed encounter between two voices—Ardant's and Callas's—as a fall of Callas into her present state.

The film presents yet another vocal pair, voices employed for the creation of *character*: when Callas *speaks*, we hear Ardant's voice; when she sings, it is the voice of Callas that we hear. Indeed, speaking and singing can be so far apart in terms of timbre and rhythm that it goes unnoticed that the voice that speaks is not the voice that sings. Zeffirelli distracts our attention from any detectable differences in this vocal pair by using an overall "verbal chiaroscuro."[29] *Callas Forever* is an Italian-British-French-Romanian-Spanish production, set in Paris with English as its original language (though it was not released widely in the United States). The film makes no use of one of the more common functions of dubbing—ironing out the various languages and accents into one accent-free language. Instead, we hear French, Italian, and Spanish, and the main language, English, is heard in British, American, and South African accents.[30] Among the more noticeable accents is Ardant's heavy French accent when speaking English; there is also Bruna, the maid, who speaks and is spoken to solely in Italian, and Michael, Larry's deaf boyfriend, who has a slight intonation, as some deaf people have.[31] Zeffirelli is employing a "cauldron of voices" (a term used to describe Fellini's playful mixing of voices and accents), emphasized by the use of relativized speech, which, at times, can barely be understood.[32] The film's opening sequence, for instance, is shot from a distance, accompanied by loud airport noises and reporters speaking all at once (as they try to interview Larry). The scene is further blurred by loud rock music, perhaps played by Bad Dreams, the rock band Larry is producing while working with Callas (the band is referred to throughout the film but never appears). This band, too, like Callas, "cheats" by using prerecorded vocals to support a live concert.

While the aural chiaroscuro downplays Ardant's speaking voice in relation to "her" singing voice, it is also a reference to the real Callas. At a certain point in the film we hear that "I [Callas] don't speak correctly any language." Indeed, there are numerous accounts of (the real) Callas and her manner of speaking. Walter Legge, the head of EMI's classical division, offers this description: "At our first meeting I was taken aback by her rather fearsome New York accent.... Within months Callas was speaking what the English call the King's English.... A gifted linguist, she soon learned good Italian and French."[33] Callas is said to have had a foreign accent even when speaking Greek. It seems that she had no mother tongue or, one might say, was a native speaker in many languages. For Callas, speaking as well as singing appear to have always been a kind of performance.

The voices in *Callas Forever* work with and against one another; they are anxious, envious, mournful, and challenging, replacing or accepting the presence of other vocal inflections. The very attempt to represent Callas yields this vocal indeterminacy, not only in fictional works such as *Callas Forever* but also in documentaries about Callas.

We can turn for a moment to Tony Palmer's *Maria Callas* (1987), a documentary produced ten years after the singer's death. Palmer's film reiterates the fascination with and success of the dead diva's recordings, the appeal of a voice that had not been heard live in performance in a staged opera for over twenty years.

In an attempt to capture the secret behind the myth surrounding the diva, the film, as expected, moves back and forth among performances, newsreel footage, and interviews to reveal the private, vulnerable human being burdened by the image. It begins with footage from the singer's 1974 world tour, as does Zeffirelli's *Callas Forever*, focusing on her last public appearance, which for both directors is crucial for representing her voice. Palmer's film begins with what had come to symbolize the sound of Callas no-longer-sounding-like-Callas, or the "sound" of Callas's loss of voice. Palmer captures the vulnerability of this moment by showing the concert while silencing its music. Instead of Callas's voice, we hear the narrator telling us that, although a decade has gone by since her death, Callas has not died: "It's really like she's reaching out from the grave to grab hold of our imagination. She won't let go of it." It becomes a tale of the undead, an acoustic manifestation of the absent voice. This scene is followed by paired voices in which Callas's singing is superimposed on her speaking voice captured in an interview. These two voices accompany first her performance, then the interview, and finally go back and forth between the two. The film is uncertain about the natural source of the voices it sounds.

Body-in-Voice

The multiplicity of voices born of the representation of Callas's voice attests to a rejection of the anchoring body. Various theories postulate that the rejection of an anchoring body results from a notion that the voice itself, as it were, has "body." Such theories assume that a voice has a materiality or physicality, is not only invisible and ephemeral but is partially matter, and has something in it or belonging to it that intimates mass. In other words, it bears a presence beyond itself, a ghostly materiality that arises and disappears with the sound of the voice.

The notion of the ghostly materiality of voice is related to what Slavoj Žižek finds in the living dead or vampires, his paradoxical conception of what "undermines the duality of bodily density and spiritual transparency,"[34] and to Mladen Dolar's account of the dangerous materiality of music, which "presents carnality at its most insidious since it seems liberated from materiality," and is "the subtlest and the most perfidious form of the flesh."[35] The disembodied voice is thus seen as threatening and disruptive and, as such, it offers an attractive interpretation of the eerie presence of Callas's voice in *Callas Forever*. And yet no such theory can fully account for the singularity of Callas's voice: its very unaccount-ability appears to be inherent to it.

When it comes to Callas's voice, even Roland Barthes's notion of grain—"the body in the voice as it sings, the hand as it writes, the limb as it performs"—articulating the potential voluptuous-ness of the sound-signifiers themselves is insufficient.[36] Even if we do *not* exclude opera from Barthes's discussion—"opera is a genre in which the voice has gone over in its entirety to dra-matic expressivity"—the Callas Voice, in its absolute uniqueness, remains *sui genesis*.[37]

Thus, my claim is that in Zeffirelli's *Callas Forever*, the first attempt to bring back Callas's lost voice that centers on dubbing cannot be understood in terms of the successful matching of voice and body. Rather, it is about anxious pairs of voices map-ping each other, each striving in vain to become another voice. Image and body are inconsequential—for Ardant merely masks the acoustic engagements. So the film stages a second attempt to retrieve Callas's lost voice by offering an alternative representa-tion of it. And since Callas's voice is too elusive to settle into a body or to be accounted for in material terms, the second attempt is acoustically much more disruptive than the first. It is here that the voice is what can be imagined of it, and it is here that what can be imagined of the voice turns into its very presence.

Regaining the Lost Voice: Second Attempt
The second attempt to revive Callas's bygone voice appears to depend on matching a nearly nonexistent voice to a present body but is revealed to be about voice displacement. This attempt is

presented as Callas's own idea. She wishes to discover something novel about the role of Tosca; the new interpretation in turn will revive her voice. *Tosca* is then to be filmed using Callas's revitalized present voice rather than her past recording. The second attempt thus portrays a Callas preferring her present, nearly nonexistent voice to the cinematic tricks that would conjure her magnificent voice from the past.

Notice the choice of words in the exchange between Larry and the financial board, which is suspicious of Callas's new idea. Larry attempts to convince the board that Callas's voice "exists" even when not entirely "there"; that this voice, in effect, need not be audible to be "present," that it might be audible in some other way:

— Callas will only film *Tosca* if she can sing in her own voice?

— Exactly.

— Her voice is unusable. It's sad but it's true.

— But the voice doesn't matter. It's the performance that matters. We should film *Tosca* with Maria as she is today with the voice that she has today.

— The voice doesn't matter, Larry? There was a voice...the audience expects to hear that voice.... It's opera.... Opera is voice.... Opera is music.

— But there are other kinds of music.... There's the music in the head...there's the music in the heart...there's unnamable music.... You're all deaf....

The producers are deaf to a Callas present in the absence of her voice, which is far from absurd in the universe Zeffirelli is creating. Michael, Larry's new boyfriend, is a deaf painter. His paintings take shape while he listens to Callas singing. He "hears" her voice in the colors he paints: "I feel colors, vibrations, waves of sound woven into the air."[38] His paintings are born out of the sound of opera. One, for instance, is called Norma. In his apartment we see a photo of (the real) Callas and hear her voice for the first time in the film; disembodied, Callas's "Casta diva" emanates from a recording.[39] The deaf boyfriend explains that he "need[s] her voice whenever [he] come[s] home." And it is her past voice that is figured, through the deaf painter, as unavailable acoustically. The deaf painter is the true devotee, opting for an imagined, impossible hearing, a presence in the mind.[40] Indeed, when Callas herself, later in the film, visits him in his flat (staged, as Callas comments, as a setting for *La bohème*), only the orchestral accompaniment to "Casta diva" is heard. In other words, when Callas is absent from his flat, her voice is present; when she is present, her voice is not, and the orchestra suffices to prefigure her voice. The two scenes in Michael's apartment illustrate the potential of hearing the voice in absentia—in the double absence of singer and singer's voice.

Tosca

> When Tosca enters, Tosca returns: loved objects can never appear for the first time, they can only reappear, dragging with them a prehistory. When Callas returned to the Met in 1965 as Tosca, WELCOME HOME, CALLAS said the banners outside the opera house, and WELCOME HOME, TOSCA say the banners in the listener's imagination whenever Tosca enters.
> —Wayne Koestenbaum, *The Queen's Throat*

Callas's idea that the *role* of Tosca is endowed with the power to revive a lost voice is extraordinary. In effect, she is imagining a possibility in which even though a voice is not really there, its presence can be conjured by or through its investment in an operatic role. Before trying to account for Zeffirelli's failing this option (because of the producers' objection) as he failed the first option (because of Callas's objection), let us pause and consider the actual choice. Why *Tosca*? How are this particular opera and the role of Tosca endowed with such powers of voice revival? Could the answer lie in the complex role this opera plays in Callas's own singing career? Could the answer be that Tosca stages the passage from a fake death to a real one?

The intertextual references linking *Tosca* with Zeffirelli,

Ardant, and Callas form a complex web. The opera figured in the master classes that Callas held at the Julliard School of Music in New York in 1971–72 (though the incipit appearing in *Callas Forever* was not taught).[41] These master classes served as one of Callas's alternatives to singing after losing her voice. Then, there is Ardant portraying Callas on stage in Terrence McNally's play *Master Class*, with its final monologue serving as the last track in a recording of sample voice lessons from the famous Callas master classes.[42] Although Zeffirelli did not see Ardant in the role, it was an incentive for casting her in his film.

The 1953 recording of Callas's *Tosca* is considered to be one of the very best ever made. As John Ardoin writes: "In the special world of opera on disc, there are a handful of sets that by general consent are ideal.... In this elite company belongs de Sabata's *Tosca*. It is a complete theatrical experience."[43] This was Callas's first *Tosca* with Tito Gobbi, and preceded their performing together live.[44] And it is this recording that Zeffirelli stages when Callas, on a sleepless night in *Callas Forever*, remembers her past role.

Tosca, of course, was also the opera that brought Callas back to the stage after the long years of her seclusion with Aristotle Onassis: in 1964, Zeffirelli persuaded Callas to appear in the title role of his production of *Tosca* at Covent Garden (again with Tito Gobbi as Scarpia). It was a triumphant success. Thus, although Callas had reservations about the role, it figured as her comeback.[45] Zeffirelli's production was, in fact, Callas and Gobbi's first complete *Tosca* on stage together. Act 2 was broadcast on television and became the most famous visual documentation of her onstage theatrical presence, "the principal existing sound-visual document of Callas in actual performance."[46] It is this performance that Zeffirelli considered to be the "memorable [and] definitive interpretation of Tosca."[47]

Tosca was also Callas's last performed role in Paris, London, and New York. About the performance in New York, it is famously known that after her years of absence from the Metropolitan Opera, people stood waiting in line for four days and tickets were sold out within hours. As she appeared on stage the ovations brought the performance to a halt. The performance in London (1965) was notoriously interrupted in the middle, becoming, in effect, her last appearance on stage for eight years (until the famous concert tour with di Stefano, referred to as the Japan tour in *Callas Forever*). As Ardoin writes: "Ironically, considering her lack of enthusiasm for the role of Tosca, it was to be the principal vehicle of her last two years in opera houses in London, Paris, and New York, and her last complete operatic recording for EMI."[48]

Tosca was to become an even more significant landmark when it was recorded as a soundtrack for a cinematic version. It was the closest Callas ever came to making a screened opera, as Ardoin explains:

> The re-recording of *Tosca* in stereo was undertaken as a soundtrack for a movie of the opera planned by Zeffirelli with Callas. The idea of capturing her on film dates back to 1958 when Zeffirelli designed and produced a most personal *Traviata* for Callas and the Dallas Civic Opera. It was cinematic in concept, staged entirely as a flashback from Violetta's deathbed. From that time onward, Zeffirelli tried to persuade Callas to make a film with him, but she hesitated to enter so foreign an expressive medium. Finally, in 1964 after the successful *Toscas* at Covent Garden, she agreed to film the Puccini work. EMI made the soundtrack, and Callas began to prepare herself for this new artistic adventure. Unfortunately the project floundered because the film rights to *Tosca* had been sold by Puccini's publisher, Ricordi, to a German firm.[49]

Then the final twist: in *Callas Forever*, Zeffirelli used the 1953 sound recording rather than the *Tosca* intended as a soundtrack.

If we seek the answer in the role *Tosca* plays in Callas's career, the question "Why *Tosca*?" remains largely unanswered. The answer might lie in the very ambivalence of the role as it acquired its dramatic significance in Maria Callas's own life, as if despite herself. But why choose an opera that could never carry the full weight of the diva's meteoric career? Could the answer be that

Tosca, the heroine, is tricked into believing that she can overcome death? That she can stage death by turning it into art? The answer would thus lie in a melancholic realm, in that Tosca, herself a singer, is endowed with the Orphic powers to bring the dead back to life. Tosca would thus be a role one repeatedly returns to in the quest to undo death. In *Callas Forever*, then, it might be that Zeffirelli himself is enacting this role in his attempt to undo the death of Callas by staging her, once again, as Tosca.

Tosca also enacts a mythic fusion of role and singer, a fusion that allows Callas's presence to reemerge in the role. As Gobbi affirms: "With Maria I was Scarpia and she was Tosca.... Maria was never Maria, she was Tosca onstage."[50] Zeffirelli suggests this role-singer merging in the scene in *Callas Forever* where Callas awakens from a disturbed sleep by the sound of her own *Tosca*. The scene begins with Callas dressed in a nightgown, watching and listening to herself singing, as if she were a costumed apparition. The merging of the two Callases occurs when Callas breaks into tears: she cries not because she is acting Tosca but because she is Callas. Callas the singer and Tosca the opera heroine become one and the same.[51]

Unsightly. Unheardly

The overdetermined associations invoked by Callas's *Tosca* fail to account for its power in *Callas Forever*, fail to account for the role acquiring, as it were, a life of its own. Even in the world of opera, a world that allows for a fair amount of improbable occurrences, a voice creates a role but no role can resurrect a voice. It therefore appears that *Callas Forever* turns operatic aesthetics on its head, by implying that an operatic role can actually simulate the presence of voice, and conjure one otherwise not there.

Let us examine operatic aesthetics, the medium's conventions, and the tropes underlying the creation of a role out of a singer's voice and body.[52] Exposing Maria Callas as an extreme case of the voice-body-role affinity may perhaps put us in a better position to explicate Zeffirelli's film.

A prominent trope regarding Callas's unmatched, magnetic presence on stage draws attention to how "she involved her whole body in the dramatic import of the music and instinctively acted out its meaning."[53] Trying to explain the public obsession with Callas, Ardoin suggests that "the answer is not as difficult as you might think. It is to be found in Callas's ability to excite the imagination. Hers may not have been an easy voice to listen to, but it was an impossible one to forget. In its dark, hollow recesses, it held the essence of theatre, just as her haunting, slow-movement gestures onstage were a mirror that reflected drama and music."[54] Legge puts it as follows: "Among Callas's greatest strengths were her power of projection in the theater and communication with audiences, almost animal instincts that excited a public irrespective of her purely vocal form."[55] This trope attests to a bodily presence beyond the sheer voice as something bordering on the inhuman. The whole body—its gestures, movements, and expressions—participates in executing the music and creating the drama. Here, Callas's appearance, her performing body on stage, is essential.

Another prominent trope invokes the opposite notion of presence by focusing on the roles Callas recorded in the studio—never *appearing* in them on stage. These studio recordings are referred to as the "theatre of the imagination,"[56] the spatial "*mise-en-scène* conceived in acoustic terms, a virtual space enhanced by stereophonic sound, a music theatre without a stage."[57] Here, because the body is unseen, Callas's presence derives from her voice alone, for it is her voice that calls up the performing body. In his study of the history of recording, Michael Chanan reiterates this trope, emphasizing its paradoxical nature:

> What Callas achieves through the medium of the recording continues to thrill, and no other singer has yet come near to the same qualities. Yet at the same time, for anyone who saw Callas on stage, the recording remains an *aide-mémoire* which merely evokes the memory of an extraordinary dramatic presence. It is remarkable

enough that her magnetism was larger than her voice, so that even her late performances, when her voice was overstretched and sometimes awkward, remain more powerful in the memory than performances by others, however perfectly sung. The real meaning of this paradox is discovered in recordings of roles that she never performed on stage, that nobody has seen, but that no singer since has been able to match.[58]

Chanan alludes to the paradox that even when a Callas recording is not an *aide-mémoire*, it holds within it a presence that cannot be matched by a live performance, as though her voice conjures "stage-ness," a presence of a performance in the absence of one.[59] The two tropes surrounding the image of Callas's voice are opposed: in the first trope, the body is present and essential for delivering the music; in the second, it is absent.

The idiosyncratic operatic conventions governing the correlation between a singer's visual presence and his or her voice are further complicated when considering the embodiment of a role. As Peter Brooks observed:

> What you get in opera is a body thrust upon your attention—a costumed body, staged and lighted, representing a certain person in a certain dramatic situation. Here in fact is the glory, and also the embarrassment, of opera: the claim that visual embodiment and voice coincide in the singer. Those who dislike opera do so precisely because they prefer singing voices to be disembodied, pure voice; they cannot accept a convention that, as we all know, can lead to a knob-kneed, fifty-year-old tenor condemned to wobble around the stage in Egyptian fighting gear, or a voluminous soprano made to represent a teenage virgin. The demands made on voice and body for dramatic representation are not the same, and the claim for their coincidence will very often demand a large dose of faith on the part of the spectator/listener, a willingness to accept an as-if that would seem to be excluded from a genre that traditionally seeks, in its stage settings and effects, such a large measure of illusionism.
>
> Lovers of opera do of course accept that as-if. They do not close

their eyes as the average and overweight Radames launches into his adoration of Aida. On the contrary, they revel in the weird excess of the situation. They revel in a form that combines illusionism with clear impossibility, the height of artifice with the most natural of instruments, the human voice.[60]

The conventions governing the signification of the singer's body in relation to voice are such that the body is seen as participating in the creation of the drama; but in its absence (as in studio recordings), the voice can call up that presence. In other words, we come not "to see" the singers' bodies. It is as if their signification changes once the performance begins, music sounds, and their voices sing. We see the character embodied through the music and forget the body producing the singing of that role; the first overcoming, even canceling, the meaning born of the sight of the singer's body. Thus, although opera singers are known to have large bodies in order to produce their wondrous voices—voices are taken to reside "in" the very flesh, in the singer's physical dimensions—we "see" these bodies through what we "hear" of them. One outcome of privileging the singing voice in a predominantly acoustic domain—in which reflections and refractions are induced by the very translation of the vocal into the visual, the body being a sign of the voice—is that singers require "no body" at all. In other words, an operatic performance demands a measure of "invisibility" or, as Wayne Koestenbaum notes, opera is a performative domain in which singers' bodies are "mythically unsightly."[61]

These operatic "beings"—invisible-singers-in-visible-roles—cannot be reduced to the presence of singers, to the formative effects of the singers' dramatic roles, nor to any straightforward combination of the two. And here Zeffirelli's interpretation is incisive: by extracting from Callas a role that can retrieve the trace of her lost voice, as it were, he loses the singer. The singer becomes elusive in the matrix of voice-body-role-singer.

But Zeffirelli does not stop here. He weakens the voice itself: the "voice" in *Tosca* is not Callas's. How not? Callas's novel interpretation of Tosca in *Callas Forever* centers on Tosca's resistance to her *attraction* toward the cruel Scarpia. It is a surprising interpretation of the role, though not a new one. It is not, in fact, Callas's interpretation but *Zeffirelli*'s dramatic conception of Callas's role in his 1964 production of the opera. As he explains in his autobiography: "My Tosca would obviously be drawn to an attractive man, even one whose heart is made of steel.... Unknowingly, far from merely hating him, she's actually mysteriously attracted to him, to his power, to his cruelty. In the end Tosca kills Scarpia not merely to save her lover, but to save herself from herself."[62]

The murder scene in act 2 of Zeffirelli's 1964 production is famously documented on video; as mentioned earlier, Zeffirelli refers to this 1964 interpretation as "definitive." But in Zeffirelli's 2002 film this "definitive" interpretation is thematized as Callas's own. Zeffirelli's "voice" has been implanted in Callas's, and her revived voice turns out to be a dubbed one.

If Zeffirelli is voicing his interpretation of the role of Tosca *through* a staging of Callas's lost voice, then this very option to regain the voice is no more than a false alternative to *Carmen*. Bypassing the tricks of cinema leads only to another form of dubbing. Although it is different from being dubbed by a "former self," it is dubbing nonetheless: the "voice" of a former director makes itself sound through one who no longer sings, appearing as the diva's present, nearly nonexistent voice, disguised as a novel discovery imbued with magical powers.

There is yet a further twist. If indeed Zeffirelli's 1964 production represents a new interpretation of *Tosca*, we would expect it to differ from his 1958 production of the same opera, also starring Callas and Gobbi. There are, in fact, audio-visual recordings of *Tosca*'s act 2 from both the 1958 and 1964 productions and we soon realize, when comparing them, that there is almost no difference between them in terms of acting, staging, and costumes: a new interpretation is not visibly detectable.[63] But does Tosca's attraction to Scarpia have no visual manifestation? Does it function only as an invisible ghost-text, a spectral presence analogous to Callas's fantasized voice?

And the final twist. *Callas Forever* tells rather than shows Zeffirelli's interpretation: Callas explains but does not sing; the interpretation is presented to the audience attending the master class but is not enacted in song. Moreover, we hear and see only one short incipit from *Tosca*: Scarpia's murder, which is all the more striking in comparison to the long scenes from *Carmen*. The scene is so short and song-less that it seems a non-dubbed scene, a scene delivered by the actress herself. Callas's present voice in *Callas Forever*—the one singing Tosca—is represented without sounding Callas on the soundtrack! This had already occurred in the film when Callas sang (in Ardant's voice) over her past recordings (in Callas's voice). But here it has far more radical consequences, for Ardant's voice is a means to voice Zeffirelli's ideas. It is a form of double dub. What sneaks into the empty space left by Callas's wondrous, lost voice are the voices of Zeffirelli and his actress Ardant, thus effacing even Callas's recorded voice from the film's acoustic space.

The Voice's Afterlife

In a self-reflexive gesture, Zeffirelli inserts the title of his film into the narrative when Larry brings Callas a film script entitled *Callas Forever*. But the project Larry offers Callas, to mime her old recording, requires no script, for the script would simply be a libretto. Callas laughs at the intimations of her immortality evoked by the title of the film. Is this a laughing matter? Is Callas's immortality inconceivable? Is this what Zeffirelli is trying to show us by subverting the two attempts that he presents in the film to revive her voice? Has film no advantage over sound recording? Or, put differently, cannot film offer a comeback with intimations of immortality? The quest to regain the lost voice thus raises a fundamental question about the ways the "life" of the operatic voice exists independently of the singer. Does the voice continue "to live" after the singer's death in, say, recordings? Is the recorded voice a "dead voice" or a "living voice" *of* a dead singer?

In *Callas Forever*, Zeffirelli clearly aspires to some form of afterlife, a "forever-ness," for Callas. The passage from opera to cinema, he implies, may promise immortality. Mary Ann Doane reminds us that the emergence of cinema was associated with a "technological promise to capture time: immortality, the denial of the radical finitude of the human body [and] access to other temporalities." Cinema, Doane continues, "made archivable duration itself. In that sense, it was perceived as a prophylactic against death."[64] Film scholars debate the medium's capability to animate and revive. According to Doane (following well-known accounts of Bazin, Barthes, Cavell, Metz, and Deleuze, among others), the trope of immortality wins out. Film theory, however, offers alternative accounts that stress the medium's transient, mortal nature. As photography, film shows the work of death. Garrett Stewart, for example, argues that "whether as photograph or repeated photogram, standard ocular mechanics cannot, of course, be counted on to capture (that is, represent) the otherworld of immortality.... Photochemistry can only instantiate death's flight from time.... If cinema per se ... is modern culture's new immortality machine, it relives time only in its transience."[65]

Which of the two conflicting conceptions of cinema explains Zeffirelli's poignant tale of the singer approaching her death? More specifically, how are we to reconcile the wish for "forever-ness" and the doomed tales told in the plot? Does a film that fails its own premise to relocate, re-find, revive, and regain the lost voice succeed in preserving the irretrievable presence of that voice? If so, its success would be a recognition of the essential difficulty of approaching the Callas Voice, of recalling it. Put in extreme terms: there is an inherent impossibility of actually hearing that voice. But Zeffirelli evades such a conclusion, counteracting it in the film's final images, where he returns to the disembodied, recorded voice of Callas and, with it, a promise of its eternal preservation. It is as if all that had transpired in the film, even if it failed, and despite its repeated failures, could not affect the status of voice whose presence is assured. The final images on screen are of the diva walking away, with her back to the camera: walking away from dubbing and impersonation. We hear her "Casta diva" in the background and, on the screen, the written announcement of her death appears. "Casta diva," the aria that symbolizes her unchallenged voice—holding the promise of unnamed music, of the music in the mind—does not cease to resonate. It is an imagined sound beyond any image.

But this sharp turn at the end is too hasty. The failures we have witnessed cannot be rendered irrelevant in an instant. By the end of the film we cannot hear Callas's voice as we once have. We have come to suspect voices and the images accompanying them. We are left wondering: What is it that resonates in the film's final images? Is it the voice or the sound of its loss? Callas dies yet again, and we are left in utter uncertainty as to what remains. That Callas's voice might be forever lost is too intolerable for us to bear.

Might a character in an opera fare better than a singer? Can a character have an afterlife? We now turn to the opera that serves Zeffirelli to dub Callas. In *Gianni Schicchi*, impersonation and dubbing do revive, though as a consequence the one who dubs is himself revealed to be dead. It is an opera in which death's dependence on voice acquires new signification, one specific to this very opera.

CHAPTER TWO

Sung by Death

Giacomo Puccini, *Gianni Schicchi* (1918)

> Gentlemen, if any of you would die to show me how it's supposed to
> be done, I'd be most grateful....
> —Evaristo Gherardi, *Le Théâtre italien* (1691)

The aria enacting the central paired voices in Zeffirelli's film *Callas Forever* is meticulously chosen. Puccini's *Gianni Schicchi* (1918) is employed to implant two voices in one body: it is sung with Callas's beautiful voice from the past and alternately with her present, shot voice. The dead voice from the past is seemingly brought back, acquiring an afterlife, replacing the voice that can no longer sing. As we will see, it is not accidental that this particular opera is employed to dramatize the reassignment of voices to bodies and to evoke Callas's suspicion as to the integrity of the legacy she will hand down to future generations. There are unforeseen consequences when dead voices and voices of the dead are revived, when their fit to bodies is refashioned—as with Maria Callas's bygone wondrous voice and Gianni's impersonation of the dead Buoso. Revival tricks are tried out in both works; each with its unique means deliberates an outcome undermining death.

Better End

Gianni Schicchi tells the story of a con executed by its title character to falsify a will. Impersonating the dead Buoso Donati, Gianni Schicchi dictates a new will for Donati that works to his advantage, enabling his daughter, Lauretta, and her lover, Rinuccio, to marry. The opera ends with an epilogue in which Gianni Schicchi addresses the audience directly in speech. Here he is revealed as a dweller in hell whose story has been recounted in Dante's *Inferno*.

Commentaries on Dante's *Inferno* describe Gianni Schicchi as an expert mimic with the talent to impersonate anyone. In canto 30, Gianni and Myrrha are

> two pallid shades that I [Dante] saw biting and running like the pig when it is let out of the sty. The one came at Capocchio and fixed its tusks on his neck joint, so that, dragging him, it made his belly scratch along the solid bottom. And the Aretine, who was left, trembling said to me, "That goblin is Gianni Schicchi, and he goes rabid mangling others thus." (*Inferno* 30, ll. 25–33)[1]

Gianni in hell has been transformed into a rabid animal who runs hungrily on all fours in every direction, biting at everything, trying to devour all. So complete is his metamorphosis that he needs to be identified for Dante. In hell he is unrecognizable as Gianni Schicchi—a punishment well suited to the crime of falsely representing himself as other people. Giovacchino Forzano, Puccini's librettist for *Gianni Schicchi*, constructed a libretto from the few lines Dante devoted to Gianni Schicchi in the *Inferno*, supplemented by information from Pietro Fanfani's 1866 edition of a fourteenth-century Dante commentary written by Anonimo Fiorentino, which includes in its appendix other details about Gianni's falsification of Buoso's will.[2] In his memoirs, Forzano writes that the ending gave him some trouble but that the solution he ultimately reached was favorably received by the composer. Forzano, well versed in theatrical traditions, proposed ending the opera in the way that old-fashioned plays end: "An actor finishes the performance by coming to the front of the stage and saying farewell to the audience without singing."[3] Forzano thus devises a spoken epilogue for *Gianni Schicchi*.

An ending with an epilogue is also found in Ravel's *L'heure espagnole* (1911). Here, all the singers on stage address the audience. The epilogue presents an altered consciousness—or is outright absurd: all five singers—including husband and lover—praise the erotic encounter of the wife with her new muleteer lover. All five characters step out of their roles: "The conclusion...consists...of *vocalises* sung by actors who stand in a row facing the public."[4] In Ravel's work, all the opera's characters come forth as singers and, for the only time in the opera, join in a quintet. *Gianni Schicchi* does not opt for this sort of solution; Forzano does not bring in the relatives for the epilogue but presents Gianni alone, and without song. On the face of it, it would seem that both Ravel's and Puccini's operas employ an epilogue to introduce a substantial break in characterization. I will show, however, that in *Gianni Schicchi* the epilogue is employed for the purpose of achieving a contrary effect: portraying continuity between Gianni in the opera and Gianni in hell. Here is the ending Forzano devises:

> Gianni:
> La masnada fuggì!
> (*Vede gli innamorati, sorride e si volge al pubblico.*)
> Ditemi voi, signori,
> Sei i quattrini Buoso
> Potevan finir meglio di così.
> Per questa bizzarria
> M'han cacciato all'inferno,
> E così sia;
> Ma, con licenza del gran padre Dante,
> Se stasera vi siete divertiti,
> Concedetemi voi
> (*Fa il gesto di applaudire.*)
> l'attenuante.
>
> [Gianni:
> The gang of thieves has gone!
> (*He sees the two lovers and, smiling, turns to the audience.*)
> Tell me, ladies and gentlemen,
> If Buoso's money

Could have had a better end than this.
For this prank
They sent me to hell,
And so be it;
But, with the permission of the great old man Dante,
If you've been entertained this evening,
Allow me
(*He claps his hands.*)
extenuating circumstances.]

What this ending conveys bears on our conception of Gianni. Is the epilogue Gianni's afterlife, a spoken address from hell? Is his appearance from hell external to the opera? Does it introduce a break with what has earlier taken place? Or does it rather establish continuity with his presence in the opera? In other words, the epilogue raises the question whether Gianni is dead or alive. I take this to be the central question raised by an opera that contains an address from hell as its epilogue.

How Comedy Ends

At the core of even the most frivolous comedies lies a heart of darkness.
—Erich Segal, *The Death of Comedy*[5]

In the scholarship devoted to *Gianni Schicchi*, the opera's ending has not drawn much attention. The epilogue is considered an homage to various theatrical or operatic comic traditions or regarded as a convention of sorts, typical of early-twentieth-century operas. But before dismissing the epilogue as some sort of uninspired, conventional ending, let us remind ourselves of the conventions alluded to in this kind of epilogue, and ask what they might convey for *Gianni* and Gianni.

Zvi Jagendorf, writing about the happy endings of comedy, cites the turn to the spectator as the simplest and most ancient way of announcing the end of a play. Applause, the sign of the audience's pleasure, is vital for comedy:

Epilogues are an elaboration of the plain Roman request for applause. But on the Elizabethan stage they have a more subtle status. There epilogues often occupy the interesting half-light between the illusion of the stage and the clarity of day. In the comic practice of Shakespeare and Jonson the epilogue is usually spoken by the trickster, whose wit has spun out the comic action ... and it is therefore both an apology and a claim for his art, which is also that of the comic poet.... Asking us to approve of a character's art (Face), make[s] us accomplices in it. Through epilogue applause becomes a consciously purposeful act.... Epilogues are then a way of delaying ending, like encores. They extend the illusion beyond the stage and invite the spectator's conscious participation in the comic world at the moment of its disappearance.[6]

Applause may provide a different judgment from that offered by the play. Epilogues can prompt a reevaluation and reconsideration of characters, revealing something novel about the plot. They might upset the happy ending by giving voice to unsettling attitudes or observations, such as the looming shadow of death.[7] An epilogue serves as final mirror image of the characters just before everything on the stage vanishes. The ending, writes Jagendorf,

> juxtaposes in time the make-believe of the spectacle and the spectator's return to himself and the everyday.... Actors ... are in their role one moment and out of it the next. In comedy the return to ordinary experience may be guided wittily by the actor who drops his mask, by the clever or moral epilogue, or by the direct call for applause.... Comic endings are in themselves a convention, an agreement between poet and spectator rather than a necessary outcome of the material.... This kind of clash between convention and material is characteristic of comedy and emerges as a complicating factor, disturbing the smooth symmetries of denouement.[8]

Numerous scholars have remarked on *Gianni Schicchi*'s debt to the world of *commedia dell'arte*, which served as an attractive source for other early-twentieth-century operas.[9] *Commedia* conventions, including several types of epilogues, might have served as the

source for *Gianni Schicchi*'s epilogue. Indeed, *commedia* characteristics dominate *Gianni Schicchi*, with Gianni, of course, recalling
a shrewd, mischievous, inventive Arlecchino.[10] Gianni's talent
to disguise himself and impersonate others unfolds within this
world of images—he wears, as it were, a *commedia* mask.[11] Indeed,
for the opera's central scene, that of Gianni's impersonation of the
dead, a masking scene is inserted:

> In testa la cappellina,
> Al viso la pezzolina,
> Fra cappellina e pezzolina un naso

> [On his head is the night-cap,
> Round his mouth, the handkerchief.
> Between cap and handkerchief is a nose]

A mask is Arlecchino's essence; it manifests an identification with
the character enacted.[12] Nina Da Vinci Nichols views Arlecchino
as embodying a true spirit of transformation—he becomes the
role he plays.[13] Even in abstract renderings, or when the mask is
invisible, the archetypal Arlecchino retains his nature as imita-
tor, trickster, and impersonator. Arlecchino is also known to
change shape and to rise from the dead.[14] He is associated with
hell.[15] Antonio Scuderi traces Arlecchino's origins to demonic
sources,[16] specter-devils, and clown-devils:[17] "Carnival masks
represent beings of the nether regions, of demons and spirits of
the dead.... With his origins as a subterranean spirit, Arlecchino
has qualities that we may define as non human or otherworldly."[18]
"As a consequence of his not being in any one world," Scuderi
continues, "he often maintains a metatheatrical dialogue with
the audience, as if he is simultaneously in and out of the play." An
epilogue for an Arlecchino-type character, say a Gianni Schicchi,
may be an unmasking that reveals yet one more mask—that of
an impersonator. Rather than disclose what hides behind a mask,
an epilogue performs a trick that draws the audience deeper into
fantasy and into the depths of the impersonator's doings. With an

Arlecchino-like figure, the spectral and an association with hell are never fully left behind.

A *licenza* is another candidate for the source for the opera's epilogue. A *licenza*, in the sense it bore in the seventeenth and eighteenth centuries, is an insertion by a performer, or an epilogue meant to honor a patron or a festivity.[19] Indeed, Mosco Carner views the ending of *Gianni Schicchi* as a *licenza*. It ends similarly to Ben Jonson's *Volpone* (1605), which served, Carner argues, as a model for *Gianni Schicchi*.[20] In a *licenza*, the audience is addressed and invited to censure or praise the show. It indicates that the performance has ended and the audience is about to be dismissed. This may be combined with the staging of a couple's union, the recitation of a moral from those surviving the punishment of the protagonist (as in *Don Giovanni*), or the ascension of the hero to the heavens (*Orfeo*).[21] A *licenza* usually involves an ensemble or chorus, and serves as an ending for *opera buffa* by bringing all its characters on stage.[22] *Gianni Schicchi*'s epilogue shares some features with those of the *licenza*, but it is rare to have the stage empty for the epilogue, as happens in *Gianni Schicchi*.[23]

Some of the features of *Gianni Schicchi*'s epilogue might refer to a layer beneath that of *commedia dell'arte*. Those, for instance, in which the chorus leader, on behalf of the other members of the play, causes rupture in the drama. In Aristophanic comedy, at a certain point (often in the middle of the play) while the characters are offstage, the chorus or chorus leader addresses the audience, and all action is suspended. This is called a *parabasis*. The dramatic status of the chorus's utterance is ambivalent. The members of the chorus remain who they were but now it is as if they were not involved in the fictional situation. The chorus leader may speak on behalf of the poet or remain in character; he may be critical of the play, the poet, or the poet's rivals; he may offer advice, teach, praise, and so on.[24] In K. J. Dover's view, the chorus and the characters in an Aristophanic comedy may at any moment create a "rupture of dramatic illusion" by stepping out of their dramatic roles and making reference to the theater, the audience, or the festival.[25] G. M. Sifakis, on the other hand, argues against this assumption of rupture, because there is no illusion in Old Comedy: all is played to the audience as a form of "narration by means of imitation."[26] The address to the public comes from the point of view of the role, the actor, or the poet; and it is made in quick alteration of personalities, or by confusing the role with impersonation. The actor, being free to overstep the boundaries of his role, allows tensions and disjunctions to develop between actor and role, and superimposes the two personae in conflicting ways in order to attain a comic effect, praise the performance, or direct a message from the poet.[27] Often the poet and the merits of his art are praised; older poets or the poetic genre itself are addressed, and applause is requested. The *parabasis* manipulates levels of fiction and makes it difficult to situate the speaking voice. The *parabasis*, writes Simon Goldhill, is "the play in miniature," a self-exposure, and an exhibition of artistry.[28] Goldhill sees Aristophanes's plays, and the *parabasis* in particular, to be posing questions:

> How seriously, how comically, how literally to take (the) play[?] And how far to go with such questions.... Negotiating the license and limits of comedy is drawing the line (somewhere), that is, framing a response.... The *parabasis*, a chorus stepping forward to address the audience, does not obviate but rather emphasizes the audience's involvement in negotiating the boundaries and transgressions of comedy.[29]

In *Gianni Schicchi*, there exists only one moment of confusion among role, singer, and impersonator, and only one such moment that makes it difficult to situate the voice. Moreover, in the opera there are no quick alterations of personalities, but only one in the epilogue. What is evident, then, from the discussion of the conventions of epilogues is that Puccini and Forzano's homage to or play on one or more of these conventions unsettles rather than predetermines our understanding of the opera's ending and the fate allotted Gianni. Does the epilogue suspend the stage illusion? Change the character's perspective? Does it follow from the material, fracture it, stress artificiality and artistry? The epilogue might be daring Dante or challenging the sympathy Gianni has raised in us—now that the fate allotted him in the *Inferno* is revealed. None of the conventions offers a sufficient explanation in and of itself. It is unclear which convention the opera is attuned to, and none provides a full account of *Gianni*'s epilogue. It is an epilogue, in fact, that rules out basic features of all the conventions. The question remains: What does *Gianni Schicchi*'s epilogue wish to achieve? What does it mean that in the epilogue Gianni addresses us from the perspective of hell?

Clues about Life and Death

Not only does the ending destabilize the protagonist's subjectivity, but throughout the opera clues are spread that blur distinctions between a living Gianni in the opera and a dead Gianni in the epilogue. What we come to realize is that there is an awareness, from beginning to end, of the continuity of subjectivity: an awareness that Gianni in hell has seeped into the opera earlier than what is accounted for in the epilogue.

Clue One: Dramatic and Musical Continuity

The break between the opera and the epilogue—between Schicchis alive and dead—is supported by dramatic and musical *continuity*. The stage directions describe Gianni rushing down the stairs and coming back up again—but never *leaving*. Grabbing as much silverware as possible, he chases the relatives out of the house. The orchestra imitates the sound of him dumping the silverware on the ground. It is an onomatopoetic sound outlining an event prior to the onset of the epilogue—and Gianni's first words when he reenters the stage follow from this sound, establishing an acoustic and visual continuity among the lovers, the view of Florence in the distance, and Gianni's address from hell.

Clue Two: Curious Dating of the Tale in the Libretto

The time when the opera is purportedly set does not correspond to that of the historical Gianni since he, a member of the Florentine Cavalcanti family, was dead by 1280. Thus, patently, he was already dead on September 1, 1299 – the date given in the libretto. Did Forzano and Puccini know that Gianni, and obviously Donati – the dead body in Gianni's tale – were long dead by 1299? They might not have. But a question still remains as to why they chose September 1, 1299.[30] We can speculate. The year 1299 is just before Dante embarked on his journey to hell, and 1300 is a year all Italians are familiar with.[31] It would also place Rinuccio and Lauretta's hoped-for wedding day on May 1 uncannily at the time, or even after, Gianni is in hell.[32] The libretto's dating, in fact, places Gianni on the threshold of his hellish self.

Clue Three: Inaccurate Historical References in the Libretto

There is a pronounced emphasis on historical and topographical references in the libretto.[33] The date, September 1, 1299, is not merely a stage direction but is inserted into the notary's recitation (in Latin) while he is preparing the will.[34] Michela Niccolai stresses the precision and accuracy of historical and topographical details employed to create the authentic ambience of the date chosen.[35] Indeed, references are made to Florence's "gente nova" and the war between the Ghibellines and the Guelphs. The inclusion of numerous Florentine architectural details is striking. In Rinuccio's aria alone, several sites (Piazza dei Signori, Piazza Santa Croce, the castles of Val d'Elsa) and family names (Arnolfo, Giotto, Medici) are invoked. In Lauretta's aria there is mention of Porta Rossa, Ponte Vecchio, the Arno, and the disinherited monks of Santa Reparata. But, in fact, several references are inaccurate. For instance, the construction of Santa Croce, initiated in 1294–95, had not been completed by 1299;[36] the Piazza dei Signori (Palazzo Vecchio) was also still under construction in 1299; and the Ponte Vecchio wasn't built until 1345.[37] So why create a historical context for this specific date but then fail to consistently maintain accuracy?

Clue Four: Symmetrical Impersonation

At a striking moment in the text of the women's trio, Gianni and the dead Buoso are positioned in symmetry to each other even though the plot does not require it.[38] The women are preparing the costume that Gianni will wear to pass as the dying Buoso Donati: "Chi vuoi che non s'inganni? / È Gianni che fa Buoso? / È Buoso che fa Gianni?" ("Who would not be fooled? / Is it Gianni playing Buoso? / Is it Buoso playing Gianni?) Obviously, Gianni is playing Buoso—but in what sense is the *dead Buoso* playing as well, as if he were impersonating Gianni?

Clue Five: Undifferentiating the Living from the Dead

> Io, Io Schicchi, con altra voce e forma.
> Io falsificio in me Buoso Donati,
> Testando e dando al testamento norma.
> O gente! Questa matta bizzarria
> Che mi zampilla nella fantasia
> È tale da sfidar l'eternità!

> [I, Schicchi, with another voice, another shape,
> Pretending to be Buoso Donati,
> Giving instructions and making a will.
> O, my people, this mad conception,
> Springing from my imagination
> Is enough to defy eternity!]

If hell were confined to the very end, why would a phrase from Dante's *Inferno* be delivered by the (living) Gianni in the opera—followed by a phrase that can be only understood if it were delivered by the *dead* Gianni in the epilogue? In other words, when Gianni describes his plan to falsify the will by impersonating Buoso, he quotes from the *Inferno*: "Io falsificio in me Buoso Donati, / Testando e dando al testamento norma";[39] the final phrase of his devilish plan, "È tale da sfidar l'eternità!" about defying eternity, makes sense only if it is uttered by someone in eternal hell. It would seem that distinctions between the living and the dead are not preserved in the opera.

It is becoming evident that the Gianni of the epilogue cannot be perceived only as a singer addressing the audience, narrating the fate of the character that he has embodied. The epilogue carries with it neither a clear-cut division between life and death nor a straightforward transformation from one state to the other.

Shades

> Io la credevo a Roma, forse ora ci sarà o sarà a Montecatini o a San Gimignano o all'inferno con Gianni.[40]

Who, how, and what is Gianni in Dante's *Inferno*?

In Dante, dead souls are represented as living bodies. "A dead soul," John Freccero writes, "is one whose vital trajectory has been turned back on itself so that it is indistinguishable from the body which it animated."[41] Dante's journey, Caroline Bynum elucidates, occurs in the "between-time of non-embodiment," moving in a "visible but non-material world."[42] The souls become somatomorphic: they have a corporeal dimension, yet the body of air that they radiate is also incorporeal. They only look like bodies. Manuele Gragnolati explains: "The union of a soul and the aerial body it radiates in the afterlife is called an 'ombra,' a shade, and it is shades—beings with an appearance but no substantiality—who inhabit the eschatological realms."[43] The shades of hell have retained the physical particularities of their living selves but their features are distorted and deformed, often beyond recognition. These souls express a movement away from form and order. They are, writes Gragnolati, "a worm in which full form is wanting, a monstrous being."[44] Ginsberg understands Dante's conception of the neither-dead-nor-alive depiction of the shades in hell as follows: "There must...be a radical gap at the center of any understanding of them [the phantasms of the damned], which corresponds to the radical emptiness of their being. Our comprehension of them must pattern itself after Dante's understanding of Satan. When Virgil points to him, Dante says in a famous simile that he did not die nor yet remain alive.... This is far more than a topos of inexpressibility; it is an exercise in non-intelligibility.... Dante [is] enjoining the reader ... to think what he became, deprived of both life and death."[45]

Dante assigns Gianni to the category of impersonators that includes examples of madness from antiquity. Within this category, impersonators are distinct because their actions are not evidence of a passive madness but a "deliberate disowning and discarding of their personalities.... They 'went out of themselves' by choice."[46] Assuming the personae of others, they are self-alienated; they falsify the impersonated *and* the impersonator.[47] According to Jeffrey Schnapp, the falsification of identity is a double sin: it makes false the identity of another and, at the same time, constitutes an alienation of the self.[48] The punishment for falsifiers is thus, by an inexorable logic, eternal falsification and distortion. They are forever metamorphosing and are constantly being transformed. Leonard Barkan sees in metamorphosis the basic set of principles upon which Dante builds hell: "Dante uses metamorphosis to blur the distinction between the living and the dead, or more specifically, the living and the damned."[49] Barkan also suggests an interchange between our world and hell. In hell, the shades continuously metamorphose into inhuman and unidentifiable forms that have neither an enduring nor a stable shape. Thus, the punishment in the eighth circle of hell (to which Gianni belongs) is incessant metamorphosis, constant mutation.[50] The material transformation of the shades in this circle represents, above all, a loss of what is human: bestial *and* human, they are monstrous hybrids.[51] Ginsberg views the transformation of the damned as "a metamorphosis of unbecoming," a deformation and distortion away from form and what is human, away from existence.[52] Bynum explicates the extreme metamorphosis Dante assigns this category of sinners, to which Gianni Schicchi belongs:

The metamorphosis of Dante's thieves...is...a complete loss of identity; shape does not carry story. It is story more than form that is erased. And story is erased and not only because there are no traces left but also because the metamorphosis goes nowhere except to confusion.

It is, Bynum argues, "a change in which identity does not endure."[53] Loss of story is loss of self.

Before returning to the opera, let me point out a striking fact: none of the scholarship on *Gianni Schicchi* mentions a Buoso dwelling in Dante's *Inferno*! The name Buoso is given to a shade among the thieves in canto 25; commentators have taken pains to identify the damned shades of the thieves in canto 25 since all are referred to by first names only. In Dante scholarship, the identity of Buoso (likewise referred to by first name only) has been much debated.[54] Anthony Oldcorn interprets the ambiguity of Buoso's identity in canto 25 as a deliberate obscurity on the part of Dante, who "steal[s] the thieves' textual identities even as his narrative robs them of their forms."[55] Though the information is meager, modern commentators identify the Buoso of canto 25 as Buoso di Forese Donati (died c. 1285), thus a different Buoso than the Buoso Donati in canto 30.[56] However, early commentators in major Dante editions—Anonimo Fiorentino, Ottimo, and Pseudo-Boccaccio—have identified the Buoso of canto 25 with Buoso Donati of canto 30—the one tricked by Gianni Schicchi.[57] Thus, the edition consulted by Forzano—Anonimo Fiorentino—is one of the editions identifying the Buoso in Dante's hell (canto 25) with the Buoso impersonated by Gianni (canto 30).[58]

Buoso of canto 30 belongs to the category of thieves who, like Gianni, have been stripped of sovereignty over their bodies and are forever changing form: Buoso, "attacked by a serpent, unites with the beast but suddenly starts exchanging form with it, and the two escape in opposite directions with opposite identities."[59] What takes hold of Buoso is a complete interchange of identities, a dissolution of forms; there is an exchange of identities between species when human becomes serpent and serpent becomes human. Moreover, the serpent with which Buoso exchanges shapes was once a human being. In Barkan's formulation, there is an "eternal change and, especially *ex*change,"[60] and, in Oldcorn's analysis, what transpires is a "mutual transformation of two individuals, occurring simultaneously at a distance, in which what changes is...not merely the external form or disposition of their matter...but the 'matter' itself." It is, continues Oldcorn, a "telemorphic" transformation in which neither individual has any material existence.[61] Ginsberg, as mentioned earlier, explains the transformations of the thieves as something more than merely the sense of their becoming something else: "One cannot tell what these creatures are, since they no longer have the formal distinctions by which one could identify them as men or beasts.... [It is] unbecoming due to a failure of form."[62] They are dead and not dead. The eternal fate of both Gianni and Buoso, belonging to this category of metamorphosis, "lies precisely in the knowledge that they are eternally vulnerable, forever poised on the brink of their own bestiality, their identities precarious" and subject at any moment to "change / and rechange."[63] Not Gianni alone—eternal morphing in hell is something Buoso and Gianni share.

Indeed, the opera fashions them symmetrically: "Is it Gianni playing Buoso? / Is it Buoso playing Gianni?" Their changeable identities mirror each other in Dante's hell. Both are dead and not dead; both transform and, according to the opera, are transformed into the other. In other words, if hellish metamorphosis is identity that does not endure but is forever morphing, it is identity undone. And if falsification and loss of identity work both on the impersonated and the impersonator, then they work on both Buoso and Gianni. And if Gianni's voice sounds to everyone so much like Buoso's voice then, in a sense, it *is* Buoso's voice. In an opera that displays a corpse on stage, dresses its protagonist in a dead man's clothes (while seducing him with a nursery rhyme), places him in a dead man's bed, and lights and puts out candles for the dead, the subtext may be that both Gianni and Buoso, shades from hell, are enacting their dead selves. Impersonating the dead affects the living, distinctions no longer hold, life and death mingle. The interchangeability fashioned by the opera between Gianni and Buoso is extended to Gianni's different states. Notice how the music identifies Gianni of the opera with Gianni of the epilogue: it is one continuous Gianni throughout. Is the impersonation enacted in the opera a hellish metamorphosis? Is the living Gianni a manifestation of Gianni's hellish self? If so, then this would explain the curious dating of the opera on the threshold of Dante's journey through hell. Perhaps we have a glimpse of Puccini and Forzano's inheritance of Dante. As in Dante, the dead are indistinguishable from their embodied selves; they are somatomorphic, and such metamorphoses close the gap between the living and the dead. If the opera subordinated the very enactment of the story of impersonation to the rules governing hell, then Gianni is already dead for the duration of the opera, and he is playing out its plot as a form of extreme metamorphosis. Life becomes a metamorphosis of death.

Morphing Music

Da morte son rinato.[64]

Gianni has not one but three themes to denote him: the *fanfare*, *addio*, and *name* themes.[65] These are best characterized not as different themes, with each standing for a facet of his personality (Macdonald's suggestion), but as an overdeterminacy of sound pointing to a fluidity in characterization.[66] The themes share, as Mosco Carner observes, a fanfare-like rhythmic quality.[67] Sonic proximity emphasizes their interconnectedness, rendering all Gianni's thematic expressions tinted by his hellish sound. This is surprising since the very predilection for fanfare is novel and uncharacteristic of Puccini's style.[68] All themes also share a deficiency, in that no theme denotes Gianni directly. The *fanfare* theme, though viewed by Girardi as "the only motive that is truly his own," is, in fact, sung by Gianni only when it is heavily

Still 2. "Is it Gianni playing Buoso? / Is it Buoso playing Gianni?" still from the production of Puccini, *Gianni Schicchi* in Forlì Teatro Diego Fabbri (JCE Festival Musicale Estivo Bertinoro) and Friedberger Musiksommer 2005, Orchestra: Bruno Maderna, conductor Karl-Heinz Steffens, director Michal Grover-Friedlander, set designer Eli Friedlander. In the role of *Gianni Schicchi*: Ralph Sauerbray.

disguised (see example 1).[69] Why then designate Gianni with a trumpet call—his *fanfare* theme—which is a topos for the rising of the dead, for redemption? As Carolyn Abbate writes: "The trumpet needs no medium; it commands and the dead rise up.... There is no correct fanfare, no semiotic code, no score or particular melody that must be present for the trick to work."[70] The call is unambiguous. So why employ the acoustic icon of Judgment Day, the trumpet call, not meant for the damned souls in hell, to designate Gianni? Why a *fanfare* theme to punctuate his address from hell and all his central appearances throughout the opera? Dante's hell is for eternity: the trumpet call is, precisely, not intended for the damned. The *fanfare* theme, the figure for the trumpet call of Judgment Day, thus acts to remind us that redemption is forever out of reach for Gianni.

The *fanfare* theme is heard on three distinct occasions before it sounds for Gianni's emergence from hell in the epilogue: in Rinuccio's aria, prior to Gianni's appearance when Rinuccio introduces him in his absence, and in the two impersonation scenes when Gianni passes as the dead Buoso—before the theme acquires its ultimate hellish significance in the ending. Linking Gianni's living and dead selves more intimately than the libretto does, the *fanfare* theme represents a form of musical behavior that we encounter in the onomatopoetic sound that bypasses the break for the epilogue, and also in the overall metamorphoses of themes in this opera.

For the very final orchestral moments of the opera, following Gianni's address from hell, the *fanfare* sounds in the version that we have heard in the second dubbing scene. It is as though in its early appearances in the opera the theme already foreshadows hell, or, in fact, that hell is present early on in the opera, making it ultimately clear that there is one continuous Gianni: dead and alive, as himself and as Buoso. The sound of Gianni as Buoso reverberates underneath Gianni in hell; Gianni in hell has always perhaps reverberated underneath Gianni's voices in the opera. Opera maintains no distinctions between its living and its dead.

Gianni Schicchi

Fra cap-pel - li - na   e pez-zo   il   na

The *addio* theme, migratory and unfixed, is associated with exile from a city that had extended a dubious welcome to Gianni in the first place. The theme is heard for both Florence as paradise and as hell. Indeed, cities in the *Inferno* "seem to undergo metamorphoses like the souls," writes Joan Ferrante.[71] And John Freccero maintains that Dante models hell on Florence: "The imitation of the real world that takes place in Dante's poem is a hostile, critical imitation because it takes place in hell. One might even turn the formula around and suggest that it is hell *because* it imitates the real world—a world seen from the perspective of death."[72] The *addio* theme is a marker for both Florence as hell and as paradise. It sounds grotesque when Gianni uses it to hypnotically lull all the relatives with a threat of the city's judgment on forgery of wills: amputation and exile. The *addio* theme and its double signification encompasses the lovers' despair and their bliss, as signaled by "Addio speranza bella" (beginning three measures after rehearsal 42) and "Lauretta mia" (rehearsal 84).[73] The former echoes the famous phrase inscribed on the Gate of Hell in *Inferno*: "Lasciate ogni speranza, voi ch'intrate" ("Abandon all hope, ye who enter here"); on the latter, paradise is inscribed: "Firenze da lontano ci parve il Paradiso" ("Florence in the distance seemed to us like paradise!"). Paradise and hell are further superimposed when Gianni reenters the stage to make his address from hell on the lovers' "paradiso."

Finally, the *name* theme outlines the phonetics of Gianni's name, which is never pronounced by him in song. It is a theme that outlines his contour or silhouette, casts solely his shadow. The *name* theme appears together with the other two themes.

95

Example 2. Gianni's introduction in the opera, Puccini, *Gianni Schicchi*: **2a.** Gianni's *name* theme (rehearsal 25). **2b.** A variation on the *name* theme, a variation heard as early as the prelude (eight meausres before rehearsal 1). **2c.** Gianni's *fanfare* theme (nine measures after rehearsal 28). **2d.** Gianni's *addio* theme (rehearsal 31).

Rinuccio

Gia-nni Schic- chi!

2a.

Thus, not only is Gianni's emergence from hell with the *fanfare* theme echoed in the music with which he is introduced in the opera, but these first and last scenes sound all three themes side by side under varying degrees of disguise.[74] (See examples 2 and 3. Example 2 shows the themes when Gianni is introduced by Rinuccio, the lover of Gianni's daughter. See example 2a for Gianni's *name* theme, rehearsal 25; example 2b for a variation on the *name* theme, a variation heard as early as the prelude, eight measures before rehearsal 1, that is, prior to hearing the *name* theme itself; example 2c shows Gianni's *fanfare* theme nine measures after rehearsal 28; example 2d Gianni's *addio* theme, rehearsal 31. Example 3 shows all three Gianni themes in the epilogue when he emerges from hell. Example 3a is the *addio* theme two measures before rehearsal 85, example 3b the *fanfare* theme, seven measures after rehearsal 85 and example 3c is the disguised *name* theme, final three measures of the opera.)

It is evident that the three themes associated with Gianni do not distinguish between a living Gianni in the opera and a dead one in the epilogue. Nor do they distinguish between Buoso and Gianni. For example, when Gianni is disguised as the dying Buoso in the women's trio, a morphed version of his *name* theme is heard. And when the notary refers to Buoso by name, the morphed *name* theme reappears (see example 4). These musical themes break down any distinctions: Gianni and Gianni as Buoso are sonic equivalents, they are operatically identical; music

2b.

Fl.

Oboi

C. Ingl.

Cl.
Si♭

Fag.

Corni
Fa

Trbe.
(Fa)

Rinuccio

Mot-teg-gia - to - re! Bef-feg-gia - to - re!___ C'é da

2c.

snel - le!

2d.

Example 3. Gianni's emergence from Hell, Puccini, *Gianni Schicchi*: **3a.** The *addio* theme (two measures before rehearsal 85). **3b.** The *fanfare* theme (seven measures after rehearsal 85). **3c.** The disguised *name* theme (final three measures of the opera).

3a.

3b.

identifies Gianni with Buoso and parallels this identification with regard to *two Giannis*.

The most striking musical behavior here—because it suggests an acknowledgment of the soul's behavior in hell—is the opera's metamorphoses of themes. The three themes associated with Gianni lead one into the other and become one another; their musical distinctness is obliterated. Example 5 shows dotted rhythm and triple meter typical of the *fanfare* theme reworked into the *name* theme in the second dubbing scene. Example 6 shows the *fanfare* theme when it comes to resemble, through the incorporation of characteristic features, the *addio* theme (see example 6a for the *addio* theme in the final lovers' duet leading to the epilogue, rehearsal 84; example 3a for an alteration of the *addio* theme that leads into Gianni's spoken address; example 3b for the *fanfare* theme that inherits from the altered *addio* theme both a descending contour and a closing gesture of a descending second; example 6b for the *name* theme internalized by the *fanfare* theme, rehearsal 86. Notice the descending-third closing gesture. See example 7 for Gianni's *addio* theme in "Addio Firenze," rehearsal 64; and example 2a for the *addio* theme as an embellished *name* theme). The opera ends with a merging of the *name* and *fanfare* themes for a final metamorphic stroke: the Gianni of the opera is merged with the Gianni of the epilogue.

3-2-1 Schicchi

> The first actors separated themselves from the community by playing the role of the Dead: to make oneself up was to designate oneself as a body simultaneously living and dead.
> —Roland Barthes, *La Chambre claire*[75]

3c.

Example 4. Disguised *name* theme for disguised Gianni, Puccini, *Gianni Schicchi* (four measures after rehearsal 78).

Il Notaio

Mes-ser Buo-so, gra- zie!

Example 5. *Fanfare* theme reworked into the *name* theme, Puccini, *Gianni Schicchi* (fourteen measures after rehearsal 75).

Cl.
si♭

mf

In 1926, Forzano wrote the play *Ginevra degli Almieri*, a comedy based on a medieval Florentine legend that alludes to Dante.[76] The eponymous heroine of the play is a young woman who is declared dead by a doctor and buried alive. Managing to escape from her tomb, she is unable to convince anyone except her lover that she is truly alive. Her husband believes she is a ghost, her father conducts a philosophical inquiry into the nature of spirits in the afterlife, and her lover is accused of necromancy and raising the dead. Miraculously, and with an allusion to Dante's *Inferno*, the situation is resolved: the young woman is no longer considered dead but instead is regarded as a new creation, and the true lovers are reunited. In *Gianni Schicchi*, Forzano and Puccini foreshadow *Ginevra degli Almieri* by alluding to Dante in creating uncertainty regarding the separation of the living and the dead.

Indeed, when the dead sing, that which constitutes the dead is grotesquely altered. In the epilogue, is an already dead Gianni referring to a past self that once dubbed the dead, a ruse for which he is punished by eternal damnation in hell? Or does the ending enable a transmigration of matter, so that Gianni is alive and well in Florence during the opera, and then becomes a dweller in

Example 6. *Fanfare* theme when it comes to resemble the *addio* theme, Puccini, *Gianni Schicchi*: **6a.** The *addio* theme in the final lovers' duet (rehearsal 84). **6b.** The *name* theme internalized by the *fanfare* theme (rehearsal 86).

6a.

6b.

hell in the epilogue? Or is it the other way around, a backwards de-animation, as it were, from the perspective of death, an echo from the realm of shades: Is Gianni being dead during the opera an outcome of the epilogue's hauntedness? Can opera reveal such ghostly movements? Perhaps we should retrace our steps and question the very revelation of hell in the epilogue. Why not end the opera with Gianni as the new owner of the Donati house, and with the lovers now happily reunited? What in the epilogue lies beyond *that* ending?

Perhaps that we are exposed to more than one Gianni, and to fluctuations between the living and the dead, to the slippery gradation of forms that encompasses those neither dead nor living, those subject to ceaseless transformations. At times we have the impression that there is one Gianni, the dead one; alternately, we sense that there are two Giannis—Gianni as Gianni and Gianni as Buoso; and then there are instances in which we hold on to three Giannis: Gianni, Gianni as the dead Buoso, and the dead Gianni from hell. Is there a way to decipher which of these Giannis is present to us? An insufficient interpretation locates two Giannis by way of the division of the epilogue. In the La Scala production of *Gianni Schicchi*, for example, in the epilogue, Gianni returns on stage as a creature that has emerged from Dante's hell. Thus a choice was made to distort his appearance to an unrecognizable degree. But an uncanny interpretation, supported by the music, finds that the Gianni of the epilogue seeps into the opera and that there is the perception of one continuous Gianni from beginning to end. In this view, the Gianni we hear in the opera has all along been voiced from hell: the Gianni dubbing Buoso has been a visitor from hell; the dead dub the dead. The radical claim would then be: Gianni is dead. He is dead throughout.

The operatic medium, founded as it is on the myth of Orpheus and Eurydice, stages the voice's failure to hold on to the dead it revives. Opera throughout its history kills its inhabitants, but it is reluctant or unable to cross over to the other side and bring them back. Puccini's opera is an attempt to overcome opera's repeated unstaging of a crossing over to the other world to retrieve the dead. And Gianni's request for extenuating circumstances can be seen as a license addressed to *opera* to exercise its powers, even if provisionally, to cancel out a fatal fate, as once, in a mythic time, had been attempted for Eurydice. But matters are more complex than a simple correction or compensation of opera's inheritance of Orpheus. What transpires is that in *Gianni Schicchi*, raising the dead becomes *being* them.

Opera Ghosting

Michael Ching, *Buoso's Ghost: Comic Sequel in One Act after Puccini's* Gianni Schicchi (1996)

The difference between life and death, so crystal clear in man, is somewhat veiled in other fields.

—Peter Brook, *The Empty Space*

A ghost, in being there and not there, present and absent, mediating and substituting for something else, is that which evades determinate meaning. It is as if the dead were granted a form of being that makes life itself a nonending state marked by continuation, recurrence, and repetition. A ghost possesses, as it were, a life. Tom Gunning emphasizes that "it is in the nature of ghosts and specters to *haunt*, to linger somewhere in an unsettling manner, to be there and yet not to be there, to haunt rather than inhabit."[1] In Helen Sword's words, the ghost is "a kind of interpretive cloud cover" where everything converges.[2] "Critics...haunt texts," writes Sword; "texts haunt critics; authors haunt texts; texts haunt authors; authors haunt readers; readers haunt texts; early authors haunt later authors; later authors, according to Harold Bloom, can even haunt their precursors. Every one of us, meanwhile, is haunted by history, by time, by texts, by dead ancestors, even by ourselves. Haunting can be used as shorthand, in fact, for just about any kind of troubled or troubling relationship—physical, spiritual, emotional, literary, temporal—between one entity and another. For many literary critics, it serves as a synonym for 'intertextuality.'"[3] Works are haunted by the past and harbor the future; their replaying the past transforms the future.[4] This undermining of linear temporality is intimately connected to the structure of the ghostly. I would like to narrow down this broad field of reference to ghostly phenomena and remark briefly on the vocal ghost through the relation of two operas in which one acts as the other's afterlife.

In *Buoso's Ghost: Comic Sequel in One Act After Puccini's* Gianni Schicchi (1996),[5] Michael Ching invents an afterlife for Puccini's *Gianni Schicchi*. The opera offers a continuation of *Gianni Schicchi*'s plot and of the earlier opera's voices: in *Buoso's Ghost*, the dead Buoso in *Gianni Schicchi* becomes a ghost impersonated by Gianni. Ching's opera depends on the performance of *Gianni Schicchi* as its immediate prequel. *Buoso's Ghost* builds upon a death in another opera, bringing a dead man back as a ghost, all the while pondering the nature of voice within a matrix of ghosting. Let me, in a few words, mention some of the issues pertaining to the possibility of one work's afterlife in another.

Buoso's Ghost begins where Puccini's opera leaves off, but does so by returning to events that happened *before* the time when Puccini's opera takes place. Gianni finds out that Buoso did not die a natural death but was in fact poisoned by his relatives. Traces of poison are left behind before the time of Puccini's *Gianni*, and thus create an "after." For Buoso's Ghost, to give substance to this afterlife of Puccini's opera, Ching needs a "before," a new origin of events, an invented prequel in which events "appear" that never occurred in *Gianni*. The relatives plan to frame Gianni for the murder of Buoso and thus win back the inheritance. They want, so to speak, to force him to fake not the identity of Buoso but of Buoso's murderers. Gianni, finding out about the poison, plants a forged suicide note in Buoso's nightshirt and convinces the magistrate that Buoso has committed the sin of taking his own life. In a renewed attempt to regain the inheritance, the relatives wish to kill Gianni, have his daughter (who is married to their nephew) inherit everything, and thus, indirectly, regain what Gianni has taken from them. After different twists of the plot, Gianni, in an attempt to save himself, impersonates Buoso, this time not the living Buoso but his ghost. The ghost delivers the threat to the relatives that he will return from the dead to haunt them if they don't leave for good. Once again Gianni is saved by the dead.

Consider first the two ambiguous ghost scenes in *Buoso's Ghost*. I call them ambiguous since in one scene, the apparitions are not ghosts of the dead but spirits of the living relatives conjured by Gianni; similarly, in the second scene, Gianni himself parodies a ghost. He does not impersonate the living Buoso, as in Puccini's opera, but mimics Buoso's ghost, poking fun at what the relatives would believe to be the sound of a ghost. Through those scenes we are introduced to the full scope of Gianni's vocal acrobatics, above and beyond what was attributed to him in Puccini's opera. In the first scene, the relatives are conjured as though Gianni's imagination were sufficient to make them appear, their presence punctuated by his conjuring voice. The past re-presents itself through the agency of Gianni's voice. He visualizes in his mind a past occurrence and that itself makes it visible to us. He imagines the scene of poisoning, a scene that occurred not only in the past but also in his absence, and in doing so summons the relatives on stage to reenact the scene as apparitions. Gianni's vocal talent extends itself over time and matter to include the revival of a bygone time as well as the summoning of the living. In the second peculiar apparition or ghost scene, Gianni impersonates the ghost of Buoso by grotesquely mimicking what the relatives would think to be the voice of a ghost, his voice sounding like an otherworldy fake.

Judging from such ghost scenes, Michael Ching's work appears to be a parody of Puccini's. Ching develops a witty variation both on the framing of the plot and its central, most famous aspect, Schicchi's impersonation of Buoso. Yet the situation becomes more complex, hauntingly more real, if one considers more closely the relation between the two operas. Bear in mind that *Gianni Schicchi* is itself a one-act opera, part of the three one-act

Example 8. Mimicking a ghost. The voice of the ghost of Buoso Donati, second ghost scene, Ching, *Buoso's Ghost* (measures 913–16).

operas comprising Puccini's *Il Trittico*. In Ching's performance of his opera, Puccini's *Gianni Schicchi* is severed from its original surroundings and employed as prequel to *a performance* of Ching's opera: *Buoso's Ghost*, lasting forty minutes, is intended to be part of a double bill, *Buoso* replacing *Gianni Schicchi*'s customary pairings from *Il Trittico*. *Buoso's Ghost* negotiates an entrance into the operatic canon through another work, another composer's music, and another's plot.

In *Buoso's Ghost*, Ching also, importantly, employs music from *Gianni Schicchi*—which is to say, he quotes and reworks it. Musically, *Buoso's Ghost* is at once a repetition, a continuation, and a comic variation; it quotes, paraphrases, and refers to Puccini's opera, out of which most of its musical and dramatic gestures are recognizable recurrences. But, importantly, what is *comic* in *Buoso's Ghost* is only comprehended if Puccini's opera is heard *immediately* prior to it; everything depends on a nuanced, detailed, and fresh memory of the Puccini. (For example, in *Gianni Schicchi*, Gianni sings the tune "Addio Firenze" as a reminder to the relatives that if they disclose that he has impersonated the dead Buoso, they are risking punishment for the crime of forging a will, for which they would have one of their hands amputated and would be exiled; in *Buoso's Ghost*, the *relatives* are those that sing "Addio Firenze," and it is used as a plea to Gianni that he not disclose their murderous act. Here the threat is transformed from the cutting off of a hand to that of a leg. Or, to cite another example, "Ponte Vecchio"—the place where, in Puccini, Gianni's daughter threatens to commit suicide if she is not allowed to wed her lover—is employed in *Buoso's Ghost* in a pathetic [and comic] attempt by the relatives to prove to Gianni that they are actually his friends.) This is why it is imperative that the pieces be played together as a double bill. Thus, *Buoso's Ghost* not only overtakes Puccini, but its life seems to depend on drawing its strength from the constant presence of Puccini's music.

At the end of *Buoso's Ghost*, Gianni asks forgiveness for his appropriations. In so doing, Ching replicates the gesture in *Gianni Schicchi*'s epilogue when Gianni asks the audience to consider the "extenuating circumstances" surrounding his acts. But this gesture is itself overdetermined, for at the same time it is Puccini, through the agency of his character that asks forgiveness from Dante, on whose *Inferno* his opera is based. The problem of inheritance is not just Schicchi's in relation to Buoso, but also Puccini's in relation to Dante. Ching then finds himself positioned in a long chain of overtaking an inheritance and partly refashioning the past, partly put in motion and haunted by it.

The overtaking-haunting relation between the two operas is further affected by our understanding of the nature of the ghost's voice in *Buoso's Ghost*. It is supposedly the voice of Gianni, the impersonator from Puccini's *Gianni Schicchi*. But what is Gianni's voice? As I have shown in the previous chapter, my reading of Puccini's opera hinges on the discrepancy between Gianni's selfhood in the opera (that is, Gianni alive) and Gianni's emergence from hell in the epilogue (that is, as a spirit of the dead). I also argued that the voice given at the end to the dead, in fact, permeates the opera as a whole. Puccini's *Gianni Schicchi* undermines the presupposition that hell is kept separate from the world of the living and confined to the opera's epilogue. Gianni Schicchi's afterlife in hell reflects back from the epilogue to the whole opera and refashions the character's operatic self as one that is simultaneously living and dead. If *Gianni Schicchi* is explicitly about a dead man being overtaken by a voice of the living man who dubs him—about how the dead are threatened by the living—then its implicit argument reveals the world of the living as itself permeated by death.

The assumption, supported by the music, is that Gianni is in fact *dead throughout the opera*, not just when he is speaking from hell in the epilogue. This has a far-reaching effect on the seemingly stable appropriation of Puccini's opera by Ching. It places a living/dead Gianni at the background of the apparitions in *Buoso's Ghost*. If these ghost scenes had at first something of a stable identity, particularly appearing as manipulations of Gianni to retain his achievements in the original opera, the reading I propose of Puccini's opera introduces a fundamental ambiguity into all his utterances in *Buoso's Ghost* as well. Gianni's falsification of the voice now hovers between the two operas: it is the voice of the trickster, but also of the dead, the conjurer, and the ghost. Any lasting anchoring of the voice of the character Gianni Schicchi is lost. The haunting voice comes equally to contain the impersonation of the living Buoso, the mimicking of the dead Buoso, the voice of the living Gianni, and the voice of Gianni from hell. It is as though haunting is itself marked by this constant instability, is neither here nor there. This might hint at the particular sense of the ghostly that appears as the afterlife of voice in the space opened between these two operas.

Through the matrix of one dead entity dubbing another, *Gianni Schicchi* surfaces as the red thread of our discussion up to this point. *Gianni Schicchi* serves, in the first half of this book, to reembody a singer with her dead voice and to animate a ghost with a voice of the dead from another opera. The next half of the book will reveal far more extreme cases: not a singer's voice, nor a character's impersonation of the dead or of ghosts, but a disembodied and reembodied, utterly independent song. For song to acquire such powers, a theological, mystical system is embedded into the world of opera.

CHAPTER THREE

Dybbuk: Between Voice and Song

Lodovico Rocca, *Il dibuk* (1934)

A Soul Has a Voice

Jewish tales, especially the mystic Kabbalist stories that show the spirits of the dead entering the bodies of the living, are based on beliefs in transmigration and after-death existence that blur boundaries separating life, death, and the spirit world. Gershom Scholem explains that the idea of *gilgul* (transmigration) predominates over the notion of retribution by punishment in hell. *Dybbuk* is the term used for a wandering dead soul who cleaves to the living.[1] The *dybbuk* inhabits the body of a living person, possesses it in a type of cohabitation. If the soul is that of a sinner, then it cleaves to the living as a means of hiding and escaping punishment, or temporarily resting the torments it is being put through. But if the soul is pious, then its purpose is to assist the living in fulfilling or completing an injunction.[2] The latter, positive case is termed not *dybbuk* but *ibbur*, meaning impregnation in Hebrew: the term brings out a sense of the living being pregnant with the dead, as if, in due course, a new life will be born from this union. The notion of the soul's impregnation (rather than its reincarnation) and the emphasis on possession by a spirit of the dead rather than by the devil are unique to Jewish conceptions of possession.[3]

One of the main signs of being inhabited by a dead soul is vocal. A *dybbuk* (most often) forces itself into another's body, which is then endowed with more than one voice. This multivocality is a sign of the body's possession by a foreign subjectivity.

A *dybbuk* does not overwhelm but rather temporarily replaces the subjectivity of the living. Its presence may take the form of a deformation of the host's voice, as when a woman acquires a male voice.[4] Often, the very presence of a *dybbuk* is detected through that change. The host still produces his or her own voice, but does so in alternation with a voice that cannot have been produced by him or her (the voice speaks another language, knows matters unknown to the speaker, has an impossible timbre or an alien temperament). These changes may be accompanied by bodily signs other than such vocal indications, but clearly a *dybbuk* is a manifestation of the dead in uniquely vocal terms.

There are observable signs of the residence of the dead soul. A body part (tongue, throat, belly, for example) is distorted, resulting in an observable swelling or lump. Thus the voice may emanate from a location other than the mouth. This is an aural presence with a material manifestation, as though the dead soul possesses matter, as though, with its return, it has acquired a new sense of dimension or volume. A *dybbuk* may wander in the body of the possessed and cause different parts of the body to change shape. During the exorcism rite, the *dybbuk*, in its struggle with and resistance to attempts to make it depart, may cause damage, choking the host if departing through the throat, for example. When the exorcist sets the terms by which the soul can exit and be forgiven, he also negotiates the place of its departure so that it will cause the least damage. This is the reason that the dead soul is requested to leave through the foot's little toe.

With the *dybbuk*, we have a dead soul manifesting itself as voice, a dead soul possessing matter — voice possessing matter. We are also presented with the ability of the deceased to cause death. Possession constructs a new relationship between self and voice. Voice is not the expression of that self but its trace, an action performed upon it or altogether detached from it.[5] If a *dybbuk* were expressed operatically, if a *dybbuk* were to sing, it would expose an extremity far greater than what was opened up by Puccini's *Gianni Schicchi*. Indeed, a few years after Puccini's opera, an Italian composer, Lodovico Rocca, writing in a style not far removed from Puccini's, composed *Il dibuk*.

The Divine's Voice

Exorcising a *dybbuk* establishes communication. First and foremost, the exorcism is a vocal exchange between exorcist and *dybbuk*. The first stage of the exorcism ritual is to determine the identity of the *dybbuk*: its name, biographical details, reasons for entering the body. This is the starting point of a negotiation so that the *dybbuk* can depart the body it has entered. When a *dybbuk* refuses to leave the body, and words are no longer effective, there is a turn to the performance of rituals assisted by the congregation: prayer, the opening of the holy ark, the burning of incense, the lighting of black candles, even whipping. When all proves ineffective, the next stage is activated: excommunication. The soul is punished by expulsion from the Jewish community, from all worlds. The final stage is accompanied by the sounding of *shofarot* (the plural of *shofar*), a goat's or ram's horn. This always occurs at the final stage, and is described in *dybbuk* tales as something the spirit can never stand up to.[6] At this point in the ritual, the exchange between voices of the exorcist and *dybbuk* is replaced with an exchange between *shofar* and *dybbuk*, in which the former possesses the ultimate battling voice. The *dybbuk*: a voice that has the power to enter and remain within a living being, a wandering dead soul struggling to amend fate; the *shofar*: the blasts that counter the dead, sound that sends the dead back.

But how are we to conceive of the *shofar*'s determining power?[7] This is critical in the context of an operatic *dybbuk* since it is folded into our understanding of the operatic voice. In other words, how would the internality of death to the operatic voice be played out by the *dybbuk* in empowering it against the power of death internal to the *shofar*? What would be the effect of the power of the *shofar* over operatic singing that is itself endowed with power over death? In opera, who would have the upper hand: *shofar* or operatic voice?

Theologically, this is not, obviously, an issue: the *shofar* is endowed with divine power. Its sound mediates the path for redemption available for the lost soul (the Holy Temple, the altar, sacrifice, mediation by the High Priest are all means long unavailable). In an exorcism rite, the voice of the wandering spirit is pitched against that of the *shofar*, with everything the latter signifies. Let us outline some of these significations. The ram was sacrificed in place of Isaac, which is why, according to tradition, the *shofar* is fashioned out of a ram's horn. The *shofar* stands for the sound of the sacrificial death-cry emitted by the ram, itself a substitute for Isaac, the human sacrifice. The *shofar* replays Isaac's sacrifice as a persistent memory. It stands for both the willingness to sacrifice the son and the act of sparing him, a mythological, miraculous event: it represents the willingness to sacrifice and the sacrifice's substitution with another offering. The originating mythical moment denoted by the *shofar* is both sacrifice *and* non-sacrifice. Acoustically, in the *shofar* lies the aural memory of the event (the *dybbuk*, according to Yoram Bilu, is also a sound reiterating the past. A sound that is not only an "inner-oriented" spirit but "a *past-oriented* endeavour, the embodiment of former lives, and thus an exercise in memory").[8] The *shofar* recalls the past and is also that past's very sound: the sacrificed animal's death-cry reproduced from the body of the sacrificed. Sounding the *shofar* in the Temple when performing the sacrifice served as memory of the original event.[9] It is a sound from the past replaying its past: the past returned. It is the sole instrument that is not replaced with newer instruments that produce newer sounds.[10]

These sounds are not considered musical. The sound of the *shofar* hovers between human and animal sounds. Theological exegeses and histories of musical instruments alike stress the *shofar*'s production of unmusical sounds. In biblical times the *shofar* served for signaling purposes (war, jubilee) or was employed in ritual, and was never used to produce music. Having a rhythmic, fanfare-like quality, it produces a few notes separated by fifths, two harmonics (second and third), and no melody.[11] Its sound is referred to in human registers—sobbing (*shevarim*) and wailing (*teruah*)—and in animal terms—moans and cries of fear and helplessness. Here is an instrument, taken from an animal's body, that is heard as animal and human and as endowed with the divine.

The *shofar* is also a symbol for the world to come, a major force in the dramas of redemption and the end of days.[12] The *shofar* of the revelation at Sinai is the horn that will be blown at the end of days. Then the *shofar* will be heard—its sound will even be seen—and past events will return.[13] Pitching the sound of the *shofar* against the voice of the *dybbuk* places the dead soul of the *dybbuk* on the chain of temporal reiteration: what is replayed is the memory of the death-cry, which is the memory of the (non) sacrifice, itself the sound of death and the promise of redemption. If a *dybbuk* possesses matter,[14] then the *shofar* governs matter—as in the story of the fall of the walls of Jericho, which were brought tumbling to earth by the sounds of the *shofar*.[15] *Shofar* and *dybbuk* are both related to death and the sound of dying, within which an exorcism ritual performs what can be heard, indeed, as a death duet (the verb used to describe putting away the *shofarot* at the conclusion of the ritual is the same verb used to describe the burial of a corpse—*Hatminu*).

The *shofar* on earth echoes a *shofar* above: "The sound of the *shofar*, composed of fire, air and water intermingled, ascends to the Throne of Judgment, strikes it and causes an upper voice to be produced. These sounds arouse the compassion of God, which neutralises the power of judgment and punishment. At the same time the *shofar*, rising with extreme strength, confuses Satan and defeats the demon. Just as the compassion aroused in human fear provokes compassion in the upper region, the sound of the lower *shofar* provokes the sound of the upper *shofar*; they meet and intermingle."[16]

The *shofar* not only echoes the realm above but mediates it. After God's revelation at Sinai, all experience is mediated and, as Gershom Scholem explains, there is an experience of the voice of God rather than of God directly, a mediation that is always an "incomprehensive communication."[17] The unique event at Sinai is taken to be an endless event containing all events to come: the voice of God at Sinai has never ceased and includes in it all voices that have been and will be.[18] The voice of God is the originary event. I quote Gil Anidjar: "The originary event is a senseless occurrence of tremendous, often cataclysmic force: it is the voice of God, the mystical experience, or a catastrophe of another kind, which, in time, gives rise to a historical chain of utterances and interpretations ('traditions'). This tradition constitutes language; it is language. It is that which gives meaning to the originary voice, word, or event, and it is figured by Scholem as a kind of conversation, a linguistic interaction and communication. The constant conversation between the original event and its later interlocutors is what constitutes and maintains language, what continues to provide it with its context and to maintain it in its integrity. The originary event resonates, or, more precisely, it must resonate in the later conversation that language is, which otherwise turns into an isolated, decontextualized monologue."[19] Tradition and language maintain the silent echo and resonance of the originary event.

The *shofar* is not only a means of communicating with God but also a manifestation of his presence.[20] Theodore Reik interprets the *shofar* not as a symbol for God but as God Himself. In Reik's formulation (developed by Lacan), the sound signifies the death of God.[21] The sound of the *shofar* is the cry reminding God that He is dead. "It is the remnant of the dead father," explicates Mladen Dolar, "that part of him which is not quite dead, what remained after his death and continues to testify to his presence — his voice — but also to his absence: it is *a stand-in for an impossible presence*, enveloping a central void."[22] Lacoue-Labarthe offers a musical take on Reik's formulation: "Art would be the repetition of the originary murder, and the four rough sounds of the *shofar* would imitate the overwhelming and terrifying cry of the assassinated *Urvater*, his groan of agony, as well as the clamor of terror of the murderers. Music, perhaps the most primitive of all arts, would proceed from this reproduction or imitation of the most ancient moan...."[23]

The voice of the *shofar* is animalistic, human, divine, an echo of the *shofar* above, God himself, His death. It is in dialogue with the *dybbuk*, as if it were hearing, understanding, and responding to it, using a secret comprehension to drive it away. The extreme interpretation that casts the *shofar*'s sound as that which reminds God that He is dead, can be placed in direct relation to the *dybbuk*. The persecutor and the persecuted do not differ. *Shofar* and *dybbuk* are both voices that sound their presence as death. In the operatic interpretation discussed below, a *dybbuk* is not simply voice, since this would not suffice to overpower the voice of the *shofar*. Available to opera are the means to go beyond voice.

The Dybbuk, or Between Two Worlds

One of the most important and well-known Jewish-Hebrew theater pieces of the twentieth century is Scialom An-Ski's play *The Dybbuk, or Between Two Worlds—A Dramatic Legend* (which premiered in Warsaw in 1920).[24] It is based on stories collected by the author (together with the composer Yoel Engel, who composed the music for *The Dybbuk*) among Hasidic Jews in Jewish communities around Russia. An-Ski, a pseudonym of Shloyme Zanvl Rappoport (1863–1920), wrote the play in 1914. On the advice of Stanislavsky, he added the character of the messenger, a dweller residing between our world and the next. The first director of the play was Eugene Vakhtangov, who "experimented with the idea of unity of gesture, rhythm, costume, scenery and lighting...[and replaced realism with] theatrical freezes, silences, chanting, singing, ghostly makeup, and grotesque formalized movements."[25] Pearl Fishman even calls Vakhtangov's version an "opera-ballet."[26]

An-Ski's play begins in the dark. Before the curtain rises, a mysteriously hushed chant is intoned about a soul that descends to earth in order to ascend to heaven. As the chant repeats, men in a synagogue are revealed on stage. They are discussing the powers of practical Kabbalah to create a golem, to raise the dead, and to conjure spirits and Satan. They say that Ḥanan, one of the most promising students, has recently immersed himself in forbidden practical Kabbalah for the purpose of mastering mystical powers that would win him Leah, the woman he loves, in marriage.[27] Sender, Leah's father, arrives at the synagogue and, to Ḥanan's horror, announces that he has just signed the contract for his daughter's arranged marriage. Ḥanan utters something about failed and successful mystical attempts and falls to the ground dead.

Act 2 of An-Ski's play opens with the wedding of Leah and her groom. All the town's poor, old, and crippled have been invited and are given a chance to dance with the bride. This is the famous beggars' dance in which Leah, in a grotesque frenzy, dances with all the village's misshapen figures until she collapses. She then goes to the cemetery to invite her dead mother and the dead Ḥanan to her wedding. This invitation gives the dead soul the opportunity to cleave to Leah, and the act ends with Ḥanan, now a *dybbuk*, dwelling within her. Act 3 shows the attempt to exorcise the *dybbuk*, who refuses to leave Leah's body. The reason for the *dybbuk*'s appearance is revealed: Leah's father has not kept his vow to Ḥanan's father to marry their respective future offspring, if born boy and girl, once they come of age. In act 4, the *dybbuk*'s deceased father is conjured, and the spirit levels the accusation that Leah's father is responsible for his son's death and for his return in the form of a *dybbuk* (the revelation of the reason for the *dybbuk*'s appearance by the dead father is meticulously comprehended, though the father's ghost says nothing).

The *dybbuk* is ultimately driven out of Leah's body. She, however, wishes him to return and reunite with her. They are able to communicate with each other and imagine they are singing to the children they never conceived together. The *dybbuk* now enters her soul, and as a result she dies. Their souls ascend to heaven and, as at the opening of the play, chanting on the dark stage is heard.[28]

An-Ski's version of the *dybbuk* narrative departs in many ways from typical *dybbuk* tales. Though Ḥanan sinned by utilizing forbidden practical Kabbalah, he was nonetheless wronged, and transmigration is the means by which he can make amends and fulfill the oath (in a next life). This makes the dead soul in

An-Ski's play closer to an *ibbur* (the positive case when a pious soul cleaves to the living for the purpose of fulfilling or completing an injunction) than a *dybbuk*. Indeed, the possessed longs for the *dybbuk*. An-Ski's version centers more on the love story and the reunion of the lovers beyond death than on the theology of sin and punishment, which is more characteristic of *dybbuk* tales. These departures bring the play into proximity with the world of opera and its latent resounding of the afterlife.

The composer Lodovico Rocca (1895–1986) and librettist Renato Simoni (1875–1952) collaborated on the creation of the opera *Il dibuk*, which they based closely on the play. Rocca was taken by the performance of An-Ski's *The Dybbuk* in Hebrew by the Habima theater company in the Teatro di Torino in October 1929.[29] (The play also attracted the attention of Gershwin and Berg when it was performed in Vienna.)[30] Rocca's *Il dubuk* premiered at La Scala in 1934 to great success.[31] Indeed, it was one of "the biggest Italian operatic successes since Puccini's *Turandot*."[32] Performances followed in Rome in 1935; by 1937, it had been staged in Warsaw, Zagreb, Bratislava, New York, and Detroit, as well as in other Italian opera houses. However successful, it suffered the fate of its time. Rocca himself was not Jewish (though he dedicates the opera to his mother which might lead us to speculate that perhaps she was Jewish—which makes him Jewish according to Jewish law).[33] Due to the opera's Jewish content—its sounds replicating synagogue chant, its words in Hebrew, and so on—it was one of the operas banned during the fascist era, and Rocca was included in the list of Jewish composers.[34] It is unclear why the opera, regarded so highly at the time, fell nearly completely into oblivion and was never recorded commercially; only the final duet, incomplete, was released in a collection of excerpts from verismo operas sung by Augusta Oltrabella and Gino del Signore.[35]

Rocca's *Il dibuk* is not the only opera based on An-Ski's play *The Dybbuk*. David Tamkin adapted the play for an opera in 1951, as did Shulamit Ran in 1996. There are also Aaron Copland's

Vitebsk and Leonard Bernstein's ballet, among other adaptations. The operas share in common the concern with sounding a voice after death. I deal here only with Rocca's *Il dibuk*, however, since it is in the orbit of the tradition of the golden age of Italian opera, the context for thinking through opera and the operatic in this book. It is this tradition that displays the supremacy of singing, the reign of death, and the goal of a sung death for its characters. Clearly, in Rocca's work, the *dybbuk*'s afterlife is a renegotiation of opera's death song.

If we temporarily put in parentheses the reading of Gianni as the dead voicing the dead (the Gianni in the opera being already dead from the outset), then in both *Gianni Schicchi* and *Buoso's Ghost*, voicing the dead is a con. The living dub the dead. Moreover, in the two operas, the voices of the dead are problematized. Their utterances are nearly entirely devoid of song and rather resemble speech. The two operas sound the voice of the dead emanating from the living as an imitation or replacement. In *Il dibuk*, the dead entity is also given voice by the living—but it is the dead soul that has entered the living body. It is the living who are "sung through."

Indeed the dead are the central occupants in *The Dybbuk*: they are consulted in matters of the living and are invited to earthly celebrations; a messenger from the other world, a cryptic dweller residing between the realms of the living and the dead, interacts with the characters; the dead communicate by speaking through the living; the grave of a bride and groom murdered on their wedding day is placed in the center of town and, during weddings, a sigh emanates from it.[36] Both the play and the opera occupy a space between the dead and the living. Voices span a time before birth and after death.

Duet within Oneself with the Dead about the Unborn

For early Kabbalists, metempsychosis was an exception brought about by the committing of an offense, mainly against the laws and mandates surrounding procreation. We recall that a positive *dybbuk* is termed *ibbur*—impregnation—hinting at a catering to and not a rejection of the guest soul. In *Il dibuk*'s final duet we encounter an explicit reference to Leah being pregnant with another's soul, an impregnation that yields as yet unborn babies.

Impregnation can be seen as the very form that determines the power of the oath taken before Leah and Ḥanan's birth. It decides the future and brings about the transformation of Ḥanan into a *dybbuk*. The marriage of Leah and Ḥanan was decided on before their birth, and this preordained decision becomes the determining bond that shows itself stronger than the marriage arrangement contracted by the father when Leah comes of age. The magical, irrational supremacy of what occurs before birth is what determines the structure of the oath. The originating marriage arrangement decided on before the births of Leah and Ḥanan governs love unto death and creates an original identity between bride and groom before they are born as distinct subjectivities. What was wished for (obviously not by them) before they were born is what determines their identities: they are conjoined by a spirit identity that is not bound by death.[37] They cannot but be together; and, indeed, on the day that Leah is to be wed to another, her lover crosses over from the other world.

The theme of impregnation is prefigured in the prologue of the opera. As the oath is narrated, we are told that after the death of Ḥanan, there remains no heir, no name, no memorial, and no one to say *Qaddish*, the prayer for the dead. Impregnation also figures in the exorcism scene where Ḥanan imagines himself a baby in his mother's arms and inside her womb. The sense of *ibbur* is explicit in the final duet, "Ninna nanna," in which Leah and Ḥanan sing an elegiac lullaby. The lovers lament their unconsummated marriage and unborn offspring, referring to these nonexistent progeny as "departed little ones." Leah, a womb, is a vessel of the restless afterlife and the as-yet-unconceived.

The *shofar*, summoned to drive the *dybbuk* out of Leah's body in the exorcism scene, hints as well at the sense of impregnation that pertains to the *dybbuk*. Comparing the ritual of blowing the *shofar* into a pit or barrel to other rituals, Curt Sachs conjectures that this produces a more terrifying sound but is also a remnant of fertilization rituals oriented toward the union of male and female principles.[38] Lisa Edwards associates the vicissitudes of motherly experience to the sounds of the *shofar*. She traces these sounds to biblical mothers: the mother of Sisera and Sarah, mother of Isaac. The former, realizing her son will not return from battle, cries a hundred cries; the latter, upon hearing of Isaac's fate, dies.[39] The mothers sound long sighs, moans, and piercing cries which in various sources are speculatively claimed to resemble the sound of the *shofar*. In turn, the *shofar* recalls those motherly cries. Edwards locates sources that view the *shofar*'s sound as echoes of those of a mother in labor, when pain causes her to emit a cry in which she asks for her own death, to then be replaced with a cry of life: the *shofar* being both "the sound of life going out of the world...and the sound of life coming into the world."[40] The *shofar* is conceived as the *dybbuk*'s double in association with impregnation. The *shofar* battles the voice, the false pregnancy by the *dybbuk*,[41] the "death that is alive" (*hamavet hachai*) within Leah.[42]

I Am Song

One of the central scenes in An-Ski's play involving a battle with the voice of the dead is the exorcism ritual. It is the *dybbuk*'s most pronounced expression, and calls for a display of virtuosity on the part of the actress playing Leah. In this scene, she is to produce a voice impersonating the *dybbuk* within her. Her voice and body turn into sites of battling forces employed against the dead soul. This results not only in Leah having two voices, but also in Ḥanan having two: one voice for the living Ḥanan (the voice of the actor playing him) and another representing him as dead (the deformed voice of the actress playing Leah).

What are we to expect from an operatic representation of this multiplication of voice? What is surprising is that multiplicity (or splitting) of the voice, the enactment of two vocal personae by one performer, is, in fact, *not* carried over in Rocca's operatic setting. In his opera's exorcism scene, no vocal distinction is made between Leah and Leah-*dybbuk*. She does not sing in a different Leah-*dybbuk* voice when H̱anan speaks through her. There is no mimicking of H̱anan or of a male timbre or typical range. We comprehend the presence of the dead from context: the exorcist addresses Leah, "Dibuk, chi sei?" ("Dybbuk, who are you?"), and it replies.[43] The *dybbuk*'s voice is agitated, the orchestral accompaniment busy, but the singing voice is not changed. Leah and Leah-*dybbuk*—Leah and the dead H̱anan—are vocally indistinguishable: the *dybbuk* has Leah's voice. The operatic *dybbuk* is neither a foreign voice nor a trace of H̱anan detectable within her voice; it does not split Leah's voice even though its vocal expression stands for operatic subjectivity.

One might wonder why Rocca forgoes this opportunity. Is not this feature of the tale—the virtuosity of sounding several voices in one—the very attraction it would offer for setting *The Dybbuk* as *opera*? One might argue that it is technically difficult, that is, a singer would not be able to impersonate (for the duration) two full-fledged vocal personae. Or perhaps it would be possible for a singer to enact within the voice two personae, to distinguish two beings within her voice, to split/double voice. We are not referring to a local change of color found in comic scenes and the world of disguise and trickery. Clearly the aim in *Il dibuk* is not to create a humorous, amusing voice. The voice of a *dybbuk* does not belong to the family of nasal, shrieking, mocking, fake, unmelodic voices, of which Gianni Schicchi's impersonation is an example. *Il dibuk* is certainly part of the tradition of Italian opera, which has at its disposal conventions, undeniable tricks, for portraying altered states of consciousness such as madness, sleepwalking, hallucination, and the like. These devices, however, are confined to single scenes and are momentary indulgences in atypicality (virtuosity, textless vocalization, extreme tessitura, unique accompaniment-voice relationship—for example, when the character surprisingly hears the accompaniment—and quotations of previous scenes as a sign of the character's memory of the past). In Puccini's *Le villi*, discussed in the prologue, an opera which provides an example of a mixture of death-scene and afterlife characteristics, there are indeed remnants of mad-scene conventions—musical quotation, for instance—that mark not madness but the return of the dead. Moreover, they are comprehended only with the assistance of external signs. In Lady Macbeth's sleepwalking scene, for example, we know of her distorted state not from a drastic change in her voice, but from the eavesdroppers' text, her gestures, and the obsessive orchestral accompaniment (Verdi requests that the singer performing the role of Lady Macbeth have an ugly, hollow voice. This is an overall condition for portrayal, not a specific request for the execution of the sleepwalking scene). "Being" a *dybbuk*, however, does not belong, in terms of its operatic portrayal, to the realm of conventionalized altered states. Rather, it belongs to the realm of death: a *dybbuk* does not partake in portrayals on the edge but reveals the inner workings and essence of what is operatic.

What, then, is the *dybbuk* in *opera*? Rocca uses the abyss he has erected between the voices of Ḥanan and the *dybbuk* and the *identity* erected between the voices of Leah and the *dybbuk* to create the *dybbuk* in a dimension verging on, but not identical to, voice. I will show its key feature. True to the traditional association of the extremity of singing with the death scene, the opera relocates the central expression of the *dybbuk* away from the exorcism scene and portrays the multiplication of subjectivities at the end of the opera. *Il dibuk* turns the end, the death scene, into its central scene. But even here, in the scene that replaces, as it were, the *dybbuk*'s expression in voice, nothing is detected *vocally*. Only the opera's stage directions and hints in the libretto—nothing aural—inform us of the abundance of existential states: first we are aware of the *dybbuk*'s presence inside Leah, then it is outside Leah's body and thus no longer "considered" a *dybbuk*; Leah at the scene's outset is still alive, but when Ḥanan's soul unites with hers, she dies and is transformed into Ḥanan's soul-mate. But nowhere does there occur a theatricalization of the voice,

nowhere are there distinctions maintained between voices of
a soul, a *dybbuk*, the dead, and the living. Thus, it is necessary
to identify the dimension in which a distinction is drawn: not
between voice and the existential state it connotes, but between
voice and song. Song may at times reflect a primordial core that is
aspired to but remains absent in the voice. This becomes evident
once we realize that what haunts the opera, what makes the dead
present to us, is not a character's voice but something that takes
the form of song: the song to end all songs, the paradigmatic Song
of Songs. To explicate this notion, let us turn to the meaning the
Song of Songs holds for the play.

In the play, the messenger tells a wonder tale about the power
of singing: the heart of the world and a water spring, separated
from each other in two far corners of the earth, long for and
need each other for survival.[44] Thus, every day, at dawn, they
sing. Their singing spreads throughout the world and leads to its
renewal for one more day. Indeed, Ḥanan believes the Song of
Songs is endowed with mystical powers. He even takes his belief
to an extreme (sounding heretical to his friend) when he declares
that all sin, having a spark in it, can be transformed into the holiness of the Song of Songs. We are in a world where singing has
divine powers to sustain creation.

This notion partakes in the overall mode of interpreting the
Song of Songs. Thus, while scholars interpret it as ancient wedding songs, dream poetry, or women's songs, on the whole they
emphasize its allegorical meanings.[45] Some regard the Song of
Songs as part of a liturgical literature related to the myth of the
death of God, his decent into the underworld, the joining of
his Goddess to rescue him, and their joint ascent back to earth.
Other scholars associate the Song of Songs with Leah, because of
Tikkun Leah (The Rite of Leah), which symbolizes God's uniting
with the exiled *Shekhinah* in mystical nuptials. During the rite,
hymns from the Song of Songs are intoned, as they are understood allegorically as the mystical union between man's soul and
God and the union of Israel and God: "The text [of the Song of

Songs] contained God's sublimity and mystery, and those who felt it deeply could be transformed and renewed when chanting the poem or meditating on its mystical meanings."[46] In the Song of Songs, the lovers' erotic desires are expressed. It conveys a sense of timelessness and concerns the repetition of an experience (the endless seeking and finding of the lover). In the Song of Songs, the real and the imagined, the actual and the hoped-for, are indistinguishable: "The lovers are capable of experiencing past, present and future with equal intensity."[47] Their love is present from birth, from the beginning, and goes into a future filled with redemptive overtones.[48] It is thus an allegory of the love between God and Israel. Therefore, explains Freddie Rokem, we comprehend that in the play "the souls [of Ḥanan and Leah] had become unified in the heavenly spheres before they were born, and they will be after their death as well." We are in the realm of "the mystical descent of the soul to its bodily abode, in the material world, a temporary state in preparation for its renewed ascent to the heavenly spheres."[49] Rokem continues: "The Song of Songs...contains several speakers. The most important one is the woman who tells about her love and her desire for her lover in different ways. The interchange between the two lovers is rendered in several passages in a literary form where the woman is actually quoting the lover. The female voice carries or contains the male voice in a way which is actually a metaphor for the very act of making love with him."[50] The Song of Songs' appearance in the *dybbuk* play, elaborates Rokem, is the most extreme form of "absorption or integration of the male voice with the female voice."[51]

Indeed, in the play's first staging by Vakhtangov—which Rocca witnessed when the Habima theater company visited Torino in 1929—Leah sings the Song of Songs as a sign that the *dybbuk* is speaking through her. In Vakhtangov's staging, the Song of Songs is employed to mark possession. Not only is it sung by Ḥanan upon Leah's entrance into the synagogue, but Vakhtangov expands its role and adds more appearances. In his version, on the first sign of possession, when Leah is being prepared for the wedding ceremony with the groom of her father's choice, she utters (in Ḥanan's voice), "You are not my bridegroom," and begins to sing Ḥanan's Song. Leah sings the Song once again when the *dybbuk* refuses to leave her body, and preparations for the exorcism rite begin. At the end of the play, Vakhtangov inserts another instance in which Leah struggles to break out of the exorcist's spell and join the spirit of Ḥanan. The Song—now sung by Ḥanan, not by Leah—is heard for Leah, who, now dead, has joined Ḥanan.[52] In Vakhtangov's staging, the Song recurs at important junctures (at the entrance of the *dybbuk*, during its refusal to exit Leah's body, and when it merges with her soul). It is also used to signal the relationship between the lovers (when they meet, when they reunite). I will only mention here a facet of Vakhtangov's voicing that does not find expression in Rocca's work. Vakhtangov casts Ḥanan's role to be played by a *woman*.[53] Thus, when Leah sings the Song to indicate Ḥanan, it is, in fact, the voice of a *woman* that she is voicing. In other words, to signify the *dybbuk* that has entered Leah, Vakhtangov relies not on the mimicking of a man's voice but on the association of the Song with Ḥanan that has been established.

Rocca's construction of the *dybbuk* may have been influenced by Vakhtangov's staging of the play *The Dybbuk*. However, in Rocca's *Il dibuk*, the Song of Songs does not function as it does in the play—as a surrogate voice. Let us follow closely how the Song of Songs behaves in the opera. We begin with the very first sounds of the opera, the prologue.

The curtain opens slowly on a dark stage "con luce debolissima" ("with diabolic light").[54] The prologue is composed of unseen, unaccompanied, disembodied voices. They are designated in the score as voices of the characters that will enact the opera's tale. In the prologue, they are the manifestation of the messenger's narration. These disembodied voices personify the characters in his story, as if they have been released by the originating oath that propels everything. What determines the course of the opera is already present here. Nothing that will occur during the opera will change what has already been determined by these voices—though the voices in the prologue are not yet recognized as those of Leah, Ḥanan, the messenger, and so on.[55] We are not yet aware that the array of disembodied voices make up all the important figures that will determine the *dybbuk*'s fate.

The prologue fashions, as it were, its subjects as voices as such. These voices originate in a time-before-the-beginning, they come to us from before birth, from what brought about the onset of the tale. We are secretly privy to the voices, eavesdropping on them before they become embodied, before they come into existence as dramatis personae. Here, the voices show the potential they possess for returning. The prologue is a glimpse of that which will haunt.

Within the prologue, there is a distinct moment that stands out from the surrounding music. It is a brief duet sung by Leah and Ḥanan. The duet sounds like a distinct, separate, rounded-off song. The text they sing, a quotation from the Song of Songs, seems indirectly related to the story of a broken oath they are enacting within the messenger's tale. It is, however, the expression of their fate. (See example 9: Rocca's *Il dibuk*, prelude, first appearance of the Song of Songs as a duet between the disembodied voices of Ḥanan and Leah.)

In example 9, we see that the song lasts only a few measures and is surrounded, for emphasis, by voices of the chorus.[56] The selection from the Song of Songs comprising the song is initiated by the voice of Ḥanan, and Leah answers with a variation on his music. It is two measures long, built on an embellished stepwise descent from E to D, then followed by an expansion of that descent down a fifth to A. This is answered, symmetrically, for two measures, by the voice of Leah. In her reply, the framework of the descending fifth, E to A, is preserved, but through a different route. Her part begins identically to Ḥanan's, on E, but then outlines an arpeggio by descending to C and ascending up to G before returning to E. The second measure is an almost exact

Example 9. A duet between disembodied voices Rocca, *Il dibuk*, prelude (seven measures before rehearsal 11).

imitation of Ḥanan's music, with only slight melodic and rhythmic alterations. This momentary duet is simple and memorable, like an embedded song.

Unlike in the play, the Song of Songs is not employed for the purpose of establishing an ambience of occult mysticism, nor is it employed as a means to show Ḥanan's immersion in mysticism.[57] But as it originates in the prologue, before Ḥanan has come into existence, it *precedes* him. The song emerged out of the explication of what brings about the *dybbuk* in the first place. In other words, the song (an incipit from the Song of Songs) is sung "by" him— before he "is." The opera creates the song as a primal presence, preceding character. It is Ḥanan who comes to embody it—is a manifestation of it—rather than the other way around, in which a song is the expression of an operatic character's inner self. It is he who is sung by the song.

The disembodied duet takes but a moment. The voice of Ḥanan sings, "Eccoti bella" ("Hear me beautiful"), and the voice of Leah replies, "Baciami i baci della tua bocca." ("Give me of the kisses of your mouth.")[58] Indeed, later in the opera, the source of these lines in the Song of Songs will be identified. One sole modification is performed on the biblical quotation: the first word of the first line, "you are beautiful," is changed to "*hear* me beautiful," as though singing calls to be heard. The song is also peculiar in that two characters, rather than one, voice it. What is clear from the outset is that the operatic *dybbuk* will not be a voice emanating from another, nor will it be a solitary voice. The *dybbuk* in this opera will be revealed as a reconfiguration of the relationship among song, voice, and character.

The Song of Songs emerges in the prologue as a primal presence, a song that Ḥanan and Leah are sung by, originating before they come into existence as characters. It is the expression of the *dybbuk*-essence in the opera. It not only replaces the play's manifestation of *dybbuk* in a voice emanating from another with a song overtaking subjectivity, but it is a doubled voice, a duet. And moreover, the song is "musically" possessed. Let me briefly show this possession by going through salient moments in acts 1 and 3, following the *dybbuk*'s trajectory.

The Song of Songs reemerges in act 1 with the longest segment. Ḥanan, in the synagogue, informs us what he sings when Leah enters: Song of Songs 4.1, the man's first love speech.[59] The text evokes an illusion of immediacy, as if the woman were conjured, made present, and stood before him.[60] It seems as though the Song of Songs is what summons Leah.[61] For the only time in the opera, the (living) lovers meet; soon after, Ḥanan will mysteriously die. At this point, only Ḥanan sings the song. Leah is listening. She will need to "know" the song in order to recognize Ḥanan when he returns. Only in the opera, where the Song had already been invoked in the domain of souls, is the sound of their first meeting rendered as that which has returned.

The Song, established in the prelude as singing itself endowed with subjectivity, has another qualifying characteristic. This, together with its power to override character, molds it into *dybbuk*-essence. This characteristic takes the form of a distinct orchestral accompaniment, memorable, indeed vocal in quality. It resurfaces several times in the opera. It is a repetitive, insistent, compulsive, *ostinato*-like sound in the orchestral accompaniment, perceived as the Song's other voice. It is as though the Song initiates, or is initiated by, an additional voice—as though the Song instigated its own internal *dybbuk*, in the form of a restless, poignant, accompanying sound, an additional voice, a *dybbuk* within the *dybbuk*, as it were, to further qualify a *dybbuk*-essence in the opera. (See example 10.)[62]

The Song's other voice, its *dybbuk*-like accompaniment, is a persistent, nearly unchanging rhythmic-melodic figure above changing harmonies that lasts for one measure. The recurring, measure-long figure is internally obsessive in its repetitiveness and deliberation on a single note and tie, which lends a sighing-like effect and human-voice quality to the reiteration (see example 10, rehearsal 46 for Ḥanan's announcement of his song). For the last two (out of six) lines of text from the Song

135

Example 10. The Song of Song's internal *dybbuk* voice in the orchestral accompaniment, Rocca, *Il dibuk* (act 1, rehearsal 45).

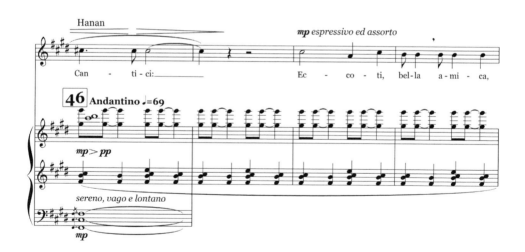

10. (cont.)

Hanan

I tuoi se - ni son co - me le gaz - zel - le che pa - sco - no tra i

Hanan

(Entrano Leah e Frade fermandosi incerte sulla soglia.)

p affettuoso

gi - gli...... O mia spo - sa, o dol - ci - ssi - ma so - rel - la......

Maier

(interrompendo)

mf

Chi ve - do? La

48

Sostenendo un poco ♩=54

p

Hanan

Maier

(con voce cerimoniosa)

fi - glia di Sen - der? Buo - na not - te, Le - ah!......

mp

10. (cont.)

of Songs, the accompaniment figuration changes twice. First, it assumes a full-fledged melodic statement—indeed, one that overrides Ḥanan's, as though he is now accompanying the accompaniment. (See example 10, nine measures after rehearsal 47.) Second, the accompaniment figuration assumes a seesaw figuration (see example 10, rehearsal 48.) This latter change in the accompaniment foreshadows Leah and Ḥanan's other song, the lullaby to their unborn offspring in act 3.[63] Both these new figurations in the accompaniment assist Leah, in the final act, to "acoustically" recognize (the invisible, ghostlike) dead Ḥanan.

The Song recurs in the final act, act 3, where it echoes its previous appearances. It is part of a duet between Leah and Ḥanan encompassing the entire act. Leah, in her reply to the sounding of the Song, tries to locate and recognize what she is hearing. It sounds to her like moaning: she hears a voice but cannot see anyone; it sounds to her like a lamenting violin at night.[64] Her search for the sound's origin and its recovery in memory is set to the Song's earlier accompaniment in the opera (see example 10 nine measures after rehearsal 47), as though she were performing a duet with the added, *dybbuk*-like voice (see example 11). In this final duet, Leah does not respond with a line from the Song, as was the case in the prelude. Rather, the duet is based on the Song through her recognition of the haunting sounds in the accompaniment. She responds to the cues in the accompaniment, the *dybbuk*'s *dybbuk* voices, until she can gradually flesh out his image in her mind. The acoustic memory of him emerges when the added voices, the *dybbuk* of the *dybbuk*—those voices encountered in the former appearance of the Song—accompany *her*.

The opera reduces the theatrical emphasis on voice by overemphasizing a register of song. Song is the source of signification. The operatic *dybbuk* is not a voice bound to character but is rather singing itself, expressed by several characters and no character. The Song voices Ḥanan—before birth, in his life, and in his transformation into a wronged and wandering soul; it also marks Leah—before birth, and after she has united with the dead soul of

Example 11. A duet with the haunting accompaniment, the *dybbuk* of the *dybbuk*, Rocca, *Il dibuk* (act 3, forty-three measures before rehearsal 26).

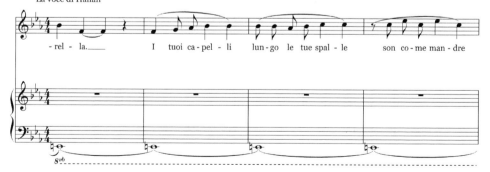

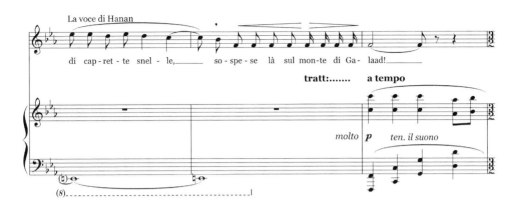

La voce di Hanan

di cap - ret - te snel - le,_____ so - spe - se là sul mon-te di Ga - laad!_____

tratt:...... a tempo

molto *p* ten. il suono

(8)

Leah

p

Chi so - spi - ra con pe - na si pro-fon - da?

La voce di Hanan

p

I - o.

come in lontananza

Leah

p

O - do la tua vo - ce,_____ ma non ti pos-so ve - der!_____

p

(pp)

11. (cont.)

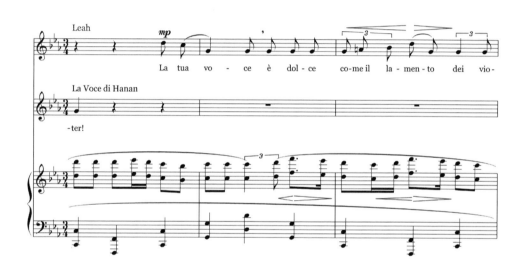

11. (cont.)

La Voce di Hanan

Non lo so più! Mi sov-vien di me so - lo se mi pen si

(Mentre Leah parla, la figura di Hanan appare prima debolmente poi sempre più chiaramente, cosa però tutta incorporea e fantomatica.)

Leah

Io ri - cor - do! Quan-te lag-ri-me dol-cis - si-me, nel bu-io ra-pi-ta da un in-

La Voce di Hanan

tu!

un poco meon sost.

sempre p e stanco

Leah

-can - to lan - gui-do e tri - ste! E semp-re in so - gno un vol - to m'ap-pa-

p e vago

più p
mf

11. (cont.)

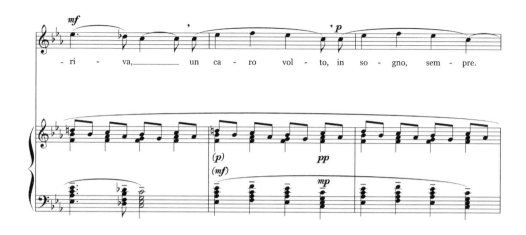

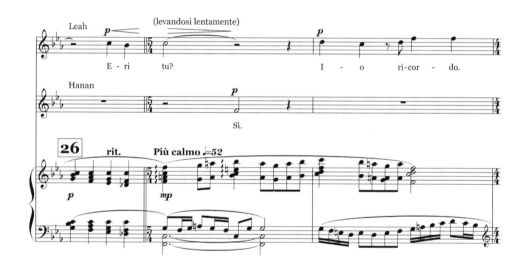

11. (cont.)

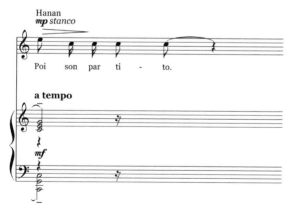

11. (cont.)

Ḥanan. As such it haunts—as a song, operatically haunting—much more effectively than would a voice emanating from another. In place of being sung, the Song gains and loses material realization. The opera has endowed song not only with subjectivity but with the power to bond several subjectivities.[65] When the opera ends, it has come full circle and has exhausted the range of the possible: it spans a time that begins before the dawn of life and extends past its termination—not the span of a lifetime, but a mythical range of singing.

Voice Replacement

Puccini, *Gianni Schicchi*, Rocca, *Il dibuk*

A comparison between an operatic *dybbuk* and an operatic impersonator of the dead, Gianni Schicchi, yields surprising results—beyond the obvious disjunctions between voices and their sources. *Il dibuk* and *Gianni Schicchi* are dissimilar, yet they offer unexpected similarities in many ways. First, the dissimilarities—since Rocca's *Il dibuk* seems to take over where *Gianni Schicchi* leaves off, the point where impersonation and dubbing lead into possession. For the damned souls in Dante's hell there is no redemption, so the granting of extenuating circumstances in Puccini's opera is thus subversive (on top of which there is Ching's opera, redeeming Gianni and countering Dante's judgment a second time); in *dybbuk* tales, on the other hand, part of the exchange in an exorcism ritual involves a promise to overturn one's posthumous fate. In *Gianni Schicchi*, the voice is meant to sound like another's, imitation and falsification being an alteration of another to become the other (in *Buoso's Ghost*, a comic effect is achieved when the impersonation of the ghost aims to sound like what the relatives would want to hear as that voice); in *dybbuk* tales, on the other hand, the voice of the *dybbuk* is precisely different from what we expect to be produced from that body—that is how a *dybbuk* is recognized in the first place. Another important difference is that Gianni is revealed to be a dead man who dubs the dead (or, in *Buoso*, who dubs a ghost); in *Il dibuk*, it is the dead soul who dwells in the living. Gianni's example offers the voice of the living emerging from the dead, while the example of the *dybbuk* shows the voice of the dead emerging from the living. One ends in hell, the other, where it began, in heaven. One opera's signification is concentrated in one edge, the epilogue; while the other lies in the other edge, the prologue.

More striking are the similarities. Both protagonists are between worlds, and in both operas, we begin and not only end in death. The dead Gianni is enacting, for the purpose of redeeming himself, his past; the *dybbuk* also seeks to redeem himself, to reclaim a stolen past. Most striking is that in *Gianni Schicchi* we detect a presence of something like a *dybbuk* in Gianni's *addio* theme. Remember that the *addio* theme serves the impersonation theme: a voice warns all that it is still Gianni, though he is voicing Buoso. The threat of punishment voiced by this theme, a severed hand, may be compared to the threat of physical damage feared by a *dybbuk*. Similarly to *Il dibuk*, the final love duet in *Gianni Schicchi* incorporates an added voice; the *addio* theme merges with the singing of the lovers. The *addio* theme provides the menacing sound of Gianni's warning; it is a coercive voice that seeps into the scene, as though the lovers incorporate the presence of Gianni's voice in theirs. And finally the *shofar* may be compared to *Gianni's fanfare* theme, the sound that opens the upper world to the trumpet call of the end of time.

CHAPTER FOUR

Singing and Disappearing Angels

Mordecai Seter, *Tikkun Ḥatsot*

(*Midnight Vigil*, 1961)

Silent Singing

In the film *I Married an Angel* (1942), Count Palaffi (Nelson Eddy) dreams he has married a perfect wife: an angel named Brigitta (Jeanette MacDonald). One of her angelic powers is her ability to sing operatically. Typical of cinema's evocation of the operatic voice, the angel sings the cadenza from *Lucia di Lammermoor*'s mad scene. The famous flute sequence, echoing the vocal acrobatics, is played by a harp, providing the angelic overtones. Brigitta sings the virtuoso, textless stretch of operatic singing without interference from plot, drama, character, or scenery. When the conductor praises her operatic virtuosity, "You sing like an angel," Brigitta, to our amusement, replies: "But I am an angel!" In the cinematic imagination, when an angel descends to earth, celestial singing is transformed into an image of operatic excess.

In a rather different theoretical context, the image of perfect operatic singing becomes associated with the ascent of the human voice toward the angelic. The fulfillment of this journey is an impossibility: the operatic voice's striving toward the angelic is what ultimately drives it to disintegration.[1] In his discussion of a medieval treatise, *The Celestial Hierarchy*, Michel Poizat writes:[2]

> In this treatise...[Pseudo-Dionysius] spells out both the role of the angel as messenger and the silence that accompanies it. At the summit of the celestial hierarchy, he explains, the seraphim dance around God while endlessly singing hymns in his praise. But these

hymns are so marvelous, so utterly beyond human language, that they are imperceptible even in the ranks of the celestial hierarchy directly below.... It is the seraphim's task to transmit these divine and silent hymns down through the celestial ranks, one sphere at a time, until the musicians of the terrestrial church, discerning the faint echo of the heavenly songs, convey them, in the form of a now audible music, to human ears. It is in this sense...that one can speak of "the angel's silent song."[3]

Poizat, echoing the author of *The Celestial Hierarchy*, formulates the angelic as a silent core within human song to which that song strives. The angelic stands for what is beyond song in song, what is sought for in song when reaching its utmost limit. Its inhuman, transsexual, unheard-of quality is epitomized in the invention of the voice of the castrato, and later is taken up by the soprano and tenor. The futile, repeated attempt to reach the angelic can lead only to a breakdown of the voice. The evocation of that moment in opera will thus be supported by a plot leading to death, thus mirroring the vicissitudes of the voice in the narrative trajectory. Death in opera stands for the apotheosis of voice. In Poizat's words: "In opera, the voice does not express the text—that is what theater is for; the text expresses the voice."[4] Opera becomes a quest for a voice detached from language or signification, a voice that ultimately turns into a vocal object: soaring higher and higher, the voice verges on the cry. The cry, in turn, is the outcome of the voice's impossible quest to turn itself into a vocal object, detached from signification and body. Angelic singing, for Poizat, rests on the notion that "an angel is a living being that is rational, immaterial, hymnological, immortal." Its role, "unceasing singing of hymns/chanting and praising of God," occupies in Poizat's matrix a place of silence: the limit of human singing.[5] Could we, perhaps, elaborate an alternative figure for angelic singing? Might it be, rather, that angelic singing echoes human song? Might the death of singing be essential to angelic singing itself? In other words, could angelic singing demand its own termination, regardless of the human striving to simulate it? And might not such termination of song be conceived as the result of an impossible striving toward the transcendent that is its dissolution, since angels themselves *are* the transcendent? Far from signaling finitude, might not such termination—singing angels that themselves die of song—be compatible with the eternal, that is, be attributed to the realms above? Can angelic singing be thought of as dying out and revived? And if so, is this an image of singing that brings together the transient and the unceasing flow of song?

Such a peculiar image of song is encountered in Plato's *Phaedrus*, where Socrates recounts the myth of the cicadas:

> The cicadas used to be human beings who lived before the birth of the Muses. When the Muses were born and song was created for the first time, some of the people of that time were so overwhelmed with the pleasure of singing that they forgot to eat or drink; so they died without even realizing it. It is from them that the race of the cicadas came into being; and, as a gift from the Muses, they have no need of nourishment once they are born. Instead, they immediately burst into song, without food or drink, until it is time for them to die. After they die, they go to the Muses and tell each one of them which mortals have honored her.[6]

In Plato's version of the myth, the humans-turned-insects die in the midst of their singing. The sound of singing, however, like the incessant vibrations of the cicadas, never ceases. A parallel account in Jewish tradition figures such an eternal cycle of dissolution and song as a metaphor for *angelic* singing. It positions dissolution within angelic singing itself as the other side of the eternity of song. Dissolution does not function as the terminal point, but rather as a perpetual, unceasing flow of singing. What catches my imagination in this Jewish tradition are the ideas of vanishing, the ephemerality of the angels, and their cycle of interrupted existence coupled with the unceasing presence of song.

Jewish theology consumes its singing angels. Angels sing and constantly disappear into the void. This is a striking and unexpected image, one that stands out among more familiar discussions of the immortality of angels. Here we have angels that die. What I want to bring to bear on music is the juxtaposition of singing and its termination, the passing and unceasing flow of song. How can such song be represented? Different from other constructions of the afterlife of singing that I have dealt with in this book, here a more extreme, inhuman form of singing confronts us with a different notion of afterlife. Thus, the overarching question: How can a musical composition enable hearing something that is always there, and yet is also always disappearing? How can it point to a presence that is beyond its compositional confines? And how might it simulate the simultaneous singing and dying out of song? How is this peculiar matrix an afterlife of singing?

Dying Singing

> The Kabbalah relates that, at every moment, God creates a whole host of angels, whose only task before they return to the void is to appear before His throne for a moment and sing His praises.
> —Walter Benjamin, "Agesilaus Santander"[7]

In Jewish theology, the cycle of singing and perishing repeats endlessly: "Every day ministering angels are created from a river of fire, and they utter a song and die." This is further elaborated:

> After these angels utter song, they immediately return to the stream of fire.... The newly created angels rush forth to sing out of order and bring immediate destruction upon themselves.[8]

And elsewhere:

> There is no company above that utters praises continually, but the Holy One, blessed be He, creates a new company of angels every day and they utter a new song in His presence, and then disappear.[9]

These angels are a favorite theme in Jewish mystical traditions, especially in the Zohar:[10]

[On the second day] were created all those angels that make accusa-
tions against their Master above, and fire consumes them and they
are burned. And so it is with all the other [angels] that pass away,
and do not survive, but are consumed by fire.[11]

These writings evoke a dynamic of cyclic dissolution and rec-
reation.[12] Singing angels are ephemeral, existing for the sole
purpose of making temporary song, after which new angels are
created to fulfill that same function.

The Zohar also presents another theme, that of a *new song*: "No
heavenly group of angels praises and repeats its praises."[13] Because
repetition is not allowed, new angels must be created to sing new
songs. Another explanation offered by the Zohar is that the angels
and their songs are perpetually regenerated: "The Lord creates a
new group of angels daily, and they say a new song and pass away."[14]

Let us pause for a moment and imagine the angels' singing: a
song of praise that must be unceasing. Indeed, the praise of God is
fundamental, and is the angels' foremost task—joined at times, as
the Zohar tells us, by the entire universe.[15] Perpetual song is constantly interrupted as these angels disappear or dissolve before
any new (or newly repeated) song sounds. This is forever the case:
the angels—the singers—are always terminated, whereas singing
is ever-present. Why this perishing of angels? Is their song dissonant or wrong, which would explain the eternal need for them
to be replaced?[16]

In Jewish sources and commentaries, the accounts of the death
and revival of angels are varied. In some, their deaths serve as
punishment for not singing correctly, not being in unison or in
harmony, for singing out of order, or jumping in to sing too soon.
Other accounts locate the demise of these angels in song's hellish
power: the angels are drawn back into an impossible proximity to
the fire that created them, the punishing, destructive fire of the
divine. There is even an account that views their renewal as not a

rebirth but as a return to the initial state of fire out of which new angels emerge.[17] In some accounts, their disintegration is viewed not as punishment for singing incorrectly, but rather as the outcome of the proximity of song to the divine.

> And they [the angels] draw near to this place (i.e., to the fire of the *Shekhinah*) ... and when they draw near to this place at the hour of song the fire flames round them and they disintegrate like tow in the fire. Afterwards, it brings them forth again as at the beginning, and they return to their stations and utter song, and when they draw near they disappear in the fire, and so it goes on every day.[18]

And elsewhere:

> These angels ... vanish after they utter their song, just as a spark vanishes from a red-hot coal, for their position is further removed, and their power is too weak for them to stand before their Maker. Then they come round and return a second time, and utter a song and disappear.

These divine entities, fulfilling their singing task, are put through an accelerated process of cyclic death. The proximity to God enabled and, indeed, called for by song becomes the reason for their annihilation. We find ourselves in a dark universe. Not plump, pink, happy, perfect, beautiful angels, but disintegrating flames. An existence briefer, more pathetic than that of the human. And the reason for this is singing.

Vertical Echoing

Singing and disappearing angels are said to form an acoustic covenant with terrestrial human singing. They complement human singing, continue, duplicate, and echo it. Angelic singing is believed to be contained in the visionary scenes in Isaiah 6.1–3 and Ezekiel 3.12. This singing, fundamentally the praise of God, is called the *Qedusha* (Sanctus) and is considered a triple repetition of the holy word by angels and humans alike.

The theme of correspondence between angelic and human singing is central to the description of the angels' song. Angels are said to transmit Israel's singing to the realms above, as they do with all prayers, and are themselves arisen with the prayers. Angels are also said to sing with Israel during the day, lending power to human song. But they also sing when Israel is silent—that is, at night—completing the twenty-four-hour cycle. Some sources view angelic hymns as the origin of human hymns, others as their outcome.[19]

In accounts of mystic visionary ascents, the mystics are said to learn their songs from the angels and to participate in the angelic chant. Those descending to the Merkavah experience mystical ecstasy when they repeat the angels' prayers, chant the angelic hymns, and base their conduct during prayer on what they learned from angels.[20] The mystics, on their return, transmit angelic song to the realms below.[21] Here singing is a manifestation of secret knowledge:

> Happy is he who is privileged to know this song, for it has been taught: He who knows this song knows matters of Torah and wisdom, and can investigate, proclaim, and contribute power and might with regard both to that which has been and to that which will be.[22]

Angels are also said to delay their song and to await the souls of the righteous who, raised to heaven at night, utter praise.[23] Angels wait to sing together with humans, as though it were the latter who knew the secrets of singing.

Angels are described as uttering song incessantly. It is also said that they say their prayers only by day, or only by night. When they are said to sing only at night, their silence is explained as respect for Israel.[24] There are also accounts describing angels singing at the same time as humans in order to add strength to their song. In yet another source, the angels are said to utter their song once or twice a day in coordination with the prayers of Israel below—intimating that God "is more fond of Israel than of the ministering angels, since [the people of] Israel say songs all day whilst the ministering angels do so only once a day." Some sources take this to an extreme: the song of the angels is sung only once a week, once a month, once a year, once in seven years, once in a jubilee, or once and for all.[25]

Angels' singing above is also said to constitute a heavenly Temple "to perpetuate the destroyed Temple and its rites in the heavenly shrines."[26] The singing angels emulate the service at the Temple: "The apex of the heavenly ceremony is a mystical metamorphosis of the earthly rite to the world of the Merkavah, a mytho-poetic abstraction of the liturgical ritual performed in the Temple."[27] The priests in the Temple maintained the bond between the realms above and below until the destruction of the Temple. Angels are conceived as "the Levites in the Temple" who would "speak in song."[28]

Angels, humans. An echo lacking an originating sound: heavenly singing echoes prayers on earth, prayers on earth echo singing in Heaven; angels are attuned to humans who are, in turn, the cue for their own song; angelic singing is a repercussion and amplifier of human voices; unceasing song is an echo of finitude. With angelic singing, the dying of song is compatible with eternity, at once dying and revived; the transience of angels is but another mode of the unceasing flow of singing. Echoes of human prayer have no limits, but are always already a before- and an after-life of song. In the duplication, transmission, and metamorphosis of singing, an unnamable form of human-angelic mimicry is in play; celestial realms impersonate the terrestrial, and vice versa. Each resonates with the other and is undecipherable, even inaudible, by itself.

Crowning

> ...the group of symbols here presented as one cluster also includes a key symbol that will be associated with the very highest supernal realms in Kabbalistic thought: the crown of God, called *Keter* or sometimes *Keter 'Elyon*.[29]

Angelic song is usually addressed in terms of circumstance and in terms of time. These songs are vocal and verbal, rarely instrumental. Angels sing the *Qedusha* in one continuous voice, or, according to other sources, in several cumulative voices:

> I have four hundred ninety six thousand myriad ministering angels standing before Me sanctifying My great name continuously all day from sunrise to sunset and saying: "Holy, holy, holy"....[30]

Or:

> There are three groups of angels singing daily: One says "*qadosh*," and another says "*qadosh*," and the third says "*qadosh*, Lord of Hosts."

Or, in another account:

> One says "*qadosh*," the second says "*qadosh*, *qadosh*," and the third, "*qadosh*, *qadosh*, *qadosh*, Lord of Hosts."[31]

Arthur Green explains how Kabbalist language works around "associative clusters" in which "each member of the cluster [is] identified with all the others.... Within a given cluster all the symbols...are supposed to bear the same valance."[32] Green shows how the term *Keter* (crown) works to represent the prayer of Israel and the people of Israel themselves, "who collectively ascend...to become a crown upon the holy head of the Kavod."[33] *Keter* is also a term for the *Shekhinah*; for *Bat Kol* (heavenly voice); a general term for an angel; and a term used to designate the tenth *Sefirah*. The coronation of God sung by angels and humans is a daily, some sources say constant, offering, representing nothing less than the resonance of the *Qedusha* above and below.

Lamenting

> Exile is the fundamental and exclusive—albeit hidden—mode of all existence.
>
> —Gershom Scholem, *Sabbatai Sevi*[34]

159

Incessant celestial singing suffers from another kind of fissure, not unlike the angels' own interrupted existence. That fissure occurs around midnight, when lament is heard amid the unceasing song of praise. Though the lament occupies merely a few hours around midnight, it is an overpowering sound. There is a fable in which God mourns His destruction of the Temple. God cries, "Oy-li, what have I done?"—and the angel Metatron, hearing God crying, falls on his face and asks that God allow him to cry in God's place. God replies that if Metatron does not let Him cry, He will go into a dwelling where Metatron is forbidden to enter and will cry there.[35]

Indeed, in the Zohar, there is another account that shows the three angelic watches incorporating lament. The first camp of angels, appointed to sing during the first four hours of the evening, sings praises, but then:

> The second camp are appointed for the succeeding four hours, they sing [their song is a lament over the destruction of the Temple] only during the two hours before midnight.... They are the mourners of Zion, who weep over the destruction of the Temple. The commencement of this middle four-hour period they begin by saying "By the rivers of Babylon, there we sat down and also wept...." It is they who wept by the rivers of Babylon together with Israel.... They [the angels] accompanied the *Shekhinah* to Babylon, and there they wept with Israel.... Then the Holy One, blessed be He, is aroused throughout all His degrees, and shakes the firmaments...and He roars and weeps...and He remembers Israel and drops two tears into the Great Sea.[36]

Around midnight, the song of grief emerges and seems to override other sounds, possessing cosmic powers over God's creation.

Dying Out of Song: Midnight Vigil

Mordecai Seter's composition *Tikkun Hatsot* (*Midnight Vigil*, 1961) sounds the angelic, not by representing the song of angels but by alluding to their disappearance, sounding their recurrent vanishing. Can a composition convey a simultaneity of singing and un-singing? Can it sound evanescence? Can it echo inaudible singing?

Seter's *Tikkun Ḥatsot* creates sounds that bring about a fleeting awareness of what is always potentially audible but not listened to; always present, but heard only through its temporary correspondence with human singing, when one kind of singing enables the hearing of the other. What I take to be the fundamental question raised by *Tikkun Ḥatsot* is the potential of a musical composition to enable hearing what is always present, yet always also beyond the work's own confines; what serves as the source of the sounds of the work and as after-echoes; the potential for impossible echoes.

Tikkun Ḥatsot is an oratorio with a libretto based primarily on the Kabbalistic mystic prayer, *Tikkun Ḥatsot*. Angels indeed appear toward the end of the piece, in the "Hallelujah," yet they do not sing in it: more than that, I would say that the angels manifestly do not sing. It is not just the appearance of the angels at the end; the entire work shows angelic thematics. Their singing is not represented as localized in a particular moment, in a particular delimited song, but, as I will demonstrate, it is always potentially there to be heard in or through fleeting moments of other singing.

Unlike much contemporary Israeli art music, *Tikkun* has benefited from illuminating discussions of its music; prominent among these are the insights of Avner Bahat, William Elias, Dalia Golomb, and Ronit Seter.[37] Previous scholarship on *Tikkun* has dealt with its integration of "Eastern" and "Western" musical styles; its use of liturgical music in relation to folkloristic or ethnic music; and the work's formative place in Israeli art music. Following the penetrating writings of Carolyn Abbate on the notion of the voice, I would like to offer a novel perspective that brings *Tikkun* into a new orbit and raises questions about its treatment of *voices*. None of the existing scholarship has attempted to listen to its angels. Surely, it is not the first topic that comes to mind, but then, no scholar has ever seriously considered the

Kabbalistic text and its relationship to music, nor thought about its unique and novel aesthetics of voice. It is the latter, filtered through the former, that reveals the work's angelic thematics. In order to understand Seter's preoccupation with the singing of evanescence, I must first provide some background about the *Tikkun Hatsot* prayer, which serves as the work's libretto.

Allowing a Voice to Be Heard

The Kabbalists have allotted prayer the power to influence cosmic events. Isaiah Tishbi explains that

> the term "*Tikkun*" (repair, restoration, amendment) occurs very frequently in the Zohar, and thenceforward it developed into a central concept in the history of Kabbalah. It signifies both the positive function that man fulfills generally when he serves God, and also the purpose of prayer in particular.... The worshipper, the physical world, the world of the angels, and the sefirotic system...can all be restored by human prayer.[38]

Tikkun Hatsot is a Jewish tradition of rising at midnight to allow for the lamenting heavenly voice, *Bat Kol* (literally, "the daughter of voice" in Hebrew, meaning "heavenly voice") of the *Shekhinah*, God's presence, to be heard.[39] Tradition has it that this voice is a reverberating sound, always present but unnoticed.[40] One has to "allow" its audibility by responding to it, as it were, in kind, as in the legend about King David being called by invisible sounds:

> There was a harp suspended above David's bed. As soon as midnight arrived, a north wind came and blew upon it, and it played by itself. He immediately arose and engaged in Torah until the break of dawn.[41]

For that very purpose, a ritual, a midnight prayer has been devised. This is the Midnight Vigil, predominantly a lament for the exile and a yearning for redemption, a lament amid the otherwise constant, universal praise. Through this ritual, one identifies with the sorrow of the *Shekhinah* and joins in her lament.[42] Around midnight, the entire cosmos laments.

Underlying this ritual are inaudible voices made audible. Through *Tikkun Hatsot*, one hears celestial sounds. It is a prayer based on the notion that all voices are already a response to, or echoes of, the heavenly lament, audible at the time of the prayer. Indeed, all voices return the voice of the one voice that is always already there. This *Ur*-voice is the voice of grief, and it echoes with every other voice since, as tradition has it, the voice of grief can never be done away with. The Zohar recounts the story of the echo:

> I wish to know [the mystery of] the returning sound.... [This is then explained:] There are three voices that never disappear, apart from the voices of Torah and prayer, for these ascend on high and split firmaments. But there are other voices that do not ascend, do not disappear either, and they are three in number. The voice of the woman...when she is in labor...the voice of the man when his soul leaves his body...the voice of the snake when he sheds his skin.... What happened to these voices, and where do they come to rest? These are the voices of grief, and they travel through the air from one end of the world to the other, and they find their way into crevices and holes in the earth, and hide there. And when a man shouts they are aroused by the sound.[43]

The voice of grief is concealed, hiding as a potential echo, waiting. When called, it responds in kind. It is always there. The human voice only brings out its audibility: it is an echo but only through it can the original sound be heard.

Mystic Sounds

> In none of their systems did the Kabbalists fail to stress the interrelation of all worlds and levels of being. Everything is connected with everything else, and this interpenetrating of all things is governed by exact though unfathomable laws. Nothing is without its infinite depths, and from every point this infinite depth can be contemplated.... For in the Kabbalistic view, everything not only *is in* everything else but also *acts upon* everything else.
> —Gershom Scholem[44]

Tikkun Ḥatsot was devised by the group of Kabbalists in Safed, Palestine, beginning in the mid-sixteenth century.[45] Gershom Scholem discusses *Tikkun Ḥatsot* as an example of the Kabbalist notion of human actions' influence on the cosmos. Isaiah Tishbi emphasizes that the purpose of all prayer is the *Tikkun* of the Godhead in the unification of its feminine and masculine aspects. The *Shekhinah* is most affected by the prayers in the process of *Tikkun*, since in her "exile" she is separated from her "husband." Prayers can help her in this unwanted state:

> The main purpose of prayer is to bring the Shekhinah out of her solitude in exile and to return her to her place and her status in the divine realm, in order to demonstrate that she is not divorced from her husband.[46]

Scholem describes a mythical-mystical unity above, and below, and within God Itself. For, according to the Kabbalists, this inherent rupture did not originate with man but is inherent in the divine itself. *Tikkun* is an attempt to restore the original unity. Michael Lodahl suggests that in *Tikkun Ḥatsot*,

> a hermeneutic of exile displaced the dominant rabbinic hermeneutic of certainty and divine power. . . . [It is] a mythically tragic vision of the world. . . . In a sense, [the Kabbalists'] writings represented something of a revival of the darkness and ambiguity in deity.[47]

Tikkun Ḥatsot shows, as Lodahl puts it, "a darkly tragic, wildly symbolic, almost nightmarish vision of reality." The Kabbalists' challenge to traditional interpretations borders on heresy, as it "attempts to uncover suppressed suspicion about God, creation, humanity and evil." God and humanity share the same tragic story, continues Lodahl, as both yearn for "a lost cosmic unity." As the notion of exile is fundamental, the *Shekhinah* is vulnerable to human actions. It is a myth at "the very heart of existence" since it defines God Himself as alienated from within; God Himself is in exile.[48] This

becomes the primary cosmological fact which underlies all historical or existential experiences of *glut* [exile].... Already in the first
moment of creation, there is a postponement of divine presence,
an exile of God which is simultaneously both from and into God's
own self in order to "make space" for creation, to give birth to a
creative space.[49]

All beings are in a state of exile and are not where they should be.
Existence is itself exilic:

The exile of the *Shekhinah* in this world is yet another metaphor
for postponed presence. God as the exiled presence wanders on the
edge between presence and absence, for "exile" signifies a presence which is not fully "here" or "there," but ever "outside" and
"beyond"...—and yet which is nonetheless also "present."[50]

Tikkun is the human *role* in repairing this state of exile, a task first
given to Adam, one that he failed to fulfill.

The special midnight prayer in Kabbalah rests upon the power of
prayers over the divine realm. Here the angels join in, interrupt-
ing their incessant praise to lament. In some accounts, all follow
the lead of the weeping God Himself, as He refuses the angels'
lament as a substitute for His. It is God who most fundamentally
laments.[51]

Scholem emphasizes the ritual's eschatological implications
and its relation to redemption. In *Tikkun Ḥatsot* the exile of the
Shekhinah is dramatized and lamented.

The historical experience of the Jewish people merged indistin-
guishably with the mystical vision of a world in which the holy
was locked in desperate struggle with the satanic. Everywhere and
at every hour the simple and yet so infinitely profound fact of
exile provided ground enough for lamentation, atonement, and
asceticism.[52]

According to Scholem, *Tikkun Ḥatsot*, the rite of midnight lamentation, is one of the rites that gave concrete expression to the myth of exile. There is a Talmudist saying about the three watches of the night: in each, God roars like a lion over the destruction of the Temple and the exile of the people. The rite is a combination of lamenting during all three watches (as God laments) and rising at midnight to perform hymns and songs. In the Zohar, midnight is described as a time when God enters Paradise to rejoice with the righteous, a time when all begin to sing. This is also when the pious rise and study the Torah, as did King David; it is a time of mercy. The Zohar relates this to the exile of the Shekhinah: at midnight, God sheds two tears and breaks into lamentation that shakes the worlds.

This hermeneutics of exile has a parallel in acoustic terms: as a result of the Shekhinah's descent, a lamenting voice is heard; the sound of the exilic condition is simultaneously the source, response, and echo of the cosmic state of grieving.

Composing a Hearing

Seter's *Tikkun Ḥatsot* begins with the notion of hearing the *Shekhinah*'s voice. A prologue introduces a fable about hearing a heavenly voice. The fable is narrated by a persona called the *Aggadah*, meaning in Hebrew "the Legend," which is derived from the act of "telling" or "narrating," and which also stands for a compilation of history, narratives, and folklore not strictly concerned with religious law. The purpose of the *Aggadah* is to personify the relationship to God, "to bring Heaven down to earth and to elevate man to Heaven."[53] Seter's *Aggadah* is taken from traditional compilations of *Aggadot* (plural of *Aggadah*). It is the composer's, rather than the librettist's, addition to a libretto otherwise largely based on fragments from the *Tikkun Ḥatsot* prayer. The text from the *Aggadah* is delivered in *Tikkun Ḥatsot* by the *Aggadah*, who tells a story about entering a ruined synagogue:

Aggadah: So said Rabbi Yossey: One night as I was walking on the road, I saw nearby one of the ruins of Jerusalem and went into it to pray. Then to me came Elijah the blessed, and he kept watch by the entrance till I had ended my supplication. And after I had ended my supplication, said to me: Peace be with you, Master. And I replied: Peace be with you, holy Master and Teacher. Then said he: My son, tell me why you entered into this ruin? And I replied: I was afraid that the passers-by would interrupt my praying. Then said he: My son, what voice was it you heard in this ruin: And I replied: I heard a sweet heavenly voice [*Bat Kol*] sighing like a dove, and 'twas saying:

> "Woe [oy], that I have destroyed my House,
> And that I have burnt down my Temple,
> And that I exiled my children
> Among all the nations...."

Heavenly Voice: Alas, Alas [oy-li oy-li]....

The People: The love of Hadassah is implanted in my heart.

Aggadah: My son, as surely as you live and breathe, not at this hour alone are these words spoken, but daily, day after day, three times a day, the heavenly voice is heard. And not only then but every time that the children of Israel enter their synagogues and their houses of learning and proclaim: "Amen, O blessed be the name of the Lord"—the Holy One most blessed shakes His head, so to speak, when He hears them and says: "Happy the king who is thus praised and extolled in his house. Why did the father send his sons into exile? And woe to them [*oy-lahem*], to the sons that have wandered far from their father's table."

The prologue introduces *Bat Kol*, thus setting the scene for all that follows. Her sighing initiated here is reiterated throughout the entire work. We are reminded of the spirit voices in *Il dibuk*, introduced in that opera's prologue before existing as characters. There as well, the voices were quoted in another's narration. Following the prologue, Seter's *Tikkun* proceeds with additive tableaus, visions generated by the worshipper while ecstatically absorbed in prayer. The work has no typical narrative construction of beginning, middle, and end; rather, scenes stand for conjured apparitions. The libretto derives from the assemblage of biblical and exegetical fragments, taken, as already mentioned, predominantly from the *Tikkun* prayer—itself made up of quotations from scripture. It is not built on characters' utterances but on a mosaic of voices: the *Aggadah*, the People, the Heavenly Voice. Their song represents the Worshipper's visions. Seter's preface to the score alludes to the libretto's anomalous nature:

> Seeing that this work is dramatic—although not in the accepted [common] sense of the word—it seems advisable to give a short explanation: The action takes place in the soul of a worshipper who is holding a solitary "Midnight Vigil" in a Synagogue. While his soul is uplifted in prayer, a number of visions appear before him, all connected with his own strivings for redemption.[54]

The scenes are visions conjured by the Worshipper, himself a character in the story told by the *Aggadah* in the prologue. There are visions of exile, worship in the Temple, the raising of the dead, and Jacob's Dream (referred to by Seter as "a dream within a dream"). The work culminates in a vision of a Hallelujah. In unfolding a fable about hearing a celestial voice, the very status of voices as that which is *heard* is questioned: the human response to the unheard cannot be directly aural, but entails a detour through the visual.

Vocal Ideas
Seter's preoccupation both with voices and with the paradox of composing a musical work stemming from the notion of an inaudible voice is evident in his obsessive reworking of the piece,

which went through five complete versions between 1957 and 1961.[55] The reworking shows Seter rethinking music's relationship to the text, debating whether the work's staging should be left to the imagination, and reconsidering its reliance on characters. However, the fundamental plan undergoes no major changes from version to version, and even the music, based on preexisting songs, is for the most part retained.[56] It is, above all, the genre that remains unsettled. The work started out as a dance, then became an orchestral rhapsody with the option of added voices, then a radiophonic oratorio, and finally a concert oratorio. Seter tried out different genres to suit his ideas. The different versions do not show a progressive, linear development in which each new version improves on the last; rather, they trace different options when rethinking the material.[57] The first version (1957) is a dance, in which actors-dancers-singers play Near Eastern and Western instruments. The singers in this version were not professionals and were untrained in Western music. The story about a midnight prayer is presented through four songs. The dance is cyclic, closing with a repetition of the opening song. Seter borrowed the basic dramatic idea of a solitary midnight prayer unfolding in visions from Sarah Levi-Tanai, the head artist of the Inbal dance company. Levi-Tanai, in turn, based the music predominantly on folk tunes and traditional chants.

The second and third versions (1957–58) are orchestral rhapsodies on Yemenite themes. The second version calls for no voices at all; in the third, entitled *Midnight Prayer: Cantata on Yemenite Themes*, voices are added. If, in the first version, songs are subordinate to the enactment of the narrative in dance, in the second and third versions narrative meaning is conveyed either with or without voices and text. These three versions attest to the possibility of the work's independence from text.

The fourth version (1959–60) is the most interesting for its treatment of voices. It plays with timbre, vocal emission, echoes, and after-effects, overriding any concerns with dramatization, plot, or genre. A radiophonic oratorio for a narrator, baritone, choirs, and orchestra, it is more than twice the length of either of the previous versions, lasting thirty minutes.[58] It is the only version that includes a narrator.[59] It integrates electronic effects in the recorded version, effects that cannot be reconstructed in a live performance. It is the first to use a libretto by Mordecai Tabib, a Yemenite novelist. Seter and Tabib retain the plot originating in the ballet and preserve the texts of Levi-Tanai's songs, but they add passages from the *Tikkun* prayer and other related, para-liturgical texts. The dramatis personae are abstract and symbolic—the Legend, the People, and the Heavenly Voice—and the words of each are delivered by choruses of different sizes. For the Worshipper, Seter uses a recording of a cantor, Ovadia Tuvia, as if it were a prayer overheard in a Synagogue. The part cannot be notated in the score, nor reproduced by a professional Western singer.

Characters' voices are diversified predominantly through electronic sound manipulation.[60] For example, Elijah (a character who appears once in the first fable in the prologue) is echoed by a chorus reproducing his words in a slight time lapse; his voice is distinguished from other personae in the prologue through manipulation of his voice's thickness and spatial source. The voice of *Bat Kol*, to take another example, is echoed by women's voices in canonic speech-song, later replaced by a male chorus. Seter also plays with the muffling of voices, approximations of singing and speaking, blurring of spatial sources, and vocal effects such as sighs, shrieks, or shouts, as well as blurred-gender voices (women's voices splinter into male and female voices).

The fifth and final version dates from 1961, and is the longest, lasting forty-three minutes. It is an oratorio for tenor, mixed choirs, and orchestra. A tenor replaces the baritone and cantor; recitative-like singing replaces speechlike utterances. The different versions show that the notions of utterance and character operating in the work are complex. Words are not a means for one character to address another, but are to be recited, uttered, or chanted. Distinct characterization is impossible when all characters utter the exact same words, as though they were interchangeable, or words neither originated in or belonged to any one of them. In the move from the fourth to the fifth version, for example, entire utterances are shifted around; the text is kept intact, but who says what changes. For instance, what the People say in the fourth version often becomes what the Heavenly Voice says in the fifth version.[61] Again, from the fourth to the fifth version, voices are rendered more abstract and less dependent on vocal effects for characterization. In the last version, the distinctions among parts become more subtle, indeed barely noticeable. Rabbi Yossey and Elijah, for example, characters who appear only once in the prologue within the tale told by the symbolic figure of the Legend, are not distinguished melodically. Elijah and Yossey are only faintly distinguished through vocal delivery—*sotto voce* for Rabbi Yossey and *voce naturale* for Elijah, expressing subtle nuances in dynamics and color. The ever-so-slight rhythmic nuance (the onset of each of Elijah's recitations is in eighth notes; Rabbi Yossey's is in sixteenth notes) sounds almost improvisational. Not only is there no sense of character delineation, events, actions, or intentions, but the music is not governed in any direct way by the text. The meaning conveyed by the text is undermined by the asynchrony in the libretto, instrumental accompaniment, and singing voice. The music does not set the text.

Pargod: *Celestial Veil*

> In the things I no longer have, he [the angel] resides. He makes them transparent, and behind all of them there appears to me the one for whom they are intended.
> —Walter Benjamin, "Agesilaus Santander"[62]

> To have finished with oneself, that's the veil. That's it, just that, itself in oneself. Just where you have finished with it, it will survive you, always. That's why, far from being one veil among others, example or sample, a shroud sums up the essence of the veil.
> —Jacques Derrida, *Veils*[63]

How can one speak of a veiled voice, still veiled even in song?
—*Ibid.*[64]

Let me put the preceding points in more radical terms: though
Tikkun Ḥatsot has a libretto, signification does not arise from the
setting of the text. The music, as I said before, does not set the
text; rather, music constantly yearns to reflect and reveal something internal to itself. It is an underlying and unceasing sound,
a voice overriding any character distinction, specific utterance,
or music-text correspondence. Seter develops a novel conception
in which the musical style itself *is identified* with the content of
the drama, as though the latter could enable an expression of the
essence of the *music*.

The Kabbalistic libretto places us in a plaintive, mystic universe in which one sound persists: the sigh, the voice of grief. This
voicing overrides everything else. We are in the overwhelming
presence of an interval of a descending second, which, throughout
the libretto, acquires a distinct text: "oy-li" (woe). The piece is
an elaborate lament obsessively reiterating that sound. The voice
of the sigh is never abandoned. It is an elemental sound refigured,
reinterpreted, disguised, and concealed, but always present. In
the sigh, Seter finds a musical icon born of the libretto, a topos
common to Western and Near Eastern music, a fundamental figure in Jewish Yemenite tunes and in European art music.[65]

Slightly less conspicuous—slightly more distant, as though
dimmed—are sounds of rising sighs. As Raymond Monelle
reminds us, the inversion of the descending motive, the rising figure, can also signify a sigh.[66] Interestingly, Seter, in his
personal notebook, labels the rising second *the source* and the
descending second a derivation or variation.[67] For the composer,
the inverted and less conspicuous rising musical figure is conceived as the originator. The rising sighs are the opposite of
the obsessively reiterated descending sigh: fleeting, evasive, and

ephemeral. Barely heard, they are in the shadows of the descending sigh—with its conventional association with the lament and its plaintive "oy-li." The rising gesture seeps through like a secret voicing, hidden from immediate perception: as singing behind acoustic veils.

The composition *Tikkun Hatsot* therefore simulates the condition of the Tikkun prayer: an opening through which to hear the ineffability and ephemerality of that which is always present. The image of the acoustic veil simulates the notion of a sound seeping through another. An ever-present sound is heard in the breaking-off moments. A veil conceals what is behind it, until a light shines on it, at which point is exposed a constellation—the impression is of the ever-presence of that which seems merely to pass us by.

These recurrent acoustic veils feign angelic thematics: they are flashes of angelic metamorphosis and angelic demolition—moments otherwise imperceptible. These are instances of dying out of song. Seter's acoustic veils, or curtains, are the work's means for creating acoustic flashes in which singing is distorted, as it were, by its own death. In mystical accounts of disappearing angels, new angels or new song take instant hold, immediately replacing those which have passed, such that there is no moment that is devoid of song.

Initially, *Tikkun Hatsot* acts out these veils in passing, as transitional moments that do not draw our attention. More and more, however, they become intrusive and disruptive, figuring angelic demolition as though from a human perspective. As such, they acquire menacing overtones.

Seter's secret voicing of death resonates with Scholem's reading of Benjamin's disappearing angels:

> [There is a] personal angel of each human being who represents the latter's secret self and whose name nevertheless remains hidden from him. In angelic shape, but in part also in the form of his secret name, the heavenly self of a human being (like everything else created) is woven into a curtain hanging before the throne of God.[68]

173

Angels weave prayers into crowns, and humans in angelic form are woven into the curtain that conceals God. "The *Pargod* (curtain or veil)...separates the One Who sits on the Throne from the other parts of [God's] Chariot, and upon which are embroidered the archetypes of everything that is created."[69] The *Pargod* is the screen that hides God from the world.[70] Often, God's dwelling itself is referred to as Pargod.[71] Other times, the term refers to the partition separating the *Shekhinah* from the angels.[72] In the *Hekhalot* literature, we encounter the symbol of "the curtain of souls":

> All the souls are initially woven into a curtain (*Pargod*) that hangs before the Throne of Glory.... The entire past history and future destiny of each single soul is recorded in this curtain. The *Pargod* is not just a mystical fabric composed of spiritual ether which contains or is capable of receiving a record of each man's life and works; it is in addition the abode of all those souls that have returned from below to their native land.[73]

The fabric of the *Pargod* is composed of life stories, of lives not yet lived and of souls themselves. Thus, it shares properties of celestial singing, containing all matter of wisdom and knowledge of what has been and will be.

Three kinds of veils were in the Temple: there was one at the gate of the court, another at the entrance of the tent, and "the veil of the screen" that separated the "sanctuary of the Temple from the Holy of Holies." The latter is probably the prototype for the heavenly veil that hangs before God's throne in heaven.[74] Cherubim are embroidered on the terrestrial curtain; in the heavenly temple the embroidered angels are animated, as it were, through song. But the veil also blocks the ministering angels from God's Throne, preventing them from seeing the Glory; other sources hold that some angels continue their ministry inside the *Pargod* or hear what occurs behind it.[75] Wherever the angels are located—before or behind the *Pargod*—it is of extreme interest that they are also conceived of as embroidered in it, positioned *between* revelation and hiding.

The most striking symbolic aspect of the *Pargod* is that "the souls of the burnt angels who did not sing the *Qedusha* correctly" are woven into it.[76] Dead angels are inscribed in the veil. What keeps them at a distance from God's dwelling, then, is a scar or remnant of incorrect singing. Angels effectively become mortal as they are embroidered along with humanity's destiny, the veil acting as their dwelling in death.

In Seter's *Tikkun*, a veil of rising sighs opens the piece, the first music to be heard, even before the series of descending sighs in the double bassoons and clarinets which initiate the sounds of lament.[77] The brief moment of rising sighs is made up of coupled seconds, D–E, E–F#, and A–B, simultaneously introduced horizontally and vertically in the piano and the harp and rooted in internal repetition and self-resonance (see example 12).[78] Rising sighs recur throughout the piece, usually lasting between two and three measures, appearing for a fleeting moment before disappearing. As these moments are disjointed and foreign to their musical surroundings, they sound as though they come from somewhere else.

Barely noticeable, the veil that opens the piece lasts merely one measure of the orchestral prelude and is taken over immediately by the overwhelming insistence of its inverted version (dominating measures 3–29). The prelude ends with a return to the veil (measures 30–32), now joined by ghostly, textless voices, even though none of the characters have yet been introduced. (This gesture of sounding voices as souls is more extreme than what occurs in the prelude of Rocca's *Il dibuk* since in *Tikkun Ḥatsot*, these voices do not denote anyone's presence.) The indistinct voices are those of the choir of the Heavenly Voice intoning an "Ah" in *pianissimo* (*ppp*) outlining the veil motif of ascending sighs (see example 13). This utterance is absent from the libretto; indeed, it is not taken to denote anyone's presence. The first manifestation of the Heavenly Voice is a sound from "before" or

Example 12. A veil opens the piece, Seter, *Tikkun Ḥatsot* (measure 1).

"beyond" the voices yet to be admitted into the piece — as if it had always been there, yet is not there: no account is given of it.

As in its first appearance, the veil retains its simultaneously horizontal and vertical appearance. Veils are employed as heralds of the arrival of other musical utterances, rather than being "listened to" on their own terms. The veil's second appearance (similar to its opening statement, where it was overpowered by the presence of the descending figure proceeding from it) also manifests an "in betweenness" or "on the way" nature: it is ephemeral, lasting only a few seconds, quite close to not being there at all.

The veil motif of ascending sighs recurs frequently. It is a gesture in shadow: short-lived, a transmitter of other music, disguised as a diverted figure, soft, drawing attention away from itself. It also appears in a different mode, occupying more space and acquiring a more intrusive character, becoming dissonant and shrieking. The ascending sigh becomes a screaming, alarming voice, a menacing presence. Something has been unveiled, brought to the foreground, pushed into the open in full force. Transient singing has revealed itself as ominous. Such sinister intimations are already present in the first vocal ghost, the "Ah" sounds — singing without singers.

The final veil arrives toward the very end of the piece in the midst of the "Hallelujah."[79] It is the longest and most elaborate appearance of the motif, a tail end before another tail end — the final whispering nine-voice canon that is a simile of prayer (measures 796–854). (I will discuss the ambiguous sense of the work's ending shortly.) An *ostinato* figure played on timpani leads to a "shout," marked as such in the score: a *fortissimo*, nonmelodic intonation of "A–HA" in all three choirs (the People, the *Aggadah*, the Heavenly Voice), with the full support of the wind section, also *fortissimo*, in its highest register (see example 14). It is not swiftly done away with but prolonged, lasting for several measures. The shouting comprises all twelve notes of the scale. Every few measures, an additional instrument joins in one half-step

Example 13. Voices yet to be admitted into the piece, Seter, *Tikkun Ḥatsot* (measures 30–33).

higher. There is neither melody nor rhythm, only sound—the "presence" of timeless sound. The veil has become intense, persistent, and deliberate, hyperbolic and out of control, piling higher and higher rising seconds, then becoming silent. It is as though in the shadows, yet screaming and shrieking. When the shouting is over, only the timpani remain, pounding the same rhythmic *ostinato*. The timpani then lead into a new cluster, causing the veil to billow out anew. The cluster consists of a piling up of semitones played as overtones in the strings: slowly it builds over thirty measures (measures 822–53), but at an extremely soft dynamic (*ppppp*).

Seter's work juggles impossible features. It begins by presenting us with a sound that barely seeps through the music we more acutely notice and listen to. It impersonates an "endless" sound, presenting the acoustic illusion that something is always out there which we hear or are attuned to only occasionally. Seter constructs this paradoxical effect by lacing the work with rising sighs—traces of the work's mourning gesture. We thus envision a sound that is absent-while-present, and evanescent-turned-menacing: it is the voice of ineffable demolition or death. Veils comprise flashes of shadowed singing, pointing to a covered appearance, a disappearing, an unveiling. They figure continuous singing, reviving while dying out. Singing and disappearing angels are captured in one fleeting moment: perishing as they raise their voices to sing, singing signifying unsinging. Revival and death are one single sound. If Zeffirelli's film *Callas Forever* problematizes the operatic voice's dependence on body, and Puccini's *Gianni Schicchi* extends that relationship to include a dead body, and Rocca's *Il dibuk* dispenses with a notion of embodiment and fashions an independent song taking over character, then Seter's *Tikkun Ḥatsot* is the most extreme case of all. No longer relying on characters and their utterances, music echoes and impersonates other music.

Example 14. Shouting, Seter, *Tikkun Ḥatsot* (measures 800–806).

Singing Evanescence

> ...the group of symbols here presented as one cluster also includes
> a key symbol that will be associated with the very highest super-
> nal realms in Kabbalistic thought: the crown of God, called *Keter*
> or sometimes *Keter Elyon*. The association of the crown with the
> shadow drew upon Psalm 91:1, "He dwells in the secret of the Most
> High." The Hebrew phrase is *Seter Elyon*, identified with *Keter Elyon*
> except for a single letter.
> —Arthur Green, *Keter: The Crown of God in Early Jewish Mysticism*[80]

> The definition of the character of the tone or of the sound of Keter
> in the radiophonic version of Tikkun: transparent voice. A voice
> lacking the human matter that makes it dense—like crystal—clear-
> toned, pure, lacking any sensuality.
> —Mordecai Seter, notebook, 1961[81]

> The main theme is hidden (*ne'elam*), and does not reveal itself
> even at the end. Present absence—vanishing presence (*he'adrut
> nokhahat—nokhehut ne'elemet*).
> —*Ibid.*[82]

I am not claiming that in *Tikkun Ḥatsot* angels have a specific
music, but rather that angelic themes are intimated in musical
constructions through which another presence of music and singing shines. Seter does not compose the music of the heavens even
for *Bat Kol*, who can be heard down below. The work provides
an opening to the ineffable made audible, an evasive representation heard momentarily in the sound of something else.[83] Invisible angelic acoustics in *Tikkun Ḥatsot*—what I call music's self-
setting, or veiling—is available to the piece because there are also
less invisible angels. They are in the shadows and fringes of the
libretto, wherein one finds explicit allusions to invisible and silent
entities. By the end of the composition, we know the angels are
carrying the work's interpretative weight.

The prologue, as we have seen, establishes the first allusion to
celestial sounds: the voice of the *Shekhinah*. In several sources, this

is the fire out of which angels are created, as well as the consuming fire in which they are destroyed. Indeed, some sources describe angelic singing itself as fire; coming into existence, singing, and dying are one and the same. Some sources refer to the *Shekhinah* herself as an angel. In the libretto's lamenting *Shekhinah*, the silhouette of lamenting angels can be perceived. Furthermore, commentaries on the fable in the prologue refer to the presence of angels to explain a difficult point—why Elijah did not enter the ruin with Yossey if, as seems to have been the case, it was a dangerous place to enter alone. Angels are there, invisible, unseen, explicate the commentaries; they safeguard the worshipper. In some sources Elijah himself is identified with Sandalphon, the angel who binds crowns out of Israel's prayers. Elijiah's lingering and not entering the ruin has a purpose: it allows Yossey to witness the moment when one can hear the heavenly voice.[84] This is why Elijah asks Yossey the curious question regarding the voice he hears in the ruin—as though solitary prayer brings about the possibility of hearing.

It is in the "Hallelujah," toward the very end of *Tikkun Ḥatsot*, that angels are indirectly audible. They do not sing, but are what the Heavenly Voice sings about—not exactly her song, but a presence of singing in the song. I reproduce the "Hallelujah" text in full:

Heavenly Voice: A crown shall be given Thee

The People: Hallelujah!
Praise, O ye servants of the Lord,
O praise ye the name of the Lord,
Ye that stand in the house of the Lord,
O praise ye the name of the Lord!

Heavenly Voice: By the angelic host of heaven . . .

The People: Hallelujah!
Praise, O ye servants of the Lord,

O praise ye the name of the Lord,
Ye that stand in the house of the Lord,
O praise ye the name of the Lord!
In the courts of the Almighty
Hallelujah!

Heavenly Voice: With Israel Thy nation assembled on the earth…

The People: Israel's house, O bless ye the Lord!
Aharon's house, O bless ye the Lord!
Levi's house, O bless ye the Lord!
Ye servants of God, O bless ye the Lord!
O bless ye the Lord out of Zion
Which dwells in Jerusalem
Hallelujah!

With *Aggadah*:   Praise Him in His House!
Praise Him in the heavenly heights!
Hallelujah for his mighty deeds!
Hallelujah for his greatness!
Praise, O ye servants of the Lord!
O praise ye the name of the Lord!
Ye that stand in the House of the Lord!
Hallelujah!

Heavenly Voice: And His attendants ask of Him:
O where, O where is
Thy glorious place that we may adore Thee?

The People: Hallelujah! Hallelujah!
May all that live give praise to Him!

All: Hallelujah! Hallelujah!
May all that live give praise to Him!
Hallelujah! Hallelujah!

The text of the traditional Tikkun prayer contains a dialogue
with the Heavenly Voice. Though Seter's "Hallelujah" does not

183

quote from this dialogue, it might be referring to its structure, in that the various personae are in dialogue with the Heavenly Voice. What is striking about the "Hallelujah" is not its interrupted arrangement on either a musical or textual level—since such a technique recurs throughout the work. It is rather that what the Heavenly Voice sings is affectively so incongruous. Her singing of crowning does not share the affect of the surrounding music, but carries over traces of the lament, the piece's past sound. What stands for the angelic is sound that is always there. Amid the ecstatic joy of the "Hallelujah," only the *Shekhinah*, voicing angels, is still lamenting. She is not transformed by the singing of praise, as though she is sung from a different location, "through" other music, lacking any source. The lament amid joy is the angels' arrest in that affect; at the moment when all voices in *Tikkun Ḥatsot* move into praise, the lament becomes an incessant trace, an acoustic relic of the sound of the piece's past.

This is the only moment in the work when the verbal text is not shared by all characters. The Heavenly Voice alone sings about angels. If read continuously, her part, the fragmented lines interspersed between those of the "Hallelujah," tells of a crown that shall be given to God by the host of angels and by Israel. Indeed, angels gather prayers and "form themselves into a crown upon the king's head, and a crown is made from them," raising them as they themselves ascend by the prayers.[85] In turn, tradition has it that angels themselves are crowned when they sing correctly.

Both music and text of the evocation of angels are taken from a song called "Keter" (see example 15), found in Idelsohn's collection of Sephardic liturgical music from the Eastern Mediterranean, which Seter has already used as the source for other songs in the work.[86] The "Keter" text is based on the text recited during daily service:

> A crown they give unto You, YHWH [name of God] our God, angels enthroned above and Your people Israel gathered below. All of them

together thrice proclaim Your holiness, as has been spoken by Your prophet's word: "They call out to one another, saying: Holy, holy, holy is the Lord of hosts! The whole earth is filled with His glory!"[87]

In Idelsohn's collection, the role of the cantor is provided, while the response of the congregation, *Qadosh, qadosh, qadosh* (Holy, holy, holy), is omitted from the transcription. In other words, the song skips over the actual singing of the *Qedusha*: "*Qadosh, qadosh qadosh.*" Seter then uses the continuation of the song as it picks up after the (omitted) singing of the *Qedusha*. Here is the text in *Tikkun Ḥatsot*:

> A crown shall be given Thee / By the angelic host of heaven ... / With Israel Thy nation assembled on the earth ... / And His attendants ask of Him: O where, O where is Thy glorious place that we may adore Thee?

Seter's setting replaces the singing of the *Qedusha* found in the service (and the allusion to it in Idelsohn) with the angels' search for God's dwelling. Indeed, according to tradition, even the angels do not know God's dwelling.

Seter's "Keter" is a variation on the tune found in Idelsohn's collection, but it is also a variation on a song that already appears in *Tikkun Ḥatsot*, "Ahavat Hadassah," the song that originated the angelic veils.[88]

The first phrase of "Keter" is a barer, slower version of the first phrase of "Ahavat Hadassah" (see examples 16a and 16b). The final phrase of "Keter" is the same as that of "Ahavat Hadassah" but in transposition, while the rhythmic profile remains intact. Indeed, a measure of eighth notes amid whole notes in "Keter" clearly recalls a similar figure in "Ahavat Hadassah" (see example 16c). In addition, the conspicuous setting of the words "Aye" ("O where")—the angels' search for God's dwelling, noted by seven measures of recitation on a single note—is a reworking of the sigh gesture as it appears in "Ahavat Hadassah." Even the prolonged recitation in "Keter" over the syllables "Aye" is a play on the sigh motif's text—"oy-li." (See example 16d for the recitation

in "Keter"; example 16e for the corresponding ornamented sigh motif in "Ahavat Hadassah"; ex. 16f for the sigh motif at the beginning of "Ahavat Hadassah" in a more melodic rendering.) As are the veils and as is all of *Tikkun Ḥatsot*, "Keter," too, is born of a sigh.

The way "Keter" punctuates the "Hallelujah" at the end of Seter's piece is analogous to the way "Ahavat Hadassah" returns to punctuate the "Hallelujah" in the work's first ballet version. Since "Keter" does not appear until the fourth oratorio version, when Seter introduces a libretto, it seems as though "Keter" is what becomes of the cyclic return of "Ahavat Hadassah" at the end of the piece. It is thus that "Keter" echoes both music already heard in the work and music from previous versions, but it sounds novel because of its dissimilarity to its immediate context. It is familiar and foreign, just like the veils foreshadowing it. The

Example 16. The angelic as sound that is never gone, Seter, *Tikkun Ḥatsot*: **16a.** Originator of veils, "Ahavat Hadassah" song (measures 35–39). **16b–c.** Echoing, "Keter" song (measures 542–44; 695–96). **16d.** Angelic search, "Keter" song (measures 700–707). **16e–f.** All is born of the sigh, "Ahavat Hadassah" song (measures 71; 58).

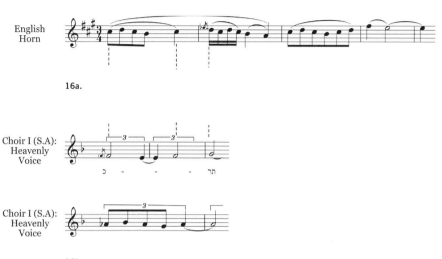

16a.

16b–c.

16d.

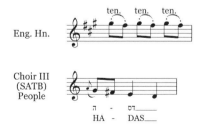

16e–f.

presence of unsinging angels is made evident by music that has already occurred in lyric form (in "Ahavat Hadassah") and in abstract form (the interval of a second, the veil motif)—but at the same time "Keter" also sounds out of place. Replacing the singing of angels, Seter introduces not only a cosmic disorientation—an eternal exilic condition, a permanent "postponed presence," in Lodahl's phrase—but one of the most overdetermined symbols in Kabbalah: *Keter*. And this is what is so intriguing about *Keter*: it is itself the very symbol of singing angels.

A double substitution is underway. The text erecting angelic singing is substituted by the quest to crown God, while *Keter* itself is already a substitute for singing as such—a clever way to have singing angels and yet not have their song. In opposition to *Il dibuk*, an opera in which singing is replaced by a song, in *Tikkun Ḥatsot*, we have singing and no song. Indeed, as Harold Bloom says, the crown is like "the source ... emptied out into a state of absence, in order for the receiver to accommodate the influx of apparent being."[89] It is thus the perfect image to denote song imaged as heard and unheard, endless and evanescent.

If one reads Seter's notebook entry from 1978,[90] where he refers to the "Misterioso" section (measures 717–46)—an insertion after the final "Keter" segment but still within the "Hallelujah"—one arrives at yet another hidden layer of angelic singing.[91] Seter writes in his diary that the "Misterioso" is an expression of the idea of *Qedusha*. And yet, this section is instrumental, with no textual hint of the *Qedusha*. The trace is in the music's derivation from the music of "Keter" itself. This, as I have shown, is a derivation of "Ahavat Hadassah," the source of the veils' music, the origin of lament (see example 17) and a hyperbolic deferral of the placement of singing: behind, in between, below, in archives underground.

Seter's music is striking in its impression of constant echoes. In Benjamin's formulation, angels are "the heavenly self of a

Example 17. Veiling angelic singing, Seter, *Tikkun Ḥatsot* (measures 721–744).

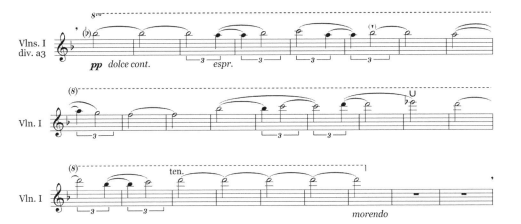

human being": they echo and are echoed in man, they are source and aftermath of the voice of man. The singing and disappearing angels are thematized as incessant ephemerality. Voice is always there but unheard; at midnight, in *Tikkun*, it is made audible. I now turn, at last, to show how the composition *Tikkun Ḥatsot* voices the imperceptible, the angelic disappearance, in a musical representation of death. The angelic is not, ultimately, an escape from death, but is its echo.

Coming to an End

> God had breathing trouble, and this trouble created the world.
> —Harold Bloom, *Kabbalah and Criticism*[92]

How does ever-presence survive a composition's end?

The end of *Tikkun Ḥatsot* is indistinct murmuring. It cannot be called singing. It is music-less. There are neither descending nor ascending seconds: we are beyond the musical language of the piece. The end immediately follows the "Hallelujah" scene. It is an epilogue, beginning with rhythm only, a repeated *ostinato* pattern on timpani that spills into a nine-voice canon. The timpani *ostinato* is the last audible sound, a rhythmic trace of the piece, with neither harmony nor melody: unsung, ultimately unmusical.

Interpretation 1: "Real" Prayer

One way to understand this ending is to notice that *Tikkun Ḥatsot*, a work about a returned lament, ends with no resonance. Seter explains in the score's preface that the epilogue represents the Worshipper's awakening to the reality of the congregational morning prayer. Following nightly visions, the epilogue is the only scene not mediated by a conjured vision and the only scene representing a congregation.

This reading is supported by the epilogue's text, which is taken from the morning prayer, and by its iconic setting: all three choirs whisper in canon, imitating the murmur of a congregational service. This seemingly straightforward reading has acoustic consequences: in the morning, *Bat Kol*'s voice can no longer be detected.

If, indeed, the ending is consumed by the morning prayer (the *Amidah* from which the text is taken), then we should consider the tradition according to which the morning prayer itself is intended to be unheard. Whispered so that it is not overheard by other prayers, the *Amidah* should be loud enough to be heard only by oneself. Hearing oneself then replaces hearing *Bat Kol*. In this reading, Seter's *Tikkun Ḥatsot* encompasses a mode of hearing. It opens echoing the heavenly voice, allowing for her audibility, and ends with the human voice and the inaudibility of *Bat Kol*'s voice.

Interpretation 2: "Real" Tikkun

Can we say about our piece, with *Tikkun* in its title and embedded in the world of *Tikkun*, that it tries to *be* an instance of *Tikkun*? Do the powers of mending granted prayer, and specifically the prayer of Midnight Vigil, transfer to the work? If only *at the end* of the work the prayer is "real," then the music beforehand is not, and is thus devoid of the power granted to prayer.

Interpretation 3: "Unreal" Prayer

Are we instead presented, at the end of *Tikkun Ḥatsot*, with the hearing of human prayer, similar to what happens to the Worshipper at the beginning when presented with the hearing of the Heavenly Voice? Have the visions through which the work unfolds enabled the chanting of the congregation to materialize and be heard, as the sound of the Heavenly Voice for the solitary prayer becomes audible? Does the piece preserve a distinction between visual and acoustic voices? Is the Worshipper himself an apparition? Has he awakened, returned to a beginning in the moment before his visions? Has he fallen asleep in this ruined synagogue, to awaken, at the end, in the same deserted ruined synagogue—with the sounds of an entire congregation surrounding him? Have the congregants simply joined him now, or have the visions transported the Worshipper to a thriving synagogue setting?

In his notebook (1961 II), in what are likely thoughts preceding the fourth oratorio version, Seter notes a "murmur of imaginary worshippers." Moreover, if we consider Seter's vocal scoring, we find that all three choruses sing the murmured prayer, including the chorus of the Heavenly Voice. The lack of stage directions also hints at an ambiguous demarcation between the Worshipper's visions and the final representation of the congregation. At the end of the First Tableau, we read: "Awakes and resumes reading of the 'Supplication.'" At the end of the second: "The vision vanishes; the Worshipper resumes reading the 'Supplication.'" In both instances, we are reminded through a framing device that we pass in and out of visions. And yet, for the final morning prayer there is no such stage direction. Is its representation of a nonvisionary scene too obvious to need instructions? And that is not all. The epilogue's text is taken from psalms which are also incorporated in the morning prayer, but these same lines also appear in all three prayers of the day, as well as in those of Sabbath and festive days. In turn, Seter's previous scene, the "Hallelujah," quotes the same psalms as do the daily prayers, and the *Tikkun* prayer also quotes these psalms. Seter's epilogue is a play on the overdetermined text. If the verbal text is not sufficient to determine whether the ending is a morning prayer or if, indeed, the Worshipper has even awakened, then perhaps the congregation is one more vision. Perhaps the worshipper is still in the midst of a nocturnal solitary prayer, and the ending is a vision of prayer. If so, the fable about entering the ruin might already have been a vision. Is there a world outside the world of visions?

Interpretation 4: Failure

> ...where God once stood now stands: Melancholy.
> —Walter Benjamin[93]

Whether "real" or "unreal," the murmuring epilogue of the oratorio versions replaces what in the ballet version constituted a return to the song "Ahavat Hadassah." The plot of *Tikkun Ḥatsot* remained essentially unchanged while Seter experimented with different genres, but there were slight alterations, one of which involved the timing of when the heavenly voice is made audible. In the ballet it occurs later. Another plot change is very telling. In the first version, the ballet, the Worshipper is near the Holy Ark while hearing the lamenting *Shekhinah*. The Holy Ark opens, and he is returned to the Temple. Then comes the "Hallelujah" scene, which is followed by the Worshipper's failed attempt to lift the Menorah. The female dancers bring the Menorah to the Cohen, and the Worshipper cries. The ballet ends with "Ahavat Hadassah," a yearning song, closing the dance in silence.

In the second version, the rhapsody with no voices, an excerpt from the program notes reads as follows:

> The content of the plot: A Yemenite [supplicant] wakes up for a midnight prayer in a synagogue. During his prayer he reaches ecstasy, and in his vision he sees the High Priest emerging out of the Holy Ark, while holding the Menorah of the Temple, the seven-arm Menorah. The High Priest gives the Menorah to the supplicant, thus connecting him to the past and blessing him for the mission.

Here breaks the Hallelujah singing, and the supplicant dances with the Menorah. But he cannot withstand the tension of his ascending soul, and he breaks down, exhausted. Before [the supplicant] falls asleep, he places the menorah, as if [it were] a *regular* lamp, on the desk next to him. At this point the music of the exposition repeats, but with an opposite meaning: not as a Hallel, but as a lament over the generation that was not worthy of redemption, since it did not withstand the mission. The High Priest takes the Menorah back and disappears, while the supplicant weeps over his failure, and the failure of the generation.[94]

A desanctified Menorah, and an illusory epiphany, are also found in a draft of a story (never completed) by Kafka. The story addresses what Scholem calls the "nonfulfillability of what has been revealed"—as do, I would claim, the early versions of Seter's work.[95] In Kafka's story, recorded in a diary entry from 1914, the narrator experiences a vision and its frustration. An angel is exposed as a lifeless thing:

> In the dim light, still at a great height, I had judged it badly, an angel in bluish-violet robes girt with gold cords sank slowly down on great white silken-shining wings, the sword in its raised arm thrust out horizontally. "An angel, then!" I thought; "it has been flying towards me all the day and in my disbelief I did not know it. Now it will speak to me." I lowered my eyes. When I raised them again the angel was still there, it is true, hanging rather far under the ceiling (which had closed again), but it was no living angel, only a painted wooden figurehead off the prow of some ship, one of the kind that hangs from the ceiling in sailor's taverns, nothing more.[96]

Seter's Menorah scene, enacting failure, is deleted from later versions. The morning prayer takes its place. "Ahavat Hadassah" then becomes a ghost song twice over: once for the angelic *Keter* and once for the deleted Menorah. Failure, perhaps, then, is the ghostly voice heard through the sound of angels, or in the faded mortal ending.

Interpretation 5: No Redemption

Can the subdued ending stand for redemption—as Seter and Tabib would have it, the formation of the state of Israel?[97] Indeed, scholars have seen these sentiments in the rising sigh motif, referring to it as the "hope motif." Or, is it one more veil, "a new myth of Judaism," as Scholem emphasizes with regard to Lurianic redemption: "The decisive innovation [of Lurianic Kabbalah]... was the transposition of the central concepts of exile and redemption from the historical to a cosmic and even divine plane."[98] Historical exile is only a reflection of divine exile. "*Tikkun* is thus an essentially spiritual activity directed at the inner side of the cosmos.... Exile, therefore, had its reason, and this reason was rooted in the nature of creation."[99] Is Seter's subdued ending not closer in spirit to Scholem's mystic redemption than to Tabib's national one? Isn't the role of the angels in the dramatic scheme of the work to downplay the effect of the "Hallelujah," as well as any potentially misleading redemptive tones of joy?

Interpretation 6: Our Death

> The population of the sky by tens of thousands of all sorts of angels ["le désir de peuple la ciel"] is an expression of the fear of the empty space, nothingness, or: death.
> —Mordecai Seter[100]

> I see myself and see an angel! and I die, and long—
> Whether the window be art or the mystical—
> To be reborn.
> —Stéphane Mallarmé[101]

At the end of the work, we recognize that we have been in the realm of singing and dying angels all along, even if only to be exposed to veiled traces of disappearances. The last audible sound of the work, its rhythmic trace—a bare timpani *ostinato*—is an emblem of the continuous presence of death. And whose death?

"Prayer is nothing other than a sacrifice in which man offers up himself. [In] the conclusion of the morning prayer . . . the devotee originally threw himself on the ground, [it] involved a mortal peril."[102] The metaphor of man's repeated death in prayer echoes the annihilation of singing angels; the worshipper, like the angels, dies with the work. Even so, this death is not the result of the impossible human quest for the angelic, for an unattainable vocal object—as advocated for in opera. Rather, in Seter's interpretation of Jewish mysticism, even in death, the human and the angelic echo each other.

Interpretation 7: Silence

When an ending is radically different from what preceded it, one may ask how such an ending bears on the composition as a whole. Do we reflect back, realizing we have been hearing something other than what we thought we've heard? We might gradually work our way backwards in search of the moment a shift took place, adjusting our sense of hearing in the process. Put in angelic terms, we may acknowledge that we have been in the realm of singing and dying angels all along: they were always somewhere singing, even if the composer never composed their music, nor we heard their song. We might also be led to acknowledge the opposite. They never sang; angels must be beyond the scope of the composition; there are no such echoes. Vladimir Jankélévitch writes: "Silence reveals a more dense, more inspiring plentitude, otherwise populated, inhabited by other voices: and thus, silence inverts the usual relationship between fullness and emptiness. . . . The other voice, the voice that silence allows us to hear, is named Music. . . . Music . . . is itself a sort of enigmatic silence."[103] A work about an imperceptible voice might be entertaining an interpretation of music as a sort of "enigmatic silence." Such silence or muteness reminds us of another trace left by angels: in the mother's womb, the unborn child is taught the entire Torah from beginning to end. As soon as it is born, an angel approaches, slaps it on its mouth, and causes it to completely forget the Torah it had learned.[104] We knew and forgot; we heard and it was silenced. If we were made to hear a beyond in the work, we were also made not to recognize it as such.

Cartoon-Animated Opera

The Whale Who Wanted to Sing at the Met

(Disney, 1946)

This book began with a chapter devoted to *Callas Forever*, a cin-ematic biopic's failed attempt to breathe life into a dead opera singer; it ends, here, reflecting on a successful attempt to immor-talize the operatic voice via animation. A cartoon renders operatic death as a proliferation of voices after death. This book opened with a prologue exploring a clash between signifying systems, that of the death song and the afterlife of singing (in *Le villi*); it ends here in an epilogue, with two signifying systems reinforcing one another. As I interpret it here, Disney's cartoon *The Whale Who Wanted to Sing at the Met* stands for the most extreme case of the afterlife of singing: it imagines operatic singing to go on forever.

In the short Disney cartoon *The Whale Who Wanted to Sing at the Met* (1946),[1] a whale named Willie sings magnificently.[2] Able to reproduce three voices simultaneously—a tenor, a baritone, and a bass—it fantasizes about becoming a famous opera singer.[3] The extraordinary whale, however, is killed by the opera impre-sario Tetti-Tatti, who, unable to believe in this singing phenom-enon, is convinced instead that the whale has swallowed not just one but three opera singers. At the end of the cartoon, the whale sings in heaven, as a voice-over informs us that "whatever heaven is preserved for creatures of the deep, Willie is still singing in a hundred voices, each more golden than before...." In heaven, singing is infinite, a coming together of all potential operatic voices. Technically, all the voices in the cartoon, including the narrator's, the whale's three voices, and the soprano parts in the

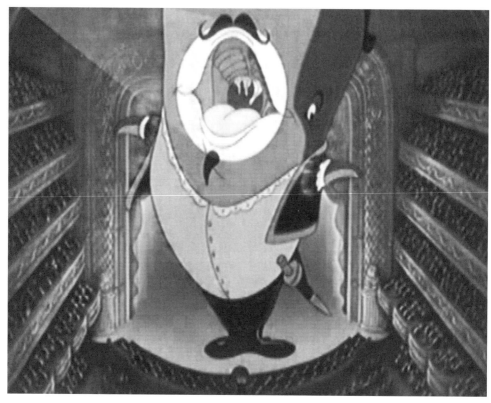

Still 3. A whale named Willie sings magnificently. Able to reproduce three voices simultaneously—a tenor, a baritone, and a bass—it fantasizes about becoming a famous opera singer. Disney's *The Whale Who Wanted to Sing at the Met*.

opera performances of Willie's fantasy, are created by overdubbing one opera singer, Nelson Eddy (most famous for the films he
made with Jeanette MacDonald).[4]

Let me begin with some all-encompassing claims. In this cartoon,
the operatic voice possesses characteristics of the cartoon body (it
extends, it multiplies, it's indestructible). *The Whale Who Wanted
to Sing at the Met* spins a fantasy about the peculiar production
and mode of embodiment of the operatic voice. The more radical claim I would like to make is that the cartoon body as such
is analogous to the operatic voice, or the idea of voice as present
in opera. I propose to open up the question of what occurs when
opera and cartoon are superimposed, as in *The Whale* cartoon.
Does the combination opera-cartoon multiply exponentially features of opera and cartoon worlds alike? Is a new "life form"
born—new to both opera and cartoon, a hybrid of sorts? In the
following, I address these issues by initially pointing to clashes
between the two media, then identifying analogies, and, ultimately, arguing for commonality, a back-and-forth movement
between the two aesthetic modes in which neither abandons its
core features.

In *The Whale Who Wanted to Sing at the Met*, the cartoon initially opens up a gap between its representation of the operatic
voice and what that voice is supposed to be in "reality." What
Willie the whale does exceeds what an opera singer can do, and,
indeed, what is anatomically possible for human beings. That
is, the cartoon is not only about an animal capable of singing
opera—a phenomenon common enough in cartoons—but about
the sort of singing that an opera singer *cannot* perform. Obviously, a cartoon opera singer, whale or otherwise, is free from
the rules of nature. But we are not simply shown how much more
magnificently operatic a cartoon world might be—featuring as it
does singing in simultaneous ranges and after death. We are also
aware that this transcendence of operatic singing is achieved by a

real, flesh-and-blood, human singer who is dubbing the cartoon voices. Nelson Eddy, the narrator, tells us that Willie's voices in heaven are more golden than even they were before he died—but we are nonetheless aware that they are *his* voice, namely Nelson Eddy's, only "more" of it.

Another clash occurs between what on the level of *plot* is taken to be unbelievable (the impresario cannot believe that a singing whale exists) and what is very believable in a cartoon world (animals in cartoons sing, and sing opera, all the time). The doubting impresario, representing the institution of opera, is pitched against the world of cartoon figures in which everything is believable, and animals, and even inanimate objects, react to music with their bodies.

Indeed, a variation on the gag in Disney's *Whale* cartoon recurs (about a decade later) in Warner Brothers' *One Froggy Evening* (1955). In this short cartoon, no one can believe a frog sings, because no one, except for the person who found him (and fantasizes making a fortune off him), can hear him sing. The frog performs only for that one man and stops whenever there is any-one else in attendance—driving that man insane, to the point of humiliation and ruin. The cartoon ends when the man disposes of the frog, someone else comes along and finds it, and the gag begins all over again. The frog is animated by a huge voice, but in the presence of anyone other than its owner, it shrinks back to its usual size and emits nothing but regular frog sounds. When the man eventually becomes a bum (resting on the customary park bench), the frog sings opera.[5]

Both the Warner Brothers and the Disney cartoons about singing pit human against animal. Both play on the rules of what is unbelievable in the plot and rudimentary for the medium. In Disney's *The Whale Who Wanted to Sing at the Met*, this unbeliev-ability is subverted in the whale's fantasy of success. Tetti-Tatti the impresario sees his mission as saving captive singers inside the belly of a whale; and yet the very same impresario—who stands for being unable to acknowledge the wonders of what he hears—appears in the whale's imagination in the role of conductor and partner on the road to success. The duality of the figure raises for us a meta-question: *Does* one believe in such inhuman, unnatural, miraculous vocality—which is opera?

Here is the place to mention the choice of animal. Why is the operatic animal a whale?[6] Obviously its size is monumental. The "anthropomorphized creature," a whale-human, toys with our sense of the size of an opera singer's body.[7] But what else is displaced onto a whale? It resides, perhaps, at a point farthest from the perch of the image customarily attached to the voice of opera—the angel. Instead of heavenly, bodiless angels symbolizing the nature of the operatic voice, we have an underwater mammal; instead of what is above the human world, we are given a figure from the depths below. The whale is not only the largest animal in the animal kingdom, but is often represented as swallowing large things, animate and inanimate, that continue to have an eventful life inside its body. Think only of Jonah, the most famous example. Indeed, Disney's *Pinocchio* (1940) was made prior to *The Whale Who Wanted to Sing at the Met*.[8] *Moby-Dick* is another obvious association when we think of the obsessive pursuit of a whale. Indeed, Sergei Eisenstein mentions Melville's work in his comments on Disney's cartoon. Finally, the choice might also be explained by the fact that whales communicate with each other via submarine whale-songs, which are heard in the deep only by other whales.

Within the world of the operatic cartoon, differences between the media of opera and cartoon are considerably less substantial than their similarities and analogies. A critical analogy can be made between the improbabilities of cartoon bodies and those of opera's voices. Paul Wells defines the characteristics of the cartoon body: it is malleable (it may stretch, compress, extend, take the shape of another, etc.); it is fragmentary (it may be broken, reassembled, conjoined); it is a contextual space: "it can be a physical environment in itself, which may be entered into and used as if it were ostensibly hollow";[9] it is a mechanism; it has impossible abilities (it can fly, it experiences no pain); it expresses explicit emotions (fragments in surprise); the normally incompatible bodies of humans and animals are rendered equal (in size, ability, etc); bodies re-determine gender and species.[10] Analogously, I would argue, the whale possesses unlimited vocal abilities. Its voice provides a model for what Sergei Eisenstein calls the "omnipotence of plasma" in cartoon behavior: it is "liquid," containing the potential to become any form.[11]

In his essay on the merits of Disney animation, Eisenstein writes about the effect achieved by a single singer, Nelson Eddy, when he narrates and sings all parts and in all ranges: "Willie not only sings, but is capable of singing in any voice range—tenor, baritone, soprano or contralto, sometimes all of them at once.... Disney uses for this phenomenal trait of Willie, *not a group* of singers of different registers, which is more than possible during the sound recording!—but gives him the voice of the singer 'phenomenon', Nelson Eddy, who sings *by himself* the whole range of voices *from soprano to bass*."[12] (Note that Eisenstein conflates Eddy's range with Willie's.) Just as the cartoon body morphs and becomes potentially any form, so are all *voices* present *in* the voice of the whale; this voice manifests itself as transformable substance: it is fire, rain, tears, smoke. Three uvulas serve as the image of such a multiple incorporation. Each uvula is, so to speak, a singer dwelling within the mammal: voice and body are not only equivalent but merge in the whale's marvelous anatomy. Indeed, the cartoon can *show* us singing in terms of such fantasized anatomy, it can show singing as cartoon anatomy; it is animation's "revelatory tool," allowing it to "evoke the internal space and portray the invisible." Thus it makes it possible, writes Wells, to "align the condition of the experience with the condition of the animated film itself."[13] Voices and their production are endowed with life, enlivened by the animated nature of the media.

The equivalence between opera and cartoon is reinforced by the multiplicity of the whale's voice and its exact correspondence in number to its audience (three seals, three sailors), as well as by the physical impact the music exerts on the audience's bodies. They become the music, as in Disney's earlier Silly Symphonies, about which Philip Brophy writes that the *body itself* becomes the musical instrument and source of musical sounds. This is part of Disney's style of perfect synch between sound and image, famously perfected in the studio's elevated attitude toward classical music in *Fantasia*. One of the important attributes of such synchronization is that signification is born of sounds as well as images.[14] In contrast, Warner Brothers developed the effect of dissociation between sound and image. As Chuck Jones puts it: "Your eye sees one thing and your ear says just the opposite."[15]

At the end of *The Whale* cartoon, the gates of heaven read "sold out," as in "sold out performance," but where is the audience? None is in sight. The narrator tells us that there are one hundred voices; but we are in fact hearing *Lucia di Lammermoor*'s sextet and watching a single whale.[16] The sextet from *Lucia* had also been used in an earlier Warner Brothers cartoon, *Notes to You* (1941), and its remake, *Back Alley Oproar* (1948). Here, a dead cat's nine lives sing the sextet's six parts. We hear six voices and watch nine dead cats singing. In one version, nine ghosts are singing; in the other, the cat's nine selves, angelically winged after death, are stationed one above the other on an ascending cloud in heaven. The discrepancy between what we are *told* is occurring with the whale's one hundred voices and the *sound* of the sextet and the *sight* of the one whale can thus be thought of as a "Warner Brothers asynchronous effect" incorporated into the world of Disney's absolute synch between image and sound. This being said, the key to understand what occurs when opera meets cartoon is located in the equivalence generated between the utterly resistant cartoon body, which withstands any attempted annihilation, and the whale's immortalized posthumous voices, its three voices that multiply and never die out. It is here that a wild and untamed meeting-place between opera and cartoon is revealed by *The Whale Who Wanted to Sing at the Met*. Neither domain lets go of its

Still 4. A dead cat's nine lives sing the sextet's six parts from *Lucia di Lammermoor* Warner Brothers, *Notes to You.*

inherent aesthetic features for the sake of the other. Rather, they conflate and morph into one another.

The whale's voice bypasses the death of its body (the analogy is not between bodies; it is *voice* that possesses characteristics of the cartoon body). After death, Willie sings with more voices, each more golden than before. In the afterlife, singing gets better (so don't be sad, the narrator tells us). Death is central to the operatic aesthetic, but here the aesthetic is cartoonlike: it does not bring singing to an end but perpetuates it as though the whale hadn't died, or he has merely suffered the "death" of a cartoon figure.

Here one senses a difference between Warner Brothers' and Disney's thematics of opera. *What's Opera, Doc?* (Warner Brothers, 1957) also ends in operatic death. At the end of the cartoon, lifeless Bugs Bunny/Brünnhilde, carried by Elmer Fudd/Siegfried, turns to us and says: "Well, what did you *expect* in an opera? A *happy* ending?" Daniel Goldmark interprets this final scene as fulfilling expectations of both cartoon and opera worlds; Bugs both dies (as in opera) and makes fun of such a death, thereby outsmarting Elmer (as in the chase cartoon). Indeed, the final line, however cartoonlike, is expressed in terms drawn from the world of opera. At the same time, opera is taking it upon itself to become a cartoon, so that its deaths will not overshadow the immortality of its singing.

The new creature dwelling in the cartoon and opera worlds simultaneously dies (unlike a cartoon figure) and sings while dead (unlike an opera character). Thus it is able, I would like to claim, to construct both operatic death and cartoon immortality at the same time—a death and a non-death. Life and death conflated, as body and voice are, invents an "opera-cartoon state of being"; dying in opera is made to mimic the undying condition of cartoon. The vehicle of conflation is song. In *The Whale Who Wanted to Sing at the Met*, operatic death does not put an end to that which is operatic. The perpetuity of the cartoon world gives body to an unending singing after death. The voice of the dead proliferates even more beautifully after death. Indeed, writes Brophy, "Disney primarily saw the technique of animation as 'bringing *images* to life,' from which he established a subsequent view that music (and to a lesser degree, sound) already has a 'life' of its own."[17] "Animation . . . is itself life-giving," add Broadfoot and Butler, who then ask: "What . . . is the form of life it creates? Is it a life that we know?"[18] By way of conclusion, I reformulate the question: Which of the media is animating which? Is opera (in being music) animating the image, or is the image animating the sounds of opera?

Traditionally, opera kills its protagonists, but it also represents a sense of the voice, of singing, or of song acquiring their own forms of lingering on, livelihood, and indestructibility. Cartoons inherit, it seems, this sense of immortality. *Through* opera the cartoon animates and revitalizes voice after paying its dues to operatic death. The voice of opera is incorporated into the world of the cartoon, perhaps through the power of what Stanley Cavell calls the very happiness of that world.[19] The cartoon invents a new being, a combo opera-cartoon, who gets the best and most absurd of both worlds: an *immortal operatic being*. Isn't this reversal of death by the power granted singing what we always imagined opera to be yearning for?

Notes

INTRODUCTION

1. Stanley Cavell, "Opera and the Lease of Voice," in *A Pitch of Philosophy: Autobiographical Exercises* (Cambridge: Harvard University Press, 1994), p. 137.

2. Cavell, *A Pitch*, p. 187.

3. Carolyn Abbate, *In Search of Opera* (Princeton: Princeton University Press, 2001), p. 179.

4. Gary Tomlinson, *Metaphysical Song: An Essay on Opera* (Princeton: Princeton University Press, 1999), p. 4.

5. Carolyn Abbate, *Unsung Voices: Opera and Musical Narrative in the Nineteenth Century* (Princeton: Princeton University Press, 1991), p. 138.

6. Abbate, *In Search*, p. xiii.

7. *Ibid.*, p. xiv.

8. Slavoj Žižek and Mladen Dolar, *Opera's Second Death* (New York: Routledge, 2002), p. 110.

9. For a detailed interpretation of this film, see my chapter "Fellini's Ashes," in *Vocal Apparitions: The Attraction of Cinema to Opera* (Princeton: Princeton University Press, 2005), pp. 131–52.

PROLOGUE: TRACES

1. See, for example, Michael Elphinstone, "*Le villi*, *Edgar*, and the 'Symphonic Element,'" in William Weaver and Simonetta Puccini (eds.), *The Puccini Companion* (New York: Norton, 1994).

2. Mosco Carner, "Puccini's Early Operas," *Music and Letters* 19, no. 3 (1938), p. 300.

3. Julian Budden, "The Genesis and Literary Source of Giacomo Puccini's

First Opera," *Cambridge Opera Journal* 1, no. 1 (1989), p. 84.

4. *Ibid.*, p. 84.

5. *Ibid.*, p. 80.

6. For details, see Elphinstone, "*Le villi.*"

7. For details, see Budden, "The Genesis," pp. 79–85.

8. *Ibid.*, especially pp. 81–82.

9. From his collection *Les Orientales* (Paris: Charles Gosselin, 1829).

10. Elphinstone, "*Le villi,*" p. 77.

11. Marian Smith, "What Killed Giselle?," *Dance Chronicle* 13, no. 1 (1990), pp. 68–81.

12. Victor Hugo, "Fantômes," in *Les Orientales*, critical edition, ed. Élizabeth Barineau (Paris: Librairier Marcel Didier, 1968), vol. 2, pp. 134–37. Translation by Henry Carrington, in Carrington, *Translations from the Poems of Victor Hugo* (London: Walter Scott, 1887), pp. 63–64. Quoted in Marian Smith, *Ballet and Opera in the Age of* Giselle (Princeton: Princeton University Press, 2000), p. 171.

13. *De l'Allemagne* (Calman Lévy edition, 1891), vol. 2, p. 60. Quoted in Marian Smith, "What Killed Giselle?," p. 80. "Elementary Spirits," in *Collected Works*, trans. Leland (New York, 1906), vol. 2, pp. 107–211 and 139–40.

14. In the many variants and changing roles the *wilis* acquired in legends and traditional accounts, one of the constants is, indeed, their love of singing and enchanting voices: "Her enchanting voice is so sweet, a man might listen to it for days without eating or sleeping." Zora Devrnja Zimmerman, "The Changing Roles of the *Vila* in Serbian Traditional Literature," *Journal of the Folklore Institute* 16, no. 3 (1979), p. 169.

15. Thus, not only do Anna and Roberto's parts in duets of both acts mirror each other but, in the first duet, their parts imitate each other and meet briefly in unison and, in the second duet, they sing long portions of the duet in strict unison, with only the text differing. The two parts of both duets are melodically nearly interchangeable.

CHAPTER ONE: THE AFTERLIFE OF MARIA CALLAS'S VOICE

This chapter was published as "The Afterlife of Maria Callas's Voice," in *Musical Quarterly*, Spring 2005, vol. 88/1: 35–62.

1. Zeffirelli's plan in 1979 to make a film about Maria Callas never materialized. See advertisement in *Corriere della sera*, Jun. 3, 1979.

2. It is widely known that, following her loss of voice, (the real) Callas explored various professional options (some less successful than others), including creating her own opera company, directing an opera, acting in a film, teaching master classes, and singing in recitals.

3. For the list of films offered to Callas, see Barth David Schwartz, "Medea and Callas," in *Pasolini Requiem* (New York: Pantheon, 1992), pp. 552–53.

4. According to Catherine Clément, to make Callas sing was a form of blackmail (*chantage*). Callas paid with her life and her privacy for singing that turned her into an idol. Clément's attack is directed at those who had turned Callas into a cult figure, a masked being. To make Callas sing amounted to undermining her vitality and destroying her life.

Pasolini, in this account, refused to idolize Callas, seeing such idolatry as a form of violence. Catherine Clément, "La cantatrice muette ou le maître chanteur démasqué," in Maria Antonietta Macciocchi (ed.), *Pasolini: Séminaire* (Paris: Grasset, 1980), pp. 265–68.

5. For a detailed interpretation of *E la nave va*, see Michal Grover-Friedlander, "Fellini's Ashes," in *Vocal Apparitions: Cinema's Attraction to Opera* (Princeton: Princeton University Press, 2005).

6. For a development of these ideas, see Grover-Friedlander, *Vocal Apparitions*.

7. Wayne Koestenbaum, *The Queen's Throat: Opera, Homosexuality and the Mystery of Desire* (New York: Poseidon Press, 1993), p. 144.

8. Franco Zeffirelli, *The Autobiography of Franco Zeffirelli* (New York: Weidenfeld and Nicholson, 1986), p. 324.

9. Callas turned down Zeffirelli's offer to appear in a film of *La Traviata* because she believed he was too inexperienced as a film director. *Ibid.*, pp. 145–46.

10. Zeffirelli "knew what the attraction of the movies was for Maria: it was her Audrey Hepburn fixation. Hepburn was the ideal and she saw herself singing Tosca while posing like Hepburn in *Roman Holiday*." *Ibid.*, pp. 207–11. However, the film rights to the opera were acquired by Herbert von Karajan, whom Callas refused to work with at the time. In addition, Callas and Zeffirelli quarreled over money matters and became estranged.

11. "Re-voicing," to my knowledge used only by one other scholar, is the best general term for denoting the procedures involving discrepancies between voices and their images on screen. For the use of this term, see Fotios Karamitroglou, *Towards a Methodology for the Investigation of Norms in Audiovisual Translation: The Choice Between Subtitling and Revoicing in Greece* (Amsterdam: Rodopi, 2000).

12. Another form is live playback as used in puppet shows and the circus, which coincides with the time of the performance — unlike playback in film, where it is delayed.

13. There is an ongoing debate regarding the relative merits of dubbing versus the use of subtitles in the translations of films (where theorizing these procedures most often takes place). Dubbing, because it separates the actor's voice from his or her image, aims at convincing the audience of the right match between the voice heard and the body shown on screen and, therefore, necessarily alters the meaning of the text. In contrast, the use of subtitles aims at conveying the meaning of the words (their number varying according to the language) and demands that the viewer's attention alternate between the image seen and the words in the subtitle. Subtitles often block parts of the images screened. On the theoretical implications of the two techniques, see "Films: To Dub or Not to Dub: Two Views" (Jack Gabriel, "Yes: It's Inevitable," and Stanley Kauffmann, "No: Whole Actors, Please"), *Theatre Arts*, October 1961, pp. 20–21, 68–69, 74–76.

14. Michel Chion, *The Voice in Cinema*, ed. and trans. Claudia Gorbman (New York: Columbia University Press, 1999), p. 155.

15. *Ibid.*, pp. 155–56.

16. Playback in American films usually refers to the dubbing of actors to singing voices rather than to a foreign language. (Some famous actors never sang the songs they are famous for, including, for example, Audrey Hepburn in *My Fair Lady*, where her songs are sung by Marni Nixon.) See Hank Kaufman, "Nobody Dubs it Better," *Attenzione*, May 1984, p. 35. Singing parts are considered easier to synchronize because of the singer's exaggerated facial movements. See István Fodor, *Film Dubbing: Phonetic, Semiotic, Esthetic and Psychological Aspects* (Hamburg: Buske, 1976), pp. 58–60.

17. Catherine Ventura, "Get the Last Word — See Roma and Dub," *Variety*, Dec. 3, 1990.

18. There are various accounts of actors reacting to different languages

emanating from their mouths on screen. See Kaufman, "Nobody Dubs," p. 36: "When *On the Waterfront* premiered in Italy, Marlon Brando stormed out of the crowded auditorium, sputtering, 'Man, I need air! Wow! When I heard that unfamiliar voice and those unknown sounds coming from *my* mouth and *my* image — well, it was too much of a shock. It was spooky.'"

19. See Daniela Bisogni, "Rub a Dub of Dante's Lingo on the Track," *Variety*, May 2, 1990, and Kaufman, "Nobody Dubs," p. 35.

20. Kauffmann in "Films: To Dub," p. 20.

21. Chion, *The Voice,* p. 85.

22. Christian Metz, "Aural Objects," and Rick Altman, "Moving Lips: Cinema as Ventriloquism," *Yale French Studies* 60, *Cinema/Sound* (1980), pp. 24–32 and 67–79.

23. This amplifies what Mary Ann Doane calls cinema's "fantasmatic body" in "The Voice in the Cinema: The Articulation of Body and Space," *Yale French Studies* 60, *Cinema/Sound* (1980), pp. 33–50.

24. Jorge Luis Borges, "On Dubbing," in Edgardo Cozarinsky (ed.), *Borges in/and/on Film*, trans. Gloria Waldman and Ronald Christ (New York: Lumen Books, 1988), p. 62.

25. Mikhail Yampolski, "Voice Devoured: Artaud and Borges on Dubbing," *October* 64 (Spring 1993), pp. 73 and 77.

26. Ginevra Bompiani argues that the Chimera should be excluded from art: "In the nineteenth century, as in the sixteenth, Chimera is once again the figure that, with its unlimited limitations, threatens art with meaninglessness.... Chimera's threat consists in her infinite impossibility.... She leads one simultaneously into the temptation of omnipotence and of nihilism: everything is possible, everything is futile." Ginevra Bompiani, "The Chimera Herself," in *Fragments for a History of the Human Body*, pt. 1, ed. Michel Feher et al. (New York: Zone Books, 1989), p. 400. And in the words of Mikhail Yampolski: "We are incapable of imagining two actors in one body, as one cannot conceive of Juana Gonzalez playing Greta Garbo playing Queen Christina. Furthermore, the voice, being only a physically perceptible, acoustical entity, has no body. It is physical yet incorporeal. In another's body it lives as a genuine Chimera." Yampolski, "Voice Devoured," p. 71.

27. For Callas's views about the state of her voice at the time of the tour, see *Callas in Her Own Words*, Pale Moon Music 1988 EKR P-14, CD 3, track 5.

28. The music is from *Madama Butterfly* and is one among many other arias ("Casta diva," "O mio babbino caro," and others) heard outside their operatic context as detachable pieces of music.

29. For the use of this term, see Michel Chion, *Audio-Vision: Sound on Screen*, ed. and trans. Claudia Gorbman (New York: Columbia University Press, 1994), p. 178.

30. The DVD market thrives on technologies of dubbing. For each language, different actors are heard speaking their native tongue. In addition, in *Callas Forever*, *Tosca* is always sung in Italian and *Carmen* always in French, regardless of dubbing.

31. For the speech of the deaf as not hearing themselves speak, see Yampolski, "Voice Devoured," p. 76.

32. See Chion, *The Voice*, p. 86, and *Audio-Vision*, p. 178.

33. Walter Legge, "Maria Callas—the Legend and the Reality," in Tom Sutcliffe (ed.), *The Faber Book of Opera* (London: Faber & Faber, 2002), p. 375.

34. Slavoj Žižek, *The Indivisible Remainder: An Essay on Schelling and Related Matters* (London: Verso, 1996), p. 152.

35. Mladen Dolar, "The Object Voice," in Renata Salecl and Slavoj Žižek (eds.), *Gaze and Voice as Love Objects* (Durham: Duke University Press, 1996), p. 21.

36. Barthes, "The Grain," p. 188.

37. Following Kristeva, Barthes calls voice in the service of dramatic expressivity "pheno-song." What attracts Barthes is an attribute of the voice itself rather than the meaning it projects through the text. The quality of the voice as such (and of music on the whole) Barthes calls "geno-song," again following Kristeva, specifying it as "a space of pleasure, of thrill, a site where language works *for nothing*, that is, in perversion." *Ibid.*, pp. 181 and 187.

38. Michael's adoration of the diva began when he was deaf. Then, following an operation, he could hear Callas with the help of a hearing aid.

39. This is a rare instance of revealing a photograph of the real Callas as neither an enactment of a role nor a remake of Ardant into Callas.

40. The deaf also figure as an unattainable ideal for hearing via lip-reading. In discussions of various forms of re-voicing, the deaf are often invoked as measuring rods: "It appears from a comparison of the cinema-goers and the deaf-mute that less than complete synchrony is enough to ensure phonetic synchrony, certainly less than is needed for a deaf person's understanding of speech

by lip reading." Fodor, *Film Dubbing*, p. 49. The comparison with the deaf shows that some dischrony will go undetected by cinemagoers. Those of us who hear can tolerate more faults that are engendered by these cinematic techniques.

The deaf painter also serves to reveal Zeffirelli's presence, hinting that Larry, the character searching for Callas's voice, is an autobiographical stand-in and that there exists a painter within and without the plot of *Tosca*. It also warmly acknowledges Fellini's *E la nave va*, another film about the legendary voice of a dead diva, in which one of the diva's eccentric admirers is a blind princess who translates the voices she hears into the colors she cannot see. The homage to Fellini is suggested by the casting of a Fellini-like director for *Carmen* (or is it Carlos Saura, as suggested by Valentí?). See Tomás Fernández Valentí, "*Callas Forever*: El compromiso del artista," *Dirigio: revista de cine* 318 (Dec. 2002), p. 13. Fellini is known to have a complex relationship with opera: on the one hand, he rejected all offers to direct an opera, yet on the other hand, his films are "operatic." See Grover-Friedlander, "Fellini's Ashes," in *Vocal Apparitions*.

41. See John Ardoin, *Callas at Julliard: The Master Classes* (New York: Knopf, 1987).

42. *Maria Callas Master Class: Le leçon de chant*, EMI Classics 1997 (EMI Music France) 7243 5 56384 2 7.

43. John Ardoin, *The Callas Legacy: The Complete Guide to Her Recordings on Compact Disc* (Portland: Amadeus Press, 1995), p. 69. For a similar opinion about this recording, see also Legge, "Maria Callas," p. 378.

44. Orchestra and chorus of Teatro alla Scala, de Sabata conducting. Recorded in Milan, Aug. 10–21, 1953, for EMI. See Ardoin, *The Callas Legacy*, p. 69.

45. "Although Callas frequently expressed her disdain for the role of Tosca as well as for the music of Puccini, the role nevertheless played a significant part in her career. It was her first major part with the Athens Royal Opera (she was only eighteen at the time), and it was as Tosca that she made her final operatic appearance (5 July 1965, at Covent Garden)." *Ibid.*, p. 17.

46. *Ibid.*, pp. 180–81.

47. *Callas: The Voice, the Story*, HighBridge Audio / HBP 56007, 4 CDs. Here CD 4, track 1.

48. Ardoin, *The Callas Legacy*, p. 180.

49. This recording was also made with Gobbi and was recorded in Paris, Dec. 3–14, 1964, for EMI. *Ibid.*, pp. 188–89.

50. *Callas: The Voice.*

51. Notice this mixture in Zeffirelli's (apparently fictional) description of Callas's corpse: "The cold body on that bed had been two people: Maria the woman who wanted to be loved and Callas the diva who was a Vestal at the altar of her art. They had seemed to battle it out within her and in the end both lost; all that had been left in those last years was little more than the shell which was laid out in that darkened room. Her maid, Bruna, stood by her body, obsessively fussing over her dead mistress: first she would gently comb her long tresses, then she would smooth her precious lace nightdress or brush away some imagined speck, then she would stop for a while and pray a little, then she would begin again, combing, combing, combing. It was a sublime image of the dead Violetta. It's a haunting scene that Zeffirelli describes, one worthy of the stage...." Nicholas Gage, *Greek Fire: The Story of Maria Callas and Aristotle Onassis* (New York: Knopf, 2000), p. 378. In fact, Franco Rossellini, the producer of Pasolini's film *Medea* (which Callas had appeared in), later reported that Bruna, Callas's maid, had refused to let Zeffirelli in when he called.

52. For a thorough account of the body in opera, see Linda Hutcheon and Michael Hutcheon, *Bodily Charm: Living Opera* (Lincoln: University of Nebraska Press, 2000).

53. Rupert Christiansen, *Prima Donna: A History* (New York: Viking, 1984), p. 312.

54. Ardoin, *The Callas Legacy*, p. 209.

55. Legge, "Maria Callas," p. 382.

56. Michael Chanan, *Repeated Takes: A Short History of Recording and Its Effects on Music* (London: Verso, 1995), p. 134.

57. Jürgen Kesting, *Maria Callas* (London: Quartet, 1992), p. 65, cited in Chanan, *Repeated Takes*, p. 136.

58. *Ibid.*

59. I would like thus to emphasize that I do not locate Zeffirelli's interpretation of the voice of Callas in the distinction between live and recorded sound.

60. Peter Brooks, "Body and Voice in Melodrama and Opera," in Mary Ann Smart (ed.), *Siren Songs: Representations of Gender and Sexuality in Opera* (Princeton: Princeton University Press, 2000), p. 121.

61. Koestenbaum, *The Queen's Throat*, p. 74. For a different view, in which bodies of singers are eroticized, see Sam Abel, *Opera in the Flesh: Sexuality in Operatic Performance* (Boulder, CO: Westview Press, 1996).

62. Zeffirelli, *The Autobiography*, p. 184.

63. *La Callas...toujours*: *Tosca (Atto II)*, Orchestre et choeurs du Théâtre National de l'Opéra de Paris, conducted by Georges Sebastian, EMI classics, Dec. 19, 1958. DVD 7243 4 92503 9 0. There are three audio-visual performances of *Tosca*, act 2: excerpts from act 2, recorded in New York, Nov. 25, 1956; act 2, the first performance with Tito Gobbi on stage, Paris, Dec. 19, 1958; a new production of Zeffirelli for television, the first time Gobbi and Callas performed the whole opera together, Covent Garden, Feb. 9, 1964. See Ardoin, *The Callas Legacy*, pp. 113, 145–46, 180–81, 217–18.

64. Mary Ann Doane, *The Emergence of Cinematic Time: Modernity, Contingency, the Archive* (Cambridge: Harvard University Press, 2002), pp. 2 and 22.

65. Garrett Stewart, *Between Film and Screen: Modernism's Photo Synthesis* (Chicago: University of Chicago Press, 1999), p. 257.

CHAPTER TWO: SUNG BY DEATH

For inspiring conversations about *Gianni Schicchi*, I would like to thank Caroline Bynum, Simone Marchesi, and Gerda Panofsky. I would like to thank all the participants in the production of *Gianni Schicchi* I directed in summer 2005 in Forli, Italy, and Friedberg, Germany, especially Karl-Heinz Steffens, Michal Friedlander, and Eli Friedlander.

1. Dante Alighieri, *The Divine Comedy, Inferno 1: Italian Text and Translation*, trans. Charles Singleton (Princeton: Princeton University Press, 1970).

2. *Commento alla Divina Commedia d'Anonimo fiorentino del secolo XIV, ora per la prima volta stampato a cura di Pietro Fanfani*, 3 vols. (Bologna: Gaetano Romagnoli, 1866), vol. 1, pp. 637–39. This source is partially transcribed in Giacomo Setaccioli, *Il contenuto musicale del Gianni Schicchi di Giacomo Puccini* (Rome: De Sanctis, 1920), pp. 17–19, and in Michele Girardi, *Puccini: His International Art*, trans. Laura Basini (Chicago: University of Chicago Press, 1994), pp. 416–17. Girardi shows that Forzano based many details on Anonimo Fiorentino's elaboration in the appendix.

3. "Il difficile era trovare il finale.... Finalmente un giorno mi venne in mente il finale delle antiche commedie musicali: *Licenziando senza cantare*. Era

l'attore che concludeva la commedia musicale venendo alla ribalte e, senza cantare, parlando, si licenziava dal pubblico." Giovacchino Forzano, *Come li ho conosciuti* (Torino: Edizioni Radio Italiana, 1957), pp. 15–16 (emphasis in original). See also the interview with Forzano in Barbara Fischer-Williams, "Forzano Remembered: A Trittico Librettist at Work and Play with Puccini," *Opera News*, Feb. 26, 1977, p. 14. (In his letter Forzano uses "Licenziando senza cantare" and "si licenziava dal pubblico"; in the libretto we find: "Ma, con licenza del gran padre Dante, / Se stasera vi siete divertiti, / Concedetemi voi / (Fa il gesto di applaudire.) / l'attenuante.")

4. Vladimir Jankélévitch, *Ravel*, trans. Margaret Crosland (New York: Grove Press, 1959), p. 52.

5. Erich Segal, *The Death of Comedy* (Cambridge: Harvard University Press, 2001), p. 13.

6. Zvi Jagendorf, *The Happy End of Comedy: Jonson, Molière, and Shakespeare* (Newark: University of Delaware Press, 1984), p. 35.

7. *Ibid.*, p. 17.

8. *Ibid.*, p. 12.

9. Including Puccini's *Tosca*, of course. On *commedia dell'arte* and *Gianni Schicchi*, see, for instance, Michela Niccolai, "Da Firenze a New York: Considerazioni sulla *mise en scène* del *Gianni Schicchi* di Puccini," *Hortus Musicus* 11 (Jul.–Sept. 2002), pp. 82–84; and John Louis DiGaetani, "*Gianni Schicchi*: The Social Synthesis," in *Puccini the Thinker: The Composer's Intellectual and Dramatic Development* (Bern: Peter Lang, 1987), p. 134. I will not discuss in any detail the many references to this tradition in *Gianni Schicchi*; I will only point out those traits relevant to my argument. On the *commedia* in the early twentieth century, much has been written. See, for instance, Gabriel Jacobs, "The commedia dell'arte in early twentieth-century music: Schoenberg, Stravinsky, Busoni and Les Six," in *Studies in the Commedia dell'arte*, eds. David George and Christopher Gossip (Cardiff: University of Wales Press, 1993). On the profound effect of *commedia* on art in general at the turn of the century and during the first few decades of the twentieth century, see, for instance, James Fisher, "Harlequinade: Commedia dell'Arte on the Early Twentieth-Century British Stage," *Theatre Journal* 41, no. 1 (1989), pp. 30–44.

10. Though not, as Arlecchino often is, a servant. For allusions in *Gianni Schicchi* to Arlecchino, see, for instance, Mosco Carner, *Puccini: A Critical*

Biography (London: Duckworth, 1992), esp. p. 497.

11. Allardyce Nicoll writes: "His [Harlequin's] sense of fun explains the eagerness with which he seizes any opportunity of popping into disguise, but he can never carry through a disguise intrigue effectively because he never forgets himself and because he lets inappropriate words slip out.... He has been described as a chameleon assuming all colours." Allardyce Nicoll, *The World of Harlequin: A Critical Study of the Commedia dell'Arte* (Cambridge: Cambridge University Press, 1963), p. 73. For details about disguise, see Derek Connon, "The Servant as Master: Disguise, Role-reversal and Social Comment in Three Plays of Marivaux," in *Studies in the Commedia dell'arte.*

12. See Bent Holm, "Harlequin, Holberg and the (In)visible Masks: Commedia dell'arte in Eighteenth-Century Denmark," *Theatre Research International* 23, no. 2 (Summer 1998), esp. p. 164.

13. Nina Da Vinci Nichols, "The Arlecchino and Three English Tinkers," *Comparative Drama* 36, no. 1–2 (Spring–Summer 2002), pp. 145–84. Here p. 162. Derek Connon, however, argues that "Arlequin cannot ever truly be disguised.... Fundamentally he is always immutably himself." Connon, "The Servant," p. 136.

14. Da Vinci Nichols, "The Arlecchino," p. 156.

15. M. A. Katritzky, "The Commedia dell'arte: An Introduction," *Theatre Research International* 23, no. 2 (Summer 1998), pp. 99–103.

16. Antonio Scuderi, "Arlechino Revisited: Tracing the Demon from the Carnival to Kramer and Mr. Bean," *Theatre History Studies* 20 (2000), pp. 143–55.

17. I am not trying to account for the many traits of Arlecchino—only those that bear on my interpretation of Gianni.

18. Scuderi, "Arlechino Revisited," pp. 145 and 150.

19. "Licenza," www.oxfordmusiconline.com.

20. In the final words of *Volpone*'s epilogue, Volpone asks for the audience's approval:

> "The seasoning of a play is the applause.
> Now, though the Fox be punish'd by the lawes,
> He, yet, doth hope there is no suff'ring due,
> For any fact, which he hath done 'gainst you;

If there be, censure him: here he, doubtful, stands.

If not, fare iouially, and clap your hands."

Mark Anderson explains: "We are literally asked to condone the actions of this villain because *we* have not been harmed. We are not allowed to separate our enjoyment of the play and its valuable exposure of vice and folly in society from an approval of *Volpone* and the brilliant deception, corrupt values, and social threat he represents. The applause for the play exposes the audience.... The play is intentionally disturbing in both the powerful corruption of Volpone and the implications of our response to his actions." Mark Anderson, "Structure and Response in *Volpone*," *Renaissance and Modern Studies* 19 (1975), p. 70.

21. See Frederick Sternfeld, "Lieto fine," www.oxfordmusiconline.com. As Northrop Frye explains, "Unlikely conversions, miraculous transformations, and providential assistance are inseparable from comedy." Northrop Frye, *Anatomy of Criticism: Four Essays* (Princeton: Princeton University Press, 1971), p. 170.

22. Girardi, *Puccini: His International Art*, pp. 433–34, n.43. See also Mosco Carner, *Puccini: A Critical Biography* (London: Duckworth, 1992), esp. pp. 495–99.

23. Jagendorf, *The Happy End*, p. 40. Forzano and Puccini do not choose to have the relatives step forward as a "chorus" to address the audience even though, as Helen Greenwald observes, *Gianni Schicchi* is "entirely an ensemble work." See Helen Greenwald, "Recent Puccini Research," *Acta Musicologica*, 65, no. 1 (Jan.–Jun. 1993), p. 46.

24. *Parabasis* has a recognizable structure, in which each part has a function. The parts are characterized by a specific poetic meter and may occur in full or in part. Parts can include, for example, a valediction to departing characters; praise of the work; denigration of rivals; an address to the gods to join the festival; advice to the audience and more. For details, see K. J. Dover, *Aristophanic Comedy* (Berkeley: University of California Press, 1972), pp. 49–53. Within any of the parts, there is freedom to change a particular point of view. See G. M. Sifakis, *Parabasis and Animal Chorus: A Contribution to the History of Attic Comedy* (London: The Athlone Press, 1971), pp. 33–52.

25. Dover, *Aristophanic Comedy*, pp. 55–56.

26. Sifakis, *Parabasis*, p. 11.

27. *Ibid.*, pp. 11–14.

28. Simon Goldhill, *The Poet's Voice: Essays on Poetics and Greek Litera-ture* (Cambridge: Cambridge University Press, 1991), pp. 196–205. Quote on p. 200.

29. *Ibid.*, p. 201.

30. Time is carefully staged in *Gianni Schicchi*: "The passage of time is cen-tral to [*Gianni Schicchi*'s] meaning…indicated by the movement of the sun in the opera from morning to noon." DiGaetani, *Puccini the Thinker*, p. 144. See also Helen Greenwald, "Realism on the Opera Stage: Belasco, Puccini, and the California Sunset," in *Opera in Context: Essays on Historical Staging from the Late Renaissance to the Time of Puccini* (Portland: Amadeus Press, 1998).

31. The journey takes place seven months later, in spring 1300.

32. Marriage on that day would assure many offspring. See Paul Zweifel, "Gianni Schicchi, Florence and Dante," http://www.supertitles.org/notes/gianni_schichi.htm.

33. For the abundance of historical and topographic references (though not references that relate to the date inserted into the libretto), see Girardi, *Puc-cini: His International Art*, p. 418. Girardi cites a letter from Puccini to Forzano dated September 20, 1918: "I received a letter from Prof. Bacci in which he says that he must urgently see us about the G. S. libretto—For goodness sake don't send it for printing until I have spoken to Forzano. What has he found that is so important, some modern flea?" *Ibid.*, n.38. Is Puccini mocking what he regards as an overemphasis on historical accuracy? There might have been a difference in attitude between Forzano and Puccini on this matter.

34. The recitation in Latin is clearly part of the overall comic makeup of the scene. It is also a reference to Dante being the first writer to use Italian rather than Latin for elevated literature.

35. Niccolai, "Da Firenze," p. 82.

36. See Pierre Antonetti, *La vita quotidiana a Firenze ai tempi di Dante, traduzione di Giuseppe Cafiero* (Milano: Rizzoli, 1983), p. 6. For construction projects done in and around the 1290s (and thus corresponding to sites in the libretto), see Ronald Martinez and Robert Durling's introduction to *The Divine Comedy of Dante Alighieri, Vol. 1, Inferno,* ed. and trans. Robert Durling (New York: Oxford University Press, 1996), p. 5. See also Zweifel, "Gianni Schicchi."

37. Zweifel, "Gianni Schicchi."

38. The trio is the only addition Puccini requested.

39. In Dante it reads: "Falsificar in sé Buoso Donati, / Testando e dando al testamento norma."

40. "I thought you were in Rome, perhaps you just got there, or else you are in Montecatini or St. Gimignano, or in hell with Gianni." Puccini, letter to Forzano, summer 1917. See Arnaldo Marchetti and Vittorio Giuliani, eds., *Puccini com'era* (Milano: Edizioni Curci, 1973), letter 442, p. 436.

41. John Freccero, "Infernal Irony: The Gates of Hell," in *Dante: The Poetics of Conversion* (Cambridge: Harvard University Press, 1986), p. 102.

42. Caroline Bynum, "Faith Imagining the Self: Somatomorphic Soul and Resurrection Body in Dante's *Divine Comedy*," in Sang Hyun Lee, Wayne Proudfoot, and Albert Blackwell (eds.), *Faithful Imagining: Essays in Honor of Richard R. Niebuhr* (Atlanta: Scholars Press, 1995), p. 104.

43. Manuele Gragnolati, *Experiencing the Afterlife: Soul and Body in Dante and Medieval Culture* (Notre Dame: University of Notre Dame Press, 2005), p. 55.

44. *Ibid.*, p. 79.

45. Warren Ginsberg, "Dante, Ovid, and the Transformation of Metamorphosis," *Traditio* 46 (1991), pp. 216–17.

46. *The Divine Comedy of Dante Alighieri 1: Inferno*, trans. John Sinclair (London: The Bodley Head, 1958), p. 379.

47. See notes to canto 30 by Ronald Martinez and Robert Durling to *The Divine Comedy*, ed. Durling, pp. 473–74.

48. Jeffrey Schnapp, "Lectura Dantis: Inferno 30," in Dana Stewart and Alison Cornish (eds.), *Sparks and Seeds: Medieval Literature and its Afterlife* (Turnhout, Belgium: Brepols Publishers, 2000), p. 78.

49. Leonard Barkan, *The Gods Made Flesh: Metamorphosis and the Pursuit of Paganism* (New Haven: Yale University Press, 1986), p. 161.

50. Ginsberg, "Dante, Ovid," pp. 221–23.

51. Gragnolati, *Experiencing the Afterlife*, p. 80.

52. See Ginsberg, "Dante, Ovid," p. 205.

53. Caroline Bynum, *Metamorphosis and Identity* (New York: Zone Books, 2001), p. 184.

54. For review of the debates on the identity of this shade, see Barbi Michele, *Problemi di critica dantesca* (Florence: Sansoni, 1934), pp. 305–22.

55. See his commentary on canto 25 in Allen Mendelbaum, Anthony Oldcorn, and Charles Ross, eds., *Lectura Dantis: Inferno: A Canto-by Canto Commentary* (Berkeley: University of California Press, 1998), p. 340.

56. See, for instance, Dante Alighieri, *The Divine Comedy*, trans. Charles Singleton, p. 445; or *The Inferno*, trans. Robert Hollander and Jean Hollander (New York: Doubleday, 2000), p. 472.

57. *Commento alla Divina Commedia d'Anonimo Fiorentino del secolo XIV, ora per la prima volta stampato a cura di Pietro Fanfani*, 3 vols. ([1400?] Bologna: Gaetano Romagnoli, 1866–74); *Benvenuto da Rambaldis de Imola Comentum super Dantis Aldigherij Comoediam* ([1375–80] Florence: G. Barbèra, 1887); [Andrea Lancia,] *L'Ottimo Commento della Divina Commedia*, ed. Alessandro Torri ([1333] Pisa: N. Capurro, 1827–29); [Anonymous author generally known as the "false Boccaccio,"] *Chiose sopra Dante*, ed. G. J. Warren Vernon ([1375] Florence: Piatti, 1846).

58. This edition employs the name "Buoso Donati" in the commentaries on cantos 25 and 30. What matters, of course, is not whether the two Buosos are historically identical but whether Forzano and Puccini thought they were the same man.

59. Barkan, *The Gods*, p. 155.

60. *Ibid.*, 158.

61. Oldcorn, *Lectura Dantis*, p. 341.

62. Ginsberg, "Dante, Ovid," p. 209.

63. Oldcorn, *Lectura Dantis*, pp. 142–43.

64. "I've come back to life": Gianni in *Gianni Schicchi*.

65. Girardi also associates Gianni with three themes, and our accounts agree on the *fanfare* and *name* themes. But Girardi replaces the *addio* theme, which I see as belonging to Gianni, with the motive in the prelude—in my account a derivative of the *name* motive.

66. Indeed, in *Gianni Schicchi* there is no simple "possession" of one's themes. Take, for instance, the appearance of the melody of "O mio babbino caro" in Rinuccio's aria prior to its appearance in Lauretta's famous aria. Should we hear it, as Ray Macdonald suggests, as *Gianni*'s "second motive" and label it "Gianni Schicchi, Faithful Parent"? I think not. This would result in a chain of deferrals: a theme in the orchestral accompaniment to Rinuccio's aria, after which it comes to dominate Lauretta's aria, would be heard as "belonging"

to Gianni—characterizing Gianni through the lovers' wish and events yet to unfold (Gianni will act fatherly and yield to his daughter's request). Neither can Rinuccio be "quoting" Lauretta since she hasn't sung yet; nor could "O mio babbino caro" *not* belong to Lauretta. See Ray S. Macdonald, *Puccini: King of Verismo* (New York: Vantage Press, 1973), p. 156.

67. Carner, *Puccini*, p. 502.

68. *Ibid.*, p. 502.

69. Girardi, *Puccini: His International Art*, p. 431.

70. Carolyn Abbate, *In Search of Opera* (Princeton: Princeton University Press, 2001), p. 39. Daniel Chua relates the Orphic trumpet as interpreted by Carolyn Abbate to Beethoven's fanfare in the *Eroica*. Chua writes: "For Abbate, Orpheus eventually turns into a 'trumpet,' becoming a 'violent force' that shakes the dead and animates their bodies as automata with its fortissimo blast, the Adornian echo forever dies away—*calando*." Daniel Chua, "Untimely Reflections on Operatic Echoes: How Sound Travels in Monteverdi's *L'Orfeo* and Beethoven's *Fidelio* with a Short Instrumental Interlude," *Opera Quarterly* 21, no. 4 (Autumn 2005), p. 579. About the *Eroica*, Chua writes: "The re-emergence of the hero's motif as an echo effectively raises the dead with a blast that has traveled from hell and back. However, this is not the resurrection of the 'Other' (Eurydice) but of the hero himself: he has become the last trumpet of his own secular Parousia, calling the recapitulation to action." *Ibid.*, p. 582. Along the lines of Chua's account, Gianni's trumpet call might cause him to be viewed as a grotesque version of Beethoven's sublime hero. The echo raising the dead, the trumpet of the end of times finds Gianni to be unavailable. Following Abbate's notion of impossible echoes in "Possente spirto" (echoes which originate not in what Orpheus sings but in unheard sound), Orpheus produces, for Chua, "a time-lag in which he hears his voice travel back through the air in slow motion.... The 'phantom song' returns as phantom, and Orpheus is confronted by his sonic doppelganger, an apparition hovering over his body. Is this the truth that unfolds in the echo—a premonition of Orpheus's own death...?" *Ibid.*, p. 576. Can Gianni's fanfare from hell be a phantom echo of the sound in the opera, the epilogue heard from the distance in the time it takes an echo to travel?

71. Joan Ferrante, *The Political Vision of the "Divine Comedy"* (Princeton: Princeton University Press, 1984), p. 181. In Ferrante's interpretation, the exile

of Blacks and Whites from different cities (in the war of the Ghibellines and the Guelphs) partakes in Dante's depiction of metamorphoses. *Ibid.*, pp. 194–97. The context is, obviously, Dante's permanent exile from Florence (from 1302 to 1321, the year of his death). Forbidden to return to the city, he wrote the *Divine Comedy* in exile. The beginning of canto 30 about *Gianni Schicchi* is a description of the Arno pervaded by Edenic images that haunt Master Adam (the central figure dealt with in the canto). For discussion of these verses, see Jeffrey Schnapp, "Lectura Dantis: *Inferno* 30," in *Sparks and Seeds*, p. 80.

72. Freccero, "Infernal Irony," p. 109.

73. There are other examples of themes whose meaning morphs. For instance, the music of the relatives' fake grief over the death of Buoso Donati is not altered for the expression of genuine grief over the loss of their inheritance.

74. It is true that the entire score of *Gianni Schicchi*, as Girardi acutely points out, is tightly knit, as it comprises three themes: the *relatives' grief* theme—from which the *addio* theme is derived in Girardi's account—the *name* theme, and the *fanfare* theme. They do not, however, appear all together. See Michele Girardi, "Strutture musicali della comicità di *Gianni Schicchi*," in *Stagione d'opera della Toscana* (Pisa: Associazione Teatro di Pisa, 1987), p. 50.

75. Roland Barthes, *La Chambre claire* (Paris: Gallimard/Seuil/Cahiers du cinéma, 1980), p. 56.

76. The play alludes to *Inferno* 28, l. 123: "Forse tu non pensavi ch'io loico fossi!" ("Perhaps you did not think that I was a logician!"). In *Ginevra*, it reads: "Tu non credevi ch'io loico fossi!" Giovacchino Forzano, *Ginevra degli Almieri* (Florence: Barbera, 1932), p. 152. *Inferno* 28, l. 123 is related to the shade of Guido da Montefeltro, a man who was thought to be the finest soldier in the service of Italy at the time. He is charged with giving false counsel and never repenting, and thus is assigned to the eighth circle of Hell. For details, see, for instance, *The Divine Comedy*, trans. Charles Singleton, pp. 472–94. For more information on the play and its contemporary reception (though not an account of its debt to Dante), see C. E. J. Griffiths, *The Theatrical Works of Giovacchino Forzano—Drama for Mussolini's Italy*, Studies in Italian Literature Volume 9 (Lewiston: The Edwin Mellen Press, 2000), pp. 61–64.

INTERLUDE: OPERA GHOSTING

This interlude is based on a talk I delivered in Hong Kong in 2007 entitled "Michael Ching's *Buoso's Ghost*: Directing Ghosts and the Impossibility of Canonizing Interpretation," as part of the symposium "New Music and the Musical Canon: A Symposium on Composition in the 21st Century."

1. Tom Gunning, "Haunting Images: Ghosts, Photography and the Modern Body," in *The Disembodied Spirit* (Brunswick, ME: Bowdoin College Museum of Art, 2003), p. 9.

2. Helen Sword, *Ghostwriting Modernism* (Ithaca: Cornell University Press, 2002), p. 165.

3. *Ibid.*

4. For more on these themes, see Gunning, "Haunting Images," p. 10.

5. Michael Ching is a composer and has been Artistic Director of Opera Memphis since 1992.

CHAPTER THREE: DYBBUK

I am grateful for the valuable assistance of Boaz Huss, Ronit Meroz, Michela Garda, and Freddie Rokem in various stages of writing this chapter.

1. Harold Bloom explains the term *zelem*, used to refer to an existence after death: it is "the divine image in every man, a modification of the later Neoplatonic idea of the astral body, a kind of quasi-material entity that holds together mind and physical body, and survives the death of the body proper." *Zelem* becomes *gilgul*, meaning transmigration of souls: "Each person can take up in himself the spark of another soul, of one of the dead, provided that he and the dead share the same root [families of souls, united by the root of a common spark]. This leads to the larger idea of a kind of Eternal Recurrence, with the saving difference that *gilgul* can be the final form of *tikkun*, in which the fallen soul can have its flaws repaired. The legend of the *dybbuk* is a negative version of the same idea." Harold Bloom, *Kabbalah and Criticism* (New York: Seabury Press, 1975), pp. 43–45. As Scholem explains: "The most terrible fate that could befall any soul—far more ghastly than the torments of hell—was to be 'outcast' or 'naked,' a state precluding either rebirth or even admission to hell. Such absolute exile was the worst nightmare of the soul." Gershom Scholem, "Isaac Luria and His School," in *Major Trends in Jewish Mysticism* (New York: Schocken, 1995), p. 250. There exists a mixture of ideas about *gilgul* and hell,

in which hell occupies a place among the stages of transmigration. *Ibid.*, p. 282.

2. For elaboration, see J. H. Chajes, *Between Worlds: Dybbuks, Exorcists, and Early Modern Judaism* (Philadelphia: University of Pennsylvania Press, 2003); Joseph Dan, "Introduction," in Matt Goldish (ed.), *Spirit Possession in Judaism: Cases and Contexts from the Middle Ages to the Present* (Detroit: Wayne State University Press, 2003); Gedalia Nigaal, "Ha 'dybbuk' bamistika hayehudit," ("The 'dybbuk' in Jewish Mysticism") in *Da'at* 4 (1980), p. 79 (in Hebrew), and *Sipure "dybbuk" besifrut Israel* (*"Dybbuk" Tales in Jewish Literature*) (Jerusalem: Rubin Mass, 1983) (in Hebrew).

3. See Tamar Alexander, "Love and Death in a Contemporary Dybbuk Story: Personal Narrative and the Female Voice," in *Spirit Possession*.

4. On *dybbuk* and dubbing, see Mikhail Yampolski, "Voice Devoured: Artaud and Borges on Dubbing," *October* 64 (Spring 1993), pp. 57–77.

5. For an expansion of these ideas, see Steven Connor, *Dumbstruck: A Cultural History of Ventriloquism* (Oxford: Oxford University Press, 2000), pp. 165–66.

6. For the narrative structure typical of *dybbuk* tales, see Tamar Alexander, "Love and Death."

7. The host, Leah, is not responsive to the sound. The *shofar* endangers only the *dybbuk*. In the film *The Man Without A World* (1991), directed by Eleanor Antin and made in the style of a 1928 Yiddish film as homage to An-Ski's play and the 1937 Yiddish film *The Dybbuk* (directed by Michal Waszynski), the *dybbuk* is depicted as physically suffering from the sound of the *shofar*. None of the others present are affected by it. It carries a specific meaning for the *dybbuk*. Perhaps the *dybbuk* hears it differently.

8. Yoram Bilu, "Dybbuk, Aslai, Zar: The Cultural Distinctiveness and Historical Situatedness of Possession Illness in Three Jewish Milieus," in *Spirit Possession*, p. 355.

9. For elaboration, see for example Avraham Volpish, "Hage'ografya hakhodesh ubetekiah bashofar umashma'uta; iyun bamishnah, bemasekhet rosh hashana uvemakbiloteha" ("The geography and meaning of blessing the month and blowing the shofar; a reading of the Mishnah, Rosh Hashanah tractate and parallel passages") (Ariel: Meḥkarey Yehuda Veshomron, 2002), vol. 11, pp. 261–62 (in Hebrew).

10. The *shofar* is the only ancient instrument preserved in Jewish worship

up through today (blown on Rosh Hashanah and Yom Kippur). In some communities, it is blown on New Moon and is still used in exorcism.

11. Curt Sachs describes the four fanfares the *shofar* can produce: *tekiah* (blast) is an appoggiatura on the tonic prefixed to a long blow on the fifth; *shevarim* (breaks) is a rapid alternation between tonic and fifth; *teruah* (din) is a quavering blow on the tonic, ending on the fifth; and *tekiah gdola* (great blast) contains a longer *sostenuto* on the fifth, always played at the end. (Their relative lengths according to tradition are: one *tekiah* = three *teruah* = nine *shevarim*). Curt Sachs, *The History of Musical Instruments* (New York: Norton, 1940), pp. 110–12. See also A. Z. Idelsohn, *Jewish Music in its Historical Development* (New York: Tudor Publishing Company, 1944), p. 9. The three different sounds of the *shofar* denote the soul in one of three different stages (purity; sin; the soul's death due to sin).

12. For elaboration, see Amnon Shiloah, "The Symbolism of Music in the Kabbalistic Tradition," in *The World of Music: Journal of the International Institute for Comparative Music Studies and Documentation (Berlin) in Association with the International Music Council (Unesco)* 20, no. 3 (1978), pp. 56–69.

13. Amnon Shiloah, *Jewish Musical Traditions* (Detroit: Wayne State University Press, 1992), pp. 142–43.

14. Steven Connor writes that "under the theatrical conditions of exorcism, the word or the voice is no longer instrumental. The voice becomes a thing in the world, with the same status as other material things: it becomes part of the order of things, rather than being the means by which things are ordered. It can be flourished and manipulated like a holy relic, or a stage property. The 'hoc est corpus' which transforms a material object into the person of the Word also transforms the word into a kind of body, the hocus pocus of vocal idolatry. Rather than being listened to, the voice is obstinately shown like an object." Connor, *Dumbstruck*, p. 166.

15. Curt Sachs, *The History*, p. 112.

16. Amnon Shiloah, "The Symbolism," p. 62.

17. Gershom Scholem, *The Messianic Idea in Judaism* (New York: Schocken, 1995), p. 294.

18. This is how interpretations of scripture, that is, tradition, are taken to be holy, though man-made. See Scholem, *The Messianic Idea*, pp. 288–300.

19. Gil Anidjar, *"Our Place in Al-Andalus": Kabbalah, Philosophy, Literature*

in Arab Jewish Letters (Stanford: Stanford University Press, 2002), p. 106. The reference to Gershom Scholem is to his "Revelation and Tradition as Religious Categories in Judaism," in *The Messianic Idea*, pp. 282–303. In Anidjar's explanation, for Scholem there are several originating events. They follow a double pattern from "an abyssal (often a-historical) event, a meaningless, even silent, voice, word, or name, which later becomes audible and resonates in language (still later, it may fall silent again).... God's voice, the inaudible utterance of his word and of his name, is the most prominent of these [originary] events." *Ibid.*, pp. 107 and 111.

20. On God's dwelling in the *shofar*, see Morkus Bockmuehl, "'The Trumpet Shall Sound': *Shofar* Symbolism and its Reception in Early Christianity," in William Horbury (ed.), *Templum Amicitiae: Essays on the Second Temple Presented to Ernst Bammel* (Sheffield: Continuum International Publishing Group, 1991), p. 210; Idelsohn, *Jewish Music*, p. 9; Yitzach Kolar, "Ha-shofar vehaḥatsotsra" ("The *shofar* and the trumpet"), *Bet Mikra Tashma, Ḥovrot pe'dalet-pe'zayin*, pp. 176–78 (Bet Mikra, Issues 84–87, 1981, pp. 176–78, in Hebrew).

21. Reik, a student and colleague of Freud, was the author of *The Haunting Melody: Psychoanalytic Experiences in Life and Music* (New York: Farrar, Straus and Young, 1953). The book dealing with the *shofar* is *Ritual: Psychoanalytic Studies*, trans. Douglas Bryan (New York: Norton, 1931).

22. Mladen Dolar, *A Voice and Nothing More* (Cambridge: The MIT Press, 2006), p. 53, emphasis in original.

23. Phillipe Lacoue-Labarthe, "The Echo of the Subject," in *Typography: Mimesis, Philosophy, Politics* (Cambridge: Harvard University Press, 1989), 204–205.

24. The play was written in Yiddish between 1912 and 1917 and was translated into Hebrew by Bialik in 1918. For illuminating discussions of the play, see, for example, Dorit Yerushalmi, "'I will not leave!' The Language of the Dybbuk in the plays of Aloni, Sobol and Levin," master's thesis, Tel Aviv University, 1997, esp. pp. 1–25 (in Hebrew); Tamar Alexander, "Dibbuk: hakol hanashi" ("Dybbuk: The womanly voice"), *Mikan* 2 (2001), pp. 165–90 (in Hebrew), among many others.

25. Pearl Fishman, "Vakhtangov's *The Dybbuk*," *The Drama Review* 24, no. 3 (1980), p. 44.

26. *Ibid.*

27. Ḥanan lacks the finances her father is looking for in a future groom. He thus turns to practical Kabbalah, which is permitted only to elders and cannot be used for purposes of personal gain.

28. Freddie Rokem finds in *The Dybbuk* a structure typical of works with comic endings, in which the destined couple transgress social and parental obstacles and ultimately unite. Freddie Rokem, "Motiv mot ha-ben — 'hadyb-buk' (1922), 'hu halakh basadot' (1948), ve 'shitz' (1975)" ("The theme of the death of the son in 'The dybbuk' [1922], 'Hu halakh basadot' [1948], and 'shitz' [1975]"), *Ninth World Congress of Jewish Studies* (Jerusalem, 1985), p. 77 (in Hebrew).

29. Habima toured Europe in 1926–28 and 1929–31 and came to Israel in 1929. On the mythologizing of the play and its reception in Europe, see Dorit Yerushalmi, "Ḥeker hate'atron ha'ivri: hadybbuk kemikre mivḥan" (*"The Dybbuk* as Case Study: The Investigation of Hebrew Theater"), *Motar* 7 (1999), pp. 89–96 (in Hebrew), and Tamar Yaron, "Hadybbuk bisde ha'efektim hadigitalim" (*"The Dybbuk* in the Field of Digital Effects") *Cinemateque*, vol. 95, May–June 1998, pp. 12–16 (in Hebrew). An-Ski's *Dybbuk* was translated into Italian by Mario Benedetti and Leo Goldfischer in 1927. See Samuele Avisar, *Teatro Ebraico* (Milano: Nuova accademica editrice, 1957), p. 71. Torino's theater manager, Riccardo Gualino, brought a wide range of repertoire to the theater, including *The Golem*. See Giorgio Pugliaro, "Lodovico Rocca," in *Ghedini e l'attività musicale a Torino fra le due guerre,* Atti del Convegno in occasione dell'Anno Europeo della Musica, Istituto Banca di Torino (Torino: 1986), esp. p. 5.

30. Giorgio Pugliaro views the interest in the *dybbuk* in the context of a wave of attraction to exotic minorities. Compositions like Stravinsky's *Firebird Suite* and Bloch's *Macbeth* create distinctly foreign ambiances. Rocca's later opera *Monte Ivnòr* (1939), written with librettist Cesare Meano, draws on Werfel's *The Forty Days of Musa Dagh*, an account of the Armenian persecution. Rocca's music in *Il dibuk* is original, and also draws on documentation of liturgical synagogue singing. Giorgio Pugliaro, "Lodovico Rocca."

31. "Rocca must be regarded as one of the few really important members of the *generazione del '90*: he stands or falls by *Il dibuk*, the central sun around which his other works revolve as planets." John C. G. Waterhouse, "The Emergence of Modern Italian Music up to 1940," Ph.D. thesis, Oxford University,

1968, p. 650. "Rocca's main output is operatic, in a style seeped in pre-war operatic conventions. His most important work is *Il dibuk*, his third opera." John C. G. Waterhouse, "Lodovico Rocca," oxfordmusiconline.com. Waterhouse sees all Rocca's output as bearing a relationship to *Il dibuk*, either as preparation or as appendix to it. And, in general, he sees Rocca as attracted to grotesque and mystical subjects. The final duet he calls "Puccinian *liebestod*." Rocca shows Russian influence drawn especially from Mussorgsky; his work is reminiscent of Bloch and Pizzetti, and clearly owes a substantial debt to Puccini. Waterhouse's verdict on *Il dibuk* is found in the following statement: "Taken as a whole *Il dibuk* may have been less historically important, and certainly much less influential, than the best operas of Pizzetti; but it occupies a striking, if isolated, position in the Italian music of its period." Waterhouse, "The Emergence," pp. 645 and 648.

32. Waterhouse, "Lodovico Rocca." The opera received a great deal of attention in newspapers and journals following its premiere. "In the May–June issue of the *Rassegna musicale*, Gavazzeni called it 'the most important artistic event of the season.'" Harvey Sachs, *Music in Fascist Italy* (New York: Norton, 1987), p. 178. One of the most enthusiastic commentaries about *Il dibuk*, and Rocca's compositions as a whole, has been voiced by Renzo Rossellini (composer, and brother of film director Roberto Rossellini). According to Rossellini, Rocca is one of the best composers of the twentieth century and, with *Il dibuk*, created a fundamental work of Italian culture. Renzo Rossellini, "Lodovico Rocca," *Polemica musicale* (Milano: Ricordi, 1962), pp. 55–57.

33. Alberto Basso, *Il Conservatorio di Musica 'Giuseppe Verdi' di Torino: Storia e documenti dalle origini al 1970* (Torino: Unione Tipografico-Editrice Torinese, 1971), esp. p. 183.

34. There is a letter of Rocca, from December 21, 1935, in which he declares his devotion to the Fascist Party and wishes the Duce would honor him with his presence during the performance of *Il dibuk* in Rome, where the opera was staged after its success in Milan. See Fiamma Nicolodi, *Musica e musicisti nel ventennio fascista* (Fiesole: Discanto Edizioni, 1984), p. 458. On style in general in Rocca (the grotesque, the mystical, the macabre, the strange, the psalmodic, the novel, and so on) see also Gianandrea Gavazzeni, "Paragrafi su Lodovico Rocca," *La musica e il teatro* (Pisa: Nistri-Lischi, 1954), pp. 261–70, and Renato Mariani, "Musicisti del nostro tempo: Lodovico Rocca," *RaM* 11

(1938), pp. 163–74.

35. The disc is entitled *Souvenirs from Verismo Operas*, vol. 4, IRCC CD 820. The duet is from the live performance recorded in 1934 by RAI.

36. Communication with the dead during weddings is a central theme in the play. It is the town's tradition to make the dead couple happy by dancing around their grave. Leah believes the dead couple join the celebrations.

37. For the development of these ideas, see Gershon Shaked, *Yetsirot venim'anehen: arba'a prakim betorat hahitkablut* (*Works and their addresses: Four studies in reception*) (Tel Aviv: Tel Aviv University, 1987), pp. 42 and 51–53 (in Hebrew).

38. Curt Sachs, *The History*, p. 112.

39. For details, see Lisa Edwards, "Lost and Found: The Presence of Women in the Observance of Rosh Hashanah," *Central Conference of American Rabbis* (Summer 1997), pp. 21–38.

40. *Ibid.*, p. 29. One hundred cries also accounts for the ninety-nine cries of a woman in labor; the hundredth is brought forth upon giving birth: "These cries are recalled by the shofar on the day of the creation (birth) of the world." The blasts of the *shofar* recall the sound of the *shofar* at the creation of the world. See p. 35, n.35.

41. For a psychoanalytic emphasis on introjection (manifested also as pregnancy), see Ira Konigsberg, "'The Only "I" in the World': Religion, Psychoanalysis, and *The Dybbuk*," *Cinema Journal* 36, no. 4 (Summer 1997), pp. 22–42, esp. p. 30.

42. For a notion of a tomb inside someone where "the objectal correlative of the loss is buried alive in the crypt as a full-fledged person, complete with its own topography," see Nicholas Abraham and Maria Torok, *The Shell and the Kernel* (Chicago: University of Chicago Press, 1994), p. 130.

43. Act 3, piano vocal score, p. 249.

44. In act 3.

45. Yair Zakovitch, *The Song of Songs: Introduction and Commentary* (Tel Aviv: Am Oved Publishers, 1992), pp. 6–15 (in Hebrew).

46. Bettina Knapp, *Theatre and Alchemy* (Detroit: Wayne State University Press, 1980), p. 166.

47. Jill Munro, "Spikenard and Saffron: A Study in the Poetic Language of the Song of Songs," *Journal for the Study of the Old Testament*, Supplement Series

203 (Sheffield: Sheffield Academic Press, 1995), p. 121.

48. Yuval Cherlow, *Song of Songs: "Let Us Run After You" A Contemporary Commentary on the Spiritual Significance of King Solomon's Love Poems* (Tel Aviv: Miskal, 2003), p. 268 (in Hebrew).

49. Freddie Rokem, "The Female Voice: 'Greek' and 'Hebrew' Paradigms in the Modern Theatre," *Journal of Dramatic Theory and Criticism* (Spring 1996), p. 90.

50. *Ibid.*, p. 86.

51. *Ibid.*

52. For accounts of Vakhtangov's interpretation, see Pearl Fishman, "Vakhtangov's *The Dybbuk*," pp. 43–58, and Eda Dobrovski, "Hamusika shel Yoel Engel lehatsagat hadybbuk shel Yod Vakhtangov" ("Music by Yoel Engel to *The Dybbuk*, directed by Vakhtangov"), *Bama* 153–54 (1999), pp. 99–110 (in Hebrew). Dan Kaynar writes that in Vakhtangov's production, the characters are spirited voices (*hanfasha*). Dan Kaynar, "Yetsirat ha'omanut hakolelet vehid-hudah etsel Hanokh Levin ve'aherim" ("The total work of art and its echoes in Chanoch Levin and Others"), *Zmanim* 79 (Summer 2002), p. 61 (in Hebrew). See also his "National Theatre as Colonized Theatre: The Paradox of Habima," *Theatre Journal* 50, no. 1 (Mar. 1998), pp. 1–20 (in Hebrew).

53. "The tall and statuesque" Miriam Elias. Fishman, "Vakhtangov's *The Dybbuk*," p. 46.

54. There are frequently distinct lighting instructions in the score, especially for the scenes of disembodied voices at the beginning and ending of the opera.

55. The voices are designated as *voce d'uomo* (the score specifies Hanan) and *voce di donna* (the score specifies Leah), sung from a distance.

56. Piano vocal score four measures before rehearsal 11, pp. 11–12.

57. In the play there is also another song, "Al ma velama" (in Hebrew, "Why and for what"), which I will not discuss, as it has no bearing on the interpretation I am presenting.

58. A line from one of the other songs from the Song of Songs. This is reminiscent of the famous love duet in Verdi's *Falstaff*.

59. "Eccoti, bella amica, eccoti, bella, / Rosa di Saron, giglio della valle, / O mia sposa dolcissima sorella. / I tuoi capelli lungo / le tue spalle son come mandrie di caprette snelle, / Sospese là sul monte di Galaad! / I tuoi seni son

come le gazzelle che pascolano tra i gigli / O mia sposa o dolcissima sorella."

60. J. Cheryl Exum, *Song of Songs: A Commentary* (Louisville: WJK Press, 2005), pp. 156–60.

61. The Song appears at this juncture also in the play. The groom chosen by the father is terrified of the wedding, feeling that he is being led to his death. He is told that it would be best if he delivered his wedding speech with a tune. This is in grave contrast to Ḥanan's Song of Songs. The groom's chant is not given at all. It has no place among powerful songs.

62. Act 1, from seven measures before rehearsal 46 to five measures after rehearsal 48, piano vocal score, pp. 59–61.

63. As act 1 progresses, less conspicuous echoes of the Song of Songs are heard. For example, when Leah leaves the synagogue, Ḥanan sings a variation, "Ecco venuta."

64. This is based on the play.

65. This resembles Marjorie Garber's notion of "moments of achieved personating." For her discussion of Hamlet's ghost, see Marjorie Garber, "Hamlet: Giving Up the Ghost," in *Shakespeare's Ghost Writers: Literature as Uncanny Causality* (New York: Methuen, 1987), p. 145.

CHAPTER FOUR: SINGING AND DISAPPEARING ANGELS

This chapter was written during my membership year at the School of Historical studies at the Institute for Advanced Study at Princeton. I would like to acknowledge the generous support provided by the E. T. Cone fellowship for musicologists while I was there. I would like to thank the participants in the "Death and Immortality" group at the IAS for their penetrating comments on a presentation about angels. I am especially grateful for the valuable assistance of Boaz Huss and Ronit Seter. I also greatly thank Carolyn Abbate, Oded Assaf, Caroline Bynum, Stanley Cavell, Assaf Nabaro, and Peter Schäfer. A very short version of this chapter, under the title "Singing and Disappearing: The Angelic in Seter's *Tikkun Ḥatsot*," was presented at the Fourteenth World Congress of Jewish Studies, Jerusalem, 2005. As "Echoed Above," this chapter was published in an issue of *Opera Quarterly* entitled "Echoed Elsewhere," ed. Michal Grover-Friedlander: *Opera Quarterly* 21, no. 4 (Autumn 2005), pp. 675–712.

1. These ideas are developed by Michel Poizat in *The Angel's Cry: Beyond the Pleasure Principle in Opera*, trans. Arthur Denner (Ithaca: Cornell University

Press, 1992).

2. The treatise is by Pseudo-Dionysius the Areopagite, fifth-century Christian Byzantine.

3. Poizat, *The Angel's Cry*, p. 127.

4. *Ibid.*, p. 145.

5. The first quotation provides the definition of angels. The second addresses the role of invisible forces or powers (angels included). Both quotations are found in what is probably a seventh-century Byzantine collection of questions and answers: Ps. Athanasios, "Quaestiones ad Antiochum ducem," in J. P. Migne, *Patrologia Graeca* (Farnborough, Hants., England: Gregg Press, 1965), vol. 28, p. 616. I would like to thank Yannis Papadoyannakis for this citation.

6. "Phaedrus," in *Plato: Complete Works*, ed. John Cooper (Indianapolis: Hackett Publishing Company, 1997), pp. 535–36. I would like to thank Vered Lev-Kenaan and Heinrich Von Staden for directing me to Plato's discussion of the cicadas. See Ferrari for an emphasis on the cicadas's pleasure in verbal virtuosity. They are Sirens, writes Ferrari, "whose seduction is in their voice.... [They represent] the seductive pleasure of language stripped down to a mantra's hum. Moreover, none show better than the cicadas themselves the dangers of this pleasure." G. R. F. Ferrari, *Listening to the Cicadas: A Study of Plato's Phaedrus* (Cambridge: Cambridge University Press, 1987), p. 28. In Ferrari's account, the cicadas are only background noise, a drone to Socrates' conversation. Ferrari is not struck by their transformation resulting from excessive singing, but by the contrast with reason, sense, and language.

7. Walter Benjamin, "Agesilaus Santander" (second version), in *Walter Benjamin: Selected Writings*, vol. 2, eds. Michael W. Jennings, Howard Eiland, and Gary Smith, trans. Rodney Livingstone (Cambridge: Belknap Press of Harvard University Press, 1999), p. 714.

8. *B. T. Hagigah* 14a.

9. *Bereshit Rabbah* 78:1.

10. The Zohar (meaning splendor, radiance in Hebrew) is considered the most important work of Kabbalah, Jewish mysticism. It is a group of books which includes scriptural interpretations, mythical cosmology, and so forth. The Zohar is a mystical commentary on the Bible, containing discussions of the nature of God, the origin and structure of the universe, the nature of the

soul, and related topics.

11. Isaiah Tishbi explains that the consuming fire is the *Shekhinah*. Grass refers to "the six hundred million angelic messengers who were created on the second day of Creation" (p. 635). "Why [are these angels called] 'grass'? Because they grow like grass in the world. They are cut down every day, and then they grow again as at the beginning" (p. 624). *The Wisdom of the Zohar: An Anthology of Texts,* vol. 2, eds. Fischel Lachower and Isaiah Tishbi, trans. David Goldstein (Oxford: Oxford University Press, 1989). Quotation from the introduction by Isaiah Tishbi to vol. 2, pt. 3, "Creation," sec. 3, "Angels."

12. There are also accounts describing their creation not out of fire but out of God's word: "Then the Holy One, blessed be he, opens his mouth, speaks one word and creates others instead of them, [others] like them, new ones. Each of them then stands in song before the throne of glory and recites 'Holy.'" Peter Schäfer, *The Hidden and Manifest God: Some Major Themes in Early Jewish Mysticism*, trans. Aubrey Pomerance (New York: State University of New York Press, 1992), pp. 131–32.

13. *Bereshit Rabbah* 78. Quoted in Ithamar Gruenwald, "Angelic songs, the *Qedusha* and the Problem of the Origin of the Hekhalot Literature," in *From Apocalypticism to Gnosticism: Studies in Apocalypticism, Merkavah Mysticism and Gnosticism* (Frankfurt am Main: Verlag Peter Lang, 1988), p. 149.

14. *Ibid.*

15. "The heavens utter a song in His presence . . . and the earth utters a song. . . . The whole world desires and rejoices to glorify their Creator." *The Wisdom*, vol. 2, p. 637. As Peter Schäfer writes, "The recital of the daily hymn, which culminates in the trishagion from Isaiah 6:3, is the angels' foremost task." Peter Schäfer, *The Hidden*, p. 131. Indeed, even the wings of the creatures and God's throne join in the singing. The idea that heavenly beings sing praise to God is found in scripture, Apocalyptic literature, Kumran, the sages, *Hekhalot* literature, and prayer. See Gruenwald, "Angelic songs," pp. 145–49.

16. I will not be able to consider the relationship between the image of celestial singing I am dealing with here and notions of the Music of the Spheres. It seems clear that the notion of ideal, perfected, or harmonious music is not the emphasis and goal of Jewish accounts; or at least not the main aim (there is the term *ketikkuno*, referring to when angels sing correctly). Plato's sirens sing harmoniously: "And on the top of each circle stands a siren, which is carried

round with it and utters a note of constant pitch, and the eight notes together make up a single scale" (Myth of Er, *Republic* 617b). Daniel Chua explains: "In Plato's account of creation, music tunes the cosmos according to the Pythagorean ratios...and scales the human soul to the same proportions. This enables the inaudible sounds of the heavens to vibrate within the earthly soul, and, conversely, for the audible tones of human music to reflect the celestial spheres, so that heaven and earth could be harmonized within the unity of a well-tuned scale.... So music, as the invisible and inaudible harmony of the spheres, imposed a unity over creation, linking everything along the entire chain of being.... Thus music was...the *rational agent of enchantment itself*.... It animated the cosmos and tuned its very being." Daniel Chua, *Absolute Music and the Construction of Meaning* (Cambridge: Cambridge University Press, 1999), pp. 15–16. With Pythagoras, music existed as a perfect numerological system in the celestial realms where stars sang and scales laddered the sky. Disenchantment, the fall into empirical reality, as it were, means imperfection. Music connected the earth to the heavens; it influenced the celestial realms: "The celestial harmony, although mute like the numbers that inscribed its being, sounded its silence as the infinite calculations that ordered the differences and affinities of the entire cosmos. It structured the world." *Ibid.*, p. 52. Music resided in the heavens, emanating from "the inaudible songs of angels and sirens or issue from the geometrical motions of the celestial spheres." *Ibid.*, p. 77. Music was a secret that could decipher the structure of the universe. It duplicated the world, mimed the forms of the celestial realms, and showed resemblances between man and the cosmos. The complex notions of the music of the heavens often render the correspondence in terms of pitches, tetrachords, and scales, while Jewish theology seems to be concerned with its cyclic time and the utterance of holy text rather than musical attributes. But what is most striking, and to my knowledge merits no comparison, is the metaphor of angelic demise—for the sake of singing.

17. See commentary on *Bereshit Rabbah* 78:1, in *Midrash Rabbah: Ḥelek rishon* (Jerusalem, 5730 [1969–1970]), p. 192.

18. Tishbi, *The Wisdom*, vol. 2, p. 625.

19. Wouldn't the correspondence with Israel make angelic singing less dissonant? This question is not raised, but tradition has it that Israel plays a trick on the angels by singing one of the *Qedushas* in Aramaic, a language the angels

do not understand. The explanation given for tricking the angels is that an additional *Qedusha* enables Israel to arrive at the angels' level of holiness. See Tishbi, *The Wisdom*, vol. 3, p. 969.

20. The students of the Merkavah (meaning chariot) had the idea to recreate Ezekiel's experience and ascend in the chariot to explore the heavens. The Merkavah texts are visionary, mystical writings about a journey through the heavens. They represent a type of mysticism aimed at ecstatic experience that would allow practitioners to make the same journey the prophets had made.

21. Elior, "From Earthly Temple," p. 230.

22. Tishbi, *The Wisdom*, vol. 2, pp. 641–42.

23. *Ibid.*, p. 827.

24. *Hagigah* 12b.

25. See Elior, "From Earthly Temple," p. 257.

26. *Ibid.*, p. 223.

27. *Ibid.*, p. 263.

28. Gruenwald, "Angelic Songs," p. 155.

29. Arthur Green, *Keter: The Crown of God in Early Jewish Mysticism* (Princeton: Princeton University Press, 1997), p. 130.

30. *Ibid.*, p. 159.

31. *Ibid.*, p. 147.

32. *Ibid.*, p. 129.

33. *Ibid.*, p. 124.

34. Gershom Scholem, *Sabbatai Sevi: The Mystical Messiah 1626–1676* (London: Routledge, 1973), p. 34.

35. Chaim Nachman Bialik and Yud Chet Ravnitzki, *Sefer HaAggada: mivhar haaggadot shebatalmud uvamidrashim, halakim alef-gimel* (Tel Aviv: Dvir, 1948), p. kof tet (The Book of *Aggadah*: Selections from Talmud and Midrash, pts. 1–3, p. 109).

36. Gershom Scholem, *On the Kabbalah and Its Symbolism* (London: Routledge, 1960), p. 148.

37. Avner Bahat, "Elementim musikaliyim mimasorot ha'edot bemusika be'Israel" ("Musical elements in traditional congregations in Israel"), master's thesis, Tel Aviv University, 1973; William Elias, "The *Ricercar* by Mordecai Seter (Musical and dramatic aspects)," master's thesis, Tel Aviv University, 1974; Dalia Golomb, "*Tikkun Hatsot*," in Dalia Golomb and ben-Zion Orgad,

eds., *Madrikh leha'azana liyetsirot israeliot* (*Listener's guide to Israeli works*) (Tel Aviv: Hamerkaz hametodi Lemusika, 1984); Ronit Seter, "Yuvalim Be-Israel: Nationalism in Jewish-Israeli Art Music, 1940–2000," ch. 4, "Mordecai Seter, Myth, and Midnight Vigil: Seter's *Tikkun Ḥatsot*," Ph.D. thesis, Cornell University, 2004.

38. Tishbi, *The Wisdom*, vol. 3, pp. 955–56.

39. "The use of the term *Shekhinah* would thus seem to range from the numinous revelation of God, as in the theophany at Sinai...to the more mundane idea that a religious act...draws man nearer to God. Sometimes the term is simply an alternative for 'God,' while at others it has overtones of something separate from the Godhead; it may be used in a personalized or depersonalized way." "*Shekhinah*," *Encyclopaedia Judaica Online* (section "In Talmud and Midrash," written by Alan Unterman). http://go.galegroup.com/ps/start. do?p=GVRL&u=tel_aviv

40. This angle on *Tikkun* tradition is found in Avraham Greenbaum, *The Sweetest Hour: Tikkun Ḥatsot* (Jerusalem: Breslov Research Institute, 1993).

41. Daniel C. Matt, *Zohar: Annotated and Explained* (Woodstock, VT: Skylight Paths Publishing, 2002), p. 94.

42. The symbolism describing the *Shekhinah* is the most developed in the Kabbalistic literature. She is considered nearest to the created world and "because of her femininity and closeness to the created world she is the first and the main target of the satanic power.... It is therefore the duty of man and the *Sefirot* to protect the *Shekhinah* from the designs of the *sitra ahra*.... In Kabbalistic theology the *Shekhinah* is the divine principle of the people of Israel. Everything that happens to Israel in the earthly world is therefore reflected upon the *Shekhinah*.... The idea of the exile of the *Shekhinah*, resulting from the initial cosmic disaster and from Adam's fall, became of great importance in Lurianic Kabbalah. To fulfill every commandment for the purpose of delivering the *Shekhinah* from her lowly state and reuniting her with the Holy One, blessed be He, became the supreme goal. The notion of redeeming the Shekhinah from exile acquired new eschatological content." "*Shekhinah*," *Encyclopaedia Judaica Online*, section "In Kabbalah," written by Joseph Dan. http://go.galegroup.com/ps/start.do?p=GVRL&u=tel_aviv

43. Tishbi, *The Wisdom*, vol. 2, pp. 672–73.

44. Scholem, *On the Kabbalah*, pp. 122–23 (emphasis in original).

45. *Tikkun* means perfecting, a betterment, correction. Scholars are divided about the degree to which earlier precursors participated in the Midnight Vigil as a more consolidated Lurianic rite.

46. Tishbi, *The Wisdom*, vol. 3, p. 957.

47. Michael Lodahl, *Shekhinah/Spirit: Divine Presence in Jewish and Christian Religion* (New York: Paulist Press, 1992), p. 83.

48. *Ibid.*, pp. 97, 102, 89, 93.

49. *Ibid.*, p. 94.

50. *Ibid.*, p. 95.

51. Shaul Magid, "Conjugal Union, Mourning and *Talmud Torah* in R. Isaac Luria's *Tikkun Hatsot*," *Daat* 36 (1995), pp. xvii–xlv.

52. Gershom Scholem, *On the Kabbalah*, p. 146.

53. The *Aggadah* comprises different voices and various layers of ancient myth, scripture, and universal folklore, encompassing a span of over one thousand years in various lands and cultural surroundings. Influences of different languages and different philosophical elements and concepts are apparent. Various views exist side by side since the editors believed that all the words in the *Aggadah* were words of God. The ideas, for the most part, have come down to us fragmented and fused with ideas of later commentators. See Cecil Roth, "Aggadah," in *Encyclopaedia Judaica* (Jerusalem: Keter Publishing House, 1972), vol. 1, pp. 354–66.

54. This seems to be a description of a monodrama, though the work was never titled as one. Mordecai Seter, *Tikkun Hatsot* (Midnight Vigil), Oratorio for Tenor, Mixed Choir, and Orchestra, 1962.

55. Minor, mostly orchestral retouches took place as late as 1984.

56. See Bahat, "Elementim musikaliyim," for details on the musical sources and their transformations.

57. For details on each of the versions see Ronit Seter, "Yuvalim Be-Israel."

58. The piece was submitted for the Prize of Italy and won it in 1962; in 1965, it won the Prize of Israel.

59. In the fifth, the text is unchanged but the narrator is eliminated.

60. These distinctions will be reduced, and utterances will become more abstract, in the final version.

61. The personae shifts occur primarily in the first and final scenes. Thus, in the epilogue of the fifth version, the chorus of the *Aggadah* is substituted by

all choruses. In the first scene, the fourth version's Heavenly Voice becomes—in the fifth version—the voice of the *Aggadah*; the Worshipper becomes the *Aggadah*; the People becomes either the Heavenly Voice or the Worshipper, or remains the People, and so on.

62. Walter Benjamin, "Agesilaus Santander," p. 59.

63. Jacques Derrida, "A Silkworm of One's Own," in Hélène Cixous and Jacques Derrida, *Veils*, trans. Geoffrey Bennington (Stanford: Stanford University Press, 2001), p. 32.

64. *Ibid.*, p. 63.

65. Seter, in fact, wrote a short essay advocating a synthesis "from within" between the musical traditions of "east" and "west." Mordecai Seter, "Mizrah uma'arav, ketsad?" ("East and West—How So?"), *Bat Kol* 1 (1941).

66. Raymond Monelle, *The Sense of Music: Semiotic Essays* (Princeton: Princeton University Press, 2000), pp. 66–77.

67. This statement is found in a notebook entry from 1978–80 (more than two decades after the initial preoccupation with the piece). While sketching the form of *Tikkun Hatsot*, Seter discusses the transformation of the sigh motif. In another entry, he adds that the twelve-note row derives from the sigh motif as a further variation. Mordecai Seter's personal notebook, 1978–80, mus. 110, D, 19, National and University Library, Jerusalem. Notebook entries have no specific dates. Thirty-two notebooks span the years 1952–94.

68. Scholem, "Walter Benjamin and His Angel" (1972), in Gary Smith (ed.), *On Walter Banjamin: Critical Essays and Recollections* (Cambridge: The MIT Press, 1995), p. 65.

69. Gershom Scholem, *Kabbalah* (Jerusalem: Keter, 1974), p. 18.

70. *Talmud Bavli: masekhet mo'ed katan gimel* (3). *Mevo'ar meturgam umenukad al-yede,* Adin Schteinzalts (ed.) (Jersusalem: Hamakhon haisra'eli lepirsumim talmudiyim, 1984).

71. *Berachot* 18b; *Hagigah* 15a; *Sanhedrin* 89b. See Sh. A. Horodetsky, *Hamistorin be'Israel, kerekh rishon: hamistorin hakadum (Mystery in Israel, vol. 1: ancient mystery)* (Tel Aviv: Shtibel tarza, kof-nun-gimel, 1961), p. 153.

72. *Hagigah* 15.

73. Scholem, *Kabbalah*, p. 159. Gruenwald writes, "This peculiar idea of the weaving of the history of the world into the ideal texture of a heavenly veil or curtain comes very close to the concept of the creation of the world

by a process of weaving." And, he continues, this might be a Jewish reminder of Gnostic texts about "the creation of matter from the shadow cast by the veil." Ithamar Gruenwald, "Jewish Sources for the Gnostic Texts from Nag Hammadi?," in *From Apocalypticism to Gnosticism: Studies in Apocalypticism, Merkavah Mysticism and Gnosticism* (Frankfurt am Main: Verlag Peter Lang, 1988), pp. 213–14.

74. Gruenwald, "Jewish Sources," pp. 210–15.

75. Scholem, *Kabbalah*, p. 18. Gruenwald's third category is found in rabbinical passages that describe "the separating element between the world above and that below by the name of *vilon.... Vilon* is mentioned [*Tal. Bab. Hagigah* 12b] as the lowest in a series of seven heavens, and it is said that 'it does not serve for anything, but enters in the morning and leaves in the evening, thus daily renewing the work of creation.'" (In *Beraita dema'aseh bereshit*, the opposite is said about the *vilon*: "It enters in the evening and leaves in the morning." [Gruenwald, "Jewish Sources," p. 214]). "And even though the Rabbinical veil is responsible for the creation of darkness, this is merely the cyclical darkness of the night and has apparently nothing to do with a shadow from which matter was created [as with the Gnostic veil]." *Ibid.*, p. 215. Here we find a common cyclic, renewed appearance reminiscent of metaphors of repeatedly disappearing angels. Scholem indeed explains that in the Zohar there is a notion of the *sitra ahra* (the "other side"), which is a demonic counterpart below the realm of the *sefirot*, like emanations of the second rank: "These emanations of the second rank are presented as 'curtains' (*pargodim*) in front of the emanations of the *sefirot*, and as 'bodies' and 'garments' for the inner souls, which are the *sefirot*." Scholem, *Kabbalah*, pp. 55–56.

76. Here is the full quotation: "The curtain before God's throne in which are woven all of the past and future acts of man, the stars and their names, the souls of the burnt angels who did not sing the *Qedusha* correctly, and the right hand of God, which he holds concealed behind his back due to the destruction of the temple and which he will bring out in the future to redeem Israel." Schäfer, *The Hidden*, p. 135.

77. Ronit Seter has a notion of curtain that pertains to the tonal framework of the piece. At the outset of the composition, it is the B–minor chord masking a D–Major chord, and at the end, before the nine-voice canon, a "curtain fall[s] after the drama is over," with an appearance of the *Tikkun* scale separating the

worshipper's vision from reality. Ronit Seter, "Yuvalim Be-Israel," p. 325. As will become evident, my usage of the term "veil" is radically different from hers.

78. Dalia Golomb sees the descending and rising seconds as two distinct motifs: the sigh motif and the expectation-hope motif. In Golomb's account they symbolize the mixture of reality and visions, exile and yearning for redemption, despair and hope. (Golomb, "*Tikkun Hatzot*," p. 223) Ronit Seter sees the lament motif and the hope (or yearning) motif as two *urmotifs*, the latter more scarce. Ronit Seter, "Yuvalim Be-Israel," pp. 278 and 299. The rising sighs are Levi-Tanai's connecting motif between the songs, a feature Seter retains. Terming the rising sighs the "hope motif" is part of the agenda found in various scholars to graph a national identity onto the piece. I will pick up this topic briefly below when sketching potential interpretations of the work's ending.

79. This is not an exhaustive account of the appearance of veils in *Tikkun*. It is important to stress that the unveiling is not a gradual process. Thus, for example, the veil in Tableau II (measures 334–35), which sounds after the climactic outcry discussed above, is subdued. It is reduced to only one semitone (A–B) with no accompaniment, and is only vocal—the modest ornamentation added to it, lending it uncharacteristic lyricism.

80. Green, *Keter,* p. 130.

81. Seter, personal notebooks, 1961, II, mus. 110, D, 5 (my translation), National and University Library, Jerusalem.

82. *Ibid.*, D, 4.

83. My concern is not with the *representation* of celestial singing. Daniel Albright, in his chapter entitled "Heaven," discusses briefly images of heaven in musical compositions. He writes that one of the intuitions about presenting heaven in music is that it conceives of "the juxtapositive and the sequential [as] one," a way of pertaining to the "convergence of the temporal" imaged as Heaven. Albright discusses the notion of immobility: "The music doesn't seem to evolve: some element simply intensifies its there-ness for a moment amid the undulations of melody, like adjustments of focal distance within an unchanging field.... A state of divine rhythmlessness...[in which] the constant elements are a little too constant, and the variable elements a little too variable: heaven is a place where absolute invariability is imagined through a displacement of the normal patterns of variation, or through such a surfeit and exhaustion of

variation that there is nothing left to vary. And heaven is a place where all boxes are open, all springs sprung: this is why Schoenberg would later (in *Moses und Aron*) find it right to depict God through simultaneous speaking and singing and playing of all twelve notes of the scale." Daniel Albright, "Heaven," in *Untwisting the Serpent: Modernism in Music, Literature, and Other Arts* (Chicago: The University of Chicago Press, 2000), pp. 312–13.

84. See Ben Yehodaya, *Berachot* 3, ch. 1.

85. "A leading role in the receipt and raising of the prayers to greater heights is placed by Metatron." Tishbi, *The Wisdom*, vol. 3, p. 956.

86. Song 41 in Abraham Zvi Idelsohn, *Otsar neginot Israel*, kerekh dalet, hasepharadim hamizrahiyim (Leipzig: Breitkopf & Härtel, 1914–32), p. 140 (A Treasure of the tunes of Israel, pt. 4: Eastern-Sephardic). (Idelsohn's four-volume project is a compilation of traditional tunes from various Jewish communities around the world). See Bahat, "Elementim musikaliyim," for a detailed account of the relationship between traditional tunes and their reworking in *Tikkun*. On "Keter" and the "Hallelujah," see pp. 118–22. However, Bahat mistakenly identifies Seter's "Keter" with another of Idelsohn's tunes bearing the same title (song 302 from the same volume). For the composer's allusion to Bahat's mistake, see Ronit Seter, "Yuvalim Be-Israel," p. 336, n.87.

87. This is the opening used for *Qedusha* in all services, but "as the Babylonian tradition evolved into the Sephardic rite,...it [became] restricted to Sabbath and festival use." Green, *Keter*, p. 12, n.2.

88. Avner Bahat has located the source of the rising seconds, our veil, in the song "Ahavat Hadassah." In Bahat's view, using the coupled rising seconds as a recurring gesture throughout the work, as connecting transitory material or a refrain device, originated with Levi-Tanai. She employed it as early as the first ballet version of *Tikkun*. Bahat's observation points to the veil being an abstraction of the song: the barren side of that which is expressive and most melodious. In other words, the dying out of song is the other side of song, and simultaneously identical to it. See Bahat, "Elementim musikaliyim," pp. 88 and 93–100.

89. Here is the full passage: "As it [crown] cannot be compared to any other image, it must be called *ayin*, a 'nothingness,' an object of quest that is also the subject of any search. As a Name of God, *Keter* is the *Ehyeh* of the great declaration of God to Moses in Exodus 3:14. God says *Ehyeh asher Ehyeh*, 'I Am That I

Am,' but the Kabbalists refused to interpret this as mere 'being.' To them, *Keter* was at once *Ehyeh* and *Ayin*, being and nothingness, a cause of all causes and no cause at all, beyond action. If Kabbalah can be interpreted, as I think it can, as a theory of influence, then *Keter* is the paradoxical idea of influence itself. The irony of all influence, initially, is that the source is emptied out into a state of absence, in order for the receiver to accommodate the influx of apparent being. This may be why we use the word 'influence,' originally an astral term referring to the occult effect of the stars upon men." Harold Bloom, *Kabbalah and Criticism* (New York: Seabury Press, 1975), pp. 28–29.

90. Seter, personal notebooks, 1978, I–IX, mus. 110, D, 18.

91. It was surprising to find, buried in a diary at the archives of Hebrew University in Jerusalem, a key to a mystery I thought I had invented.

92. Bloom, *Kabbalah and Criticism*, p. 83.

93. Gershom Scholem, ed., *The Correspondence of Walter Benjamin and Gershom Scholem, 1932–1940*, trans. Gary Smith and Andre Lefevere (Cambridge: Harvard University Press, 1992), p. 81.

94. Emphasis in the original. Concert program, Feb. 18, 1958, mus. 110, H, 23 (in Hebrew), National and University Library, Jerusalem. Reproduced and translated by Ronit Seter (translation slightly modified) in her "Yuvalim Be-Israel," pp. 284–87.

95. Letter of July 17, 1934. *The Correspondence*, pp. 126–27.

96. Franz Kafka, *The Diaries, 1910–1923*, ed. Max Brod, trans. Joseph Kresh and Martin Greenberg (New York: Schocken Books, 1948), pp. 291–92. The story is quoted and discussed in Robert Alter, *Necessary Angels: Tradition and Modernity in Kafka, Benjamin, and Scholem* (Cambridge: Harvard University Press, 1991), pp. 116–20. Quotation on p. 116.

97. I cite one example from a notebook entry from 1973. Seter, while classifying his oeuvre (a repeated undertaking throughout the diaries), writes that there are three topics present in his work. One is the Messianic ideal, wherein the eschatological equals the prophetic, which then, he writes, equals the foundation of the state of Israel. The second topic concerns mourning over the destruction of the temple. This, Seter writes, is a necessary counterpoint to, but also the foundation of, the previous topic. The third relates to the personal dimension. Seter then goes through his compositions and places them under one or more of the three categories. The oratorio *Tikkun Ḥatsot* falls under

the first (with an exclamation mark) specified as "mourning. reestablishment (*tekumah*)." A few years later, in the notebook of 1978, I–IX, Seter writes that *Tikkun* is about "destruction (*ḥurban*)–exile–redemption." He calls this "the specific Jewish national subject par excellence." He writes that this is the subject encompassing two thousand years of Judaism. And that this is "my subject"—no other composer has been or is preoccupied with it (emphasized with an exclamation mark). Obviously, it is unclear what one learns from a composer's self-reflections, but it is significant, I think, that alongside these unequivocal statements in his diaries, there are also contrary remarks, such as the comment showing the composer's excitement when finding in Scholem a notion of Messianism *other* than that expressed in national redemption. Seter supplements this observation with the revelation that he himself was think-ing this with regard to one of *Tikkun*'s songs. I am not implying that it is clear what Seter means, or, for that matter, that it is clear what to do with such testimonies. I would perhaps only like to show that against all declarations by composer, librettist, and scholars, we do not simply and contentedly awake into a redemptive reality at the end of *Tikkun Ḥatsot*.

98. Scholem, *Sabbatai Sevi*, p. 26.

99. *Ibid.*, pp. 42 and 45.

100. A quotation found in Seter, personal notebooks, 1963, mus. 110, D, 5.

101. From *Parnasse contemporain* (1866): "Je me mire et me vois ange! Et je meurs, et j'aime/ — Que la vitre soit l'art, soit la mysticité —/À renaître."

102. Scholem, *On the Kabbalah*, p. 133.

103. Vladimir Jankélévitch, *Music and the Ineffable*, trans. Carolyn Abbate (Princeton: Princeton University Press, 2003), p. 154.

104. *Babylonian Talmud: Tractate Niddah*, Folio 30b.

EPILOGUE

1. Released as *Willie the Operatic Whale* in 1954.

2. Other cartoons from the 1940s and 1950s directly dealing with opera include: *You Ought to Be in Pictures* (Warner Brothers, 1940); *Notes to You* (War-ner Brothers, 1941) and its remake *Back Alley Oproar* (Warner Brothers, 1948); *Rabbit of Seville* (Lantz, 1944); *Long-Haired Hare* (Warner Brothers, 1949); *Magical Maestro* (M-G-M, 1952); *One Froggy Evening* (Warner Brothers, 1955); *What's Opera, Doc?* (Warner Brothers, 1957).

3. In the cartoon, the enactment of operatic singing is embedded in a fantasy of the whale's success. But it is unclear who is fantasizing—is it the whale, the seagull, or is the fantasy part of the framing narrative? Notice that it immediately precedes the whale's death, as if its (imagined) life has gone by as a result of its approaching death.

4. Nelson Eddy sang the soprano, tenor, baritone, and bass parts through overdubbing. See Stuart Nicholson, "*Make Mine Music* and the End of the Swing Era," in Daniel Goldmark and Yuval Taylor (eds.), *The Cartoon Music Book* (Chicago: A Cappella Books, 2002), pp. 127–28.

5. Apart from the frog's singing, the cartoon is devoid of dialogue.

6. This question is an outcome of Jonathan Burt's discussion of animals in film: "The figure of the animal in film is generally understood in terms of some form of displacement, which, in the case of anthropomorphism and animation, would be largely metaphorical." Jonathan Burt, *Animals in Film* (London: Reaktion Books, 2002), p. 17.

7. The term is from Paul Wells, *Understanding Animation* (London: Routledge, 1998), p. 188.

8. On music in *Pinocchio*, see Ross Care, "Make Walt's Music: Music for Disney Animation, 1928–1967" in *The Cartoon*, pp. 26–30.

9. Wells, *Understanding Animation*, p. 189.

10. *Ibid.*, pp. 188–89.

11. Sergei Eisenstein, *Eisenstein on Disney*, ed. Jay Leda, trans. A. Upchurch (London: Methuen, 1988), p. 64.

12. *Ibid.*

13. Paul Wells, *Understanding Animation*, p. 122.

14. Wells calls this characteristic "mutuality." Wells, *Understanding Animation*, p. 99.

15. Chuck Jones, "What's Up Down Under?: Chuck Jones Talks At *The Illusion of Life* Conference," in A. Cholodenko (ed.), *The Illusion of Life: Essays on Animation* (Sydney: Power Publications, 1991), p. 61.

16. The *Lucia* sextet is the most popular opera ensemble piece to appear in cartoons. See Daniel Goldmark, *Tunes for 'Toons: Music and the Hollywood Cartoon* (Berkeley: University of California Press), p. 193, n.9.

17. Philip Brophy, "The Animation of Sound," in *The Illusion*, p. 74.

18. Keith Broadfoot and Rex Butler, "The Illusion of Illusion," in *The*

Illusion, p. 273.

19. Stanley Cavell, *The World Viewed: Reflections on the Ontology of Film*, enlarged edition (Cambridge: Harvard University Press, 1979), p. 171.

Index

Zone Books series design by Bruce Mau
Typesetting by Meighan Gale
Image placement and production by Julie Fry
Printed and bound by Thompson-Shore